# The Islamic Voluntary Sector in Southeast Asia

Islam and the Economic Development of Southeast Asia

# The Islamic Voluntary Sector in Southeast Asia

### Edited by
### Mohamed Ariff
*University of Malaya*

Social Issues in Southeast Asia
INSTITUTE OF SOUTHEAST ASIAN STUDIES

Published by
Institute of Southeast Asian Studies
Heng Mui Keng Terrace
Pasir Panjang
Singapore 0511

*The responsibility for facts and opinions expressed in this publication rests exclusively with the authors and their interpretations do not necessarily reflect the views or the policy of the Institute or its supporters.*

**Cataloguing in Publication Data**

Islam and the economic development of Southeast Asia: The Islamic Voluntary
    Sector in Southeast Asia/edited by Mohamed Ariff.
    1.  Economic development — Religious aspects — Islam — Asia, Southeastern.
    2.  Land trusts (Islamic law) — Asia, Southeastern.
    3.  Zakat.
    4.  Charitable uses, trusts, and foundations (Islamic law) — Asia, Southeastern.
    I.  Mohamed Ariff, 1940–
BP173.75 I831      1991      sls91-214470

ISBN 981-3016-07-8 (soft cover)
ISBN 981-3016-08-6 (hard cover)

Typeset in Singapore by Letraprint
Printed in Singapore by Kin Keong Printing Co. Pte. Ltd.

# CONTENTS

*Foreword*                                                                                    vii
*Acknowledgements*                                                                             x
*Contributors*                                                                                xi

1   Introduction                                                                               1
    *Mohamed Ariff*

2   The Role of the Voluntary Sector in Islam:
    A Conceptual Framework                                                                     6
    *Muhammad Nejatullah Siddiqi*

3   Resource Mobilization through the Islamic Voluntary Sector
    in Southeast Asia                                                                         31
    *Mohamed Ariff*

4   *Zakat* Collection and Distribution in Indonesia                                          50
    *Taufik Abdullah*

5   *Zakat* Administration in Malaysia                                                        85
    *Aidit bin Ghazali*

6   *Waqf* Management in Malaysia                                                            118
    *Syed Othman Alhabshi*

7   The Malaysian Pilgrims Management and Fund Board
    and Resource Mobilization                                                                138
    *Radiah Abdul Kader*

8   *Zakat* and *Sadaqqa* Practices among the Moros of
    the Philippines                                          168
    *Carmen A. Abubakar*

9   The Management of Muslim Funds in Singapore             192
    *Amina Tyabji*

10  Mobilization of Resources through *Waqf* in Thailand    233
    *Preeda Prapertchob*

# FOREWORD

Ethnic and religious issues have, in the last few decades, confounded many social analysts by refusing to disappear. The 'liberal expectancy' among social analysts used to be that modernization would blur ethnic distinctions, achievement would replace ascription and particularistic criteria, and wide-ranging communication and education systems would homogenize populations. The 'radical expectancy' was that differences in religions, languages, and culture would be swallowed up, perhaps even across national boundaries by emergent class consciousness. Instead, religion and ethnicity continue to cut across and envelop almost every facet of Southeast Asian life. Indeed, if anything, such divisions in many societies have become sharper, ethnic and religious interest groups more insistent, and opposition more politicized and strident. Much of this activity seems to be increasingly played on the urban stage — and this at a time when the pace of urbanization in Southeast Asia is increasing rapidly, to the extent that by the turn of the century, cities such as Manila, Bangkok, and Jakarta could have populations of more than ten million each. In these settings, Southeast Asian ethnic, religious, and linguistic complexities are likely to be even more challenging than in the past.

It was therefore only natural that among other aspects of the Southeast Asian social and cultural scene, the Institute should identify the study of contemporary religion as one of its key areas of interest. Southeast Asia is, after all, not only home to all the major religions of the world — Islam, Buddhism, Christianity, and Hinduism — but the geographical spread of these is such that the bonds that bind their adherents at one and the same time defy and accentuate political and territorial divides and boundaries. The case of Islam is especially striking in this respect, as its followers are present in significant numbers in almost every Southeast Asian country, and in several of these across constraining political borders. Acting on this, a group of Southeast

Asian scholars met in 1980 and proposed a project to increase our understanding of Islam in its regional context.

Towards this end, two clusters were identified. The first of these was centred on the nature of Islam in the region, Islam and societal change, and Islam and education. The second concentration was to be on Islam and problems of economic development.

The completion of the first cluster of research activities saw the publication of three volumes: *Readings on Islam in Southeast Asia.*, *Islam and Society in Southeast Asia*, and *Muslim Society, Higher Education and Development in Southeast Asia.*

Building on the foregoing studies, work commenced on the second cluster of research, that is, 'Islam and the Economic Development of Southeast Asia'. The research here, too, is in three phases, spread over three years. They are: Islamic banking; Islam and resource mobilization through the voluntary sector; and Islam and the role of the private sector in economic development.

The project on Islam stimulated considerable interest in not only other major religions in the region, but also issues relating to ethnicity and development, another of the Institute's long-standing and primary areas of research. Moreover, the experience gained in managing the project on Islam proved valuable in terms of co-ordinating comparative research involving numerous scholars from diverse backgrounds and disciplines — with the result that the Institute was encouraged not only to plan parallel projects on Buddhism and Christianity in Southeast Asia, but also to think in terms of developing a longer-term programme of research that would encompass all its projects on contemporary religions, together with those that might grow out of the Institute's interests in ethnicity, urbanism, and related areas.

To facilitate this, the Institute convened a meeting in 1985 of senior Southeast Asian social scientists to discuss issues of social change in Southeast Asia, in order to identify firm areas of research and a sharper focusing of such research and associated activities. The participants were unanimous in their conclusion that it was "essential and desirable" to encourage research on social issues in Southeast Asia, in particular religion, ethnicity, urbanism, and population dynamics.

To allow for proper planning and incremental research, the group felt that work in these areas could be most effectively developed within the structure and support of a programme, rather than as *ad hoc* projects. Accordingly, it was proposed there be established a programme of research to be known as the 'Social Issues in Southeast Asia (SISEA)' programme. This programme would address itself to the nature, persistence, and impact of religions, ethnicity, urbanism, and population change in terms of their intrinsic dynamism and potential for societal conflict, co-existence or co-operation in the context of development, stability, and nation-building.

SISEA would also allow for the consolidation of the various publications emanating from the Institute's work in ethnicity, religion, urbanism, and population change within a single and integrated series, Social Issues in Southeast Asia , with *The Islamic Voluntary Sector in Southeast Asia* edited by Dr Mohamed Ariff, being the latest addition to the series.

SISEA and the preparation of *The Islamic Voluntary Sector in Southeast Asia* have benefited greatly from the financial support provided by the Konrad Adenauer Foundation of the Federal Republic of Germany. The Institute would like to record its appreciation for all such help and support and to express the wish that the various numbers of Social Issues in Southeast Asia will circulate widely amongst all concerned with the social dynamics of the region.

In wishing the volumes in the Social Issues in Southeast Asia series all the best it is clearly understood that responsibility for facts and opinions expressed in them rests exclusively with the individual authors, editors, and compilers, and their interpretations do not necessarily reflect the views or policies of the Institute or its supporters.

K.S. Sandhu
Director
Institute of Southeast Asian Studies

## ACKNOWLEDGEMENTS

The chapters in this volume were first presented as papers at a workshop which was held in Singapore on 24–25 August 1987. Shamsher Ali, Syed Hamid Aljunid, Mohammad Haji Alias, Munawar Iqbal, Michael Mastura, Sidek Saniff, and Ibrahim Qureshi participated as discussants for the various papers which were presented and I would like to thank them for their stimulating contributions to the discussions at the workshop.

The generous financial support of the Konrad Adenauer Foundation is gratefully acknowledged. Due acknowledgements should also be given to Dr Sharon Siddique, then Co-ordinator of the Social Issues in Southeast Asia (SISEA) programme and presently Deputy Director at ISEAS, for her help in organizing the workshop and for facilitating work on the papers which make up this volume. Thanks also go to the staff of SISEA and the Institute's Publications Unit, for their professional assistance in the preparation of this volume. Last but not least, I would like to acknowledge gratefully the valuable help and assistance provided by Dr Ananda Rajah, Co-ordinator of SISEA, in putting this volume together.

Mohamed Ariff
University of Malaya

## CONTRIBUTORS

**Mohamed Ariff** is Professor of Analytical Economics in the Faculty of Economics and Administration, University of Malaya, Kuala Lumpur, Malaysia.

**Muhammad Nejatullah Siddiqi** is with the Islamic Research and Training Institute, Islamic Development Bank, Jeddah.

**Taufik Abdullah** is a Research Professor at Lembaga Ilmu Penelitian Indonesia (LIPI), Jakarta.

**Aidit bin Ghazali** is a Lecturer in the Faculty of Economics at the International Islamic University, Kuala Lumpur.

**Syed Othman Alhabshi** is Dean of the Faculty of Advanced Studies, International Islamic University, Kuala Lumpur.

**Radiah Abdul Kader** is a Lecturer in the Faculty of Economics and Administration, University of Malaya.

**Carmen A. Abubakar** is an Associate Professor in, and Acting Dean of, the Institute of Islamic Studies, University of the Philippines.

**Amina Tyabji** is a Senior Lecturer in the Department of Economics and Statistics, National University of Singapore.

**Preeda Prapertchob** is a Lecturer in the Department of Agricultural Economics, Khon Kaen University.

# 1 INTRODUCTION

*Mohamed Ariff*

Islam is not just a 'religion' in the Western sense. It is a way of life based on an elaborate set of codes and a myriad of socio-economic institutional arrangements which are ordained for the common good of the *ummah*. That Islam has continued to flourish, despite severe difficulties and formidable challenges in the past, is testimony to the inherent strengths of its institutions which have successfully warded off external threats and checked internal decay.

Islam is a practical religion which treads the middle path, avoiding extremes. Islam thus underscores the virtue of moderation. It calls for a balance between the spiritual and material needs of man, and between worldly life and the hereafter. A total denial of the world in a monkish fashion would amount to a rejection of God's gifts. Islam, therefore, enjoins man to enjoy the world but within limits ordained by God, lest he should lose his balance and go astray.

Islam looks upon man as a vicegerent of God on earth. Ownership, in the ultimate analysis, rests with God and nothing belongs to man who can act in trust and who is accountable to God on the Day of Judgement. Man's responsibilities as *khalifa* (trustee or representative) have been spelled out in some detail in the Qur'an and the Hadith. Freedom of man is enshrined in Islam. Man is free but not unaccountable. There is no compulsion in religion, but man is subject to rewards and punishments. All men are considered equal in so far as their human rights are concerned but man, in an Islamic social order, is judged by his moral excellences and spiritual attainments and not by his economic strength and material affluence.

Islam permits the acquisition of wealth through righteous means. Those who happen to possess greater wealth than others do so only as a trust from

God to fulfil the divine objective of providing sustenance to His creations at large. The greater a man's possessions, the heavier his social responsibilities.

The Islamic economy is a welfare economy, for Islam insists that economic pursuits of individuals through private initiatives should conform to ethical codes which would ensure that the activity of no one is consciously at the expense of any other. While Islam recognizes uneven wealth distribution as a fact of life ordained by God, it contains a system for an equitable redistribution of income and wealth, which is enforced through moral obligations and fiscal measures. The purpose is to bring about economic changes in such a way as to maximize the well-being of the community as a whole.

This brings us to the role of the voluntary sector in an Islamic economy. The Islamic economy may be broadly divided into three main sectors: the government, commercial, and voluntary sectors. In the polity of Islam, the state represents God's vicegerent, entrusted with the divine mission of upholding social justice, law, and order, so that man-to-man and man-to-God relationships can find meaningful expressions in a harmonious fashion. Although there is a general consensus with regard to the need for state intervention in an Islamic economy, opinions among scholars differ on the question of the extent of state intervention permissible in Islam. Thus, some scholars tend to view an Islamic economy as one essentially based on individual freedom with minimal state interference, while some others are inclined to assign a more dominant role to the state. Be that as it may, there is no compelling reason to be dogmatic about this, for much would depend on actual circumstances.

In any case, the Islamic state is obliged to achieve economic equity through fiscal means. Thus, it is the duty of the Islamic state to administer *zakat*. *Zakat* consists of *zakat al-mal* (wealth tax) and *zakat al-fitr* (poll tax). The latter is commonly referred to as *fitrah*, which is collected in the month of Ramadhan prior to Eid celebrations. *Zakat*, unless otherwise specified, ordinarily refers to wealth tax, although the term may be stretched to cover tax on incomes as well.

*Zakat* is leviable on (1) productive properties, (2) gold and silver, (3) goods obtained without exertion, e.g. treasures, and (4) incomes of professionals and artisans. *Zakat* on the produce of land is referred to as *ushr*, which amounts to one-tenth of the produce of rain-irrigated land. *Zakat* penalizes idle and unproductive properties, as the burden of the tax is heavier on those who do not make productive use of their assets. What makes the *zakat* institution so unique is not the tax structure as such, but the pattern of distribution. *Zakat* proceeds are earmarked for the poor (*fuqra*), the indigent (*masakin*), the public agents who collect *zakat* (*amilin*), new converts to Islam (*mullafatul qulub*), slaves (*riqab*), debtors (*gharimin*), the way of God (*fi-sabilillah*), and wayfarers (*ibn-as-sabil*). These eight categories of recipients are collectively referred to as *asnaf*.

It is important to point out that public expenditure by the state is not constrained by *zakat*. Obviously, *zakat* can only be used for the benefit of the *asnaf*. The state is empowered to tax the rich in excess of their *zakat* dues (which are levied at the rate of 2.5 per cent). Thus, it is incorrect to think of *zakat* as constituting the entire fiscal system of an Islamic economy, although *zakat* is certainly an important and integral part of it.

The commercial sector has a vital role to play in an Islamic economy. The importance of commerce, which includes production and trade, is duly recognized and endorsed by the Qur'an and the Hadith. Although there is room for state participation in certain commercial activities in the Islamic system, there is little doubt about the suitability or compatibility of the private enterprise system in the Islamic order. However, the private enterprise system in an Islamic framework is different from that in a capitalist society, as the former is subject to salutary checks imposed by *Shariah* (Islamic law). Private initiatives are exalted in Islam, as the Qur'anic verse that "man can have nothing but what he strives for" (verse 53: 39) clearly states. The Qur'an urges: "And when prayer is finished, then ye may disperse through the land, and seek of the Bounty of Allah . . . " (verse 62: 10). In Islam, righteous earning is equivalent to, and indeed is, a form of worship (*ibadat*).

The significance of the voluntary sector in the Islamic order can hardly be overemphasized. The Qur'an and the Hadith exhort the Muslims to give alms spontaneously to the poor and the needy. Such spontaneous alms are called *sadaqah*, which is prescribed as a supplementary measure in addition to the obligatory tax, i.e., *zakat*. Unlike *zakat*, which by definition involves financial or real transfers, *sadaqah* can assume various forms, ranging from cash donations to voluntary services. While *zakat* funds can only be used for the benefit of the well-defined *asnaf*, *sadaqah* proceeds can be allocated more flexibly. In the case of *zakat*, not all Muslims are liable to pay, whereas in the case of *sadaqah* all can participate.

Such voluntary contributions may be made to individual recipients or to non-profit organizations or institutions which work for the common good of all. In this regard, the institution of *waqf* (or *awqaf*, as it is sometimes referred to) plays a significant role. *Waqf* has the character of a foundation or an endowment. Such endowments provided by individuals or families often take the form of land, buildings, and money. The basic principle behind *waqf* is that the asset will remain intact, while the revenue from the asset will be used for the benefit of the people. It is not uncommon to see *waqf* properties being used to finance the construction and maintenance of mosques, religious schools, and orphanages. There are also *waqf* bodies which provide scholarships to students, undertake community projects, meet funeral expenses of the poor, finance Islamic missionary activities, and so on.

The Islamic voluntary sector has to assume greater responsibilities in non-Islamic states. This is especially so in countries where Muslims constitute a minority, for the Islamic voluntary sector has to take on the role of an Islamic state in performing certain functions for the benefit of the community. Thus, for example, it is the responsibility of the voluntary sector to mobilize and distribute *zakat* if the government is unable or unwilling to take it upon itself. In this context, the doctrine of *fard qifayah*, which refers to socially obligatory duties that help fulfil the basic individual needs and essential social needs, is extremely pertinent and instructive. According to this doctrine, a socially obligatory duty must be performed somehow (regardless of whether it is done by the state, the community, or individuals). All these devolve largely on the Islamic voluntary sector in a non-Islamic state or where Muslims constitute a minority.

In Southeast Asia, there are no Islamic states, although there are countries where Muslims account for the bulk of the population. Thus, Brunei, Indonesia, and Malaysia can be aptly described as 'Muslim' but not as 'Islamic' countries (since the governments of these countries are essentially secular in character), while there are sizeable Muslim minorities in the Philippines, Singapore, and Thailand. It is in societies such as those characterized by the Southeast Asian countries that the Islamic voluntary sector shoulders the heaviest burden and faces the toughest challenge.

An attempt is made in this volume to examine the role of the Islamic voluntary sector in Southeast Asia. Admittedly, the studies contained in this volume only manage to scratch the surface. Nonetheless, they do provide valuable insights into the mechanics of the Islamic voluntary sector in the region. The term 'voluntary sector', for present purposes, is loosely defined to include areas which are sometimes listed under the government sector. Such an approach is not indefensible. As alluded to earlier, the Islamic voluntary sector in Southeast Asia has to play a wider role in the absence of Islamic states. The discussion includes *zakat*, in spite of the fact that it represents an *obligatory* levy. Although *zakat* is obligatory in a technical sense, it is practised in a *voluntary* fashion. Even in Malaysia, where *zakat* collection is state-organized, it is not administered in the same way in which government taxes are handled — which underscores the essentially voluntary nature of *zakat* contributions. Besides, the present volume is concerned with the role of the Islamic voluntary sector in resource mobilization for community development, and is not an exercise in sectoral analysis in a macro-economic framework which would call for a tightly defined sectoral approach. In the same vein, the present volume also includes a chapter on the Malaysian pilgrims' fund, although the latter does not involve charity; the contributions to the pilgrims' fund have not only helped the members perform their *hajj*, but also mobilized substantial savings and generated sizeable *zakat* payments from investment incomes.

The present volume consists of ten chapters. The rest of this volume is structured as follows. Chapter 2 by M.N. Siddiqi discusses the principles governing the functions of the Islamic voluntary sector in an abstract fashion, so as to provide the theological and theoretical underpinnings for the chapters that follow. In Chapter 3, an attempt is made by the editor of this volume to provide an overview of the Islamic voluntary sector in Southeast Asia in terms of resource mobilization. The Indonesian *zakat* experience is analysed by Taufik Abdullah in Chapter 4. Aidit Ghazali examines the Malaysian *zakat* administration in Chapter 5. *Waqf* management in Malaysia is discussed by Syed Othman Alhabshi in Chapter 6. Radiah Abdul Kader analyses the Malaysian experience in resource mobilization for pilgrimage in Chapter 7. Carmen Abubakar, in Chapter 8, addresses *zakat* and *sadaqah* practices in the southern Philippines. In Chapter 9, Amina Tyabji takes a hard look at the management of Muslim funds in Singapore. Finally, Chapter 10 presents a survey of *waqf* properties in Thailand by Preeda Prapertchob.

It will be noticed that no serious attempt has been made to standardize the transliterations of Arabic terms in this volume, as they tend to vary from country to country. This, however, does not give rise to conceptual discrepancies.

## 2 THE ROLE OF THE VOLUNTARY SECTOR IN ISLAM: A CONCEPTUAL FRAMEWORK

*Muhammad Nejatullah Siddiqi*

### Introduction

This chapter\* discusses the role of the voluntary sector in the fulfilment of material and other needs within the family and in the provision of public goods. It focuses on the five traditional expressions of voluntary actions on the part of the Muslims: family support, *zakat* (wealth tax), gifts and grants, social service, and charitable endowments. The doctrine of *fard kifaya* (socially obligatory duties) is invoked to place voluntary action in proper perspective. The chapter emphasizes the vast potential of the voluntary sector in contributing to the welfare of Muslim societies, especially in countries with Muslim minorities. Contemporary issues in the administration of *zakat* and *waqf* (charitable endowments) are also examined in the light of *Sharia* (Islamic law). Finally, some present trends and future possibilities in the development of the voluntary sector are noted with special reference to Islamic financial institutions.

### Islam's Emphasis on Voluntary Help

A Muslim individual should care for others — for their spiritual well-being, material welfare, individual needs, and their collective or social good. Indeed, helping others is a basic rule of conduct in Islamic living. This is how a Muslim is characterized in the Qur'an.

> And the believers, men and women, are protecting friends of one another; they enjoin the right and forbid the wrong.... (IX: 71)[1]

Lo! those who believed and left their homes and strove with their wealth and their lives for the cause of Allah and those who took them in and helped them, these are protecting friends of one another.... (VIII: 72)[2]

Those who entered the city and the faith before them love those who flee unto them for refuge and find in their breasts no need for that which hath been given them but prefer [the fugitives] above them though poverty become their lot. And whoso is saved from his own avarice — such are they who are successful. (LIX: 9)[3]

And [would assign] in all that they possessed a due share unto such as might ask [for help] and such as might suffer privation. (LI: 19)[4]

So give the kins man his due, and to the needy and to the wayfarer. That is for those who seek Allah's countenance. And such are successful. (XXIX: 38)[5]

True piety does not consist in turning your faces towards the east or the west — but truly pious is he who believes in God, and the Last Day and the angels and revelation and the prophets; and spends his substance — however much he himself may cherish it — upon his near of kin, and the orphans, and the needy, and the wayfarer and the beggars and for the freeing of human beings from bondage, and is constant in prayers, and renders the purifying dues and [fully pious are] they who keep their promises whenever they promise and are patient in misfortune and hardship and in time of peril; it is they that have proved themselves true and it is they who are conscious of God. (II: 177)[6]

## Disregard for the plight of others is the hallmark of the unbelievers.

And when it is said unto them: spend of that where with Allah hath provided you, those who disbelieve say unto those who believe, shall we feed those whom Allah, if He willed, would feed? You are in naught else that error manifest. (XXXVI: 47)[7]

Hast thou observed him who belieth religion? That is he who repelleth the orphan, And urgeth not the feeding of the needy .... (CVII: 1–3)[8]

Likewise the Prophet (peace be upon him) has also emphasized the charitable nature of Muslims:

"Believers are to one another like a building whose parts support one another." He then interlaced his fingers.[9]

I am witness to the fact that all servants [of Allah] are brethren to one another.[10]

Mankind are God's dependants so the most beloved of people in the sight of Allah are those who do good to His dependants.[11]

Most liked by Allah is the man who is most beneficent to the people in general. And the most liked act is that of pleasing a Muslim or relieving him of some grief, or paying off a debt incurred by him, or saving him from hunger....[12]

The Prophet (peace be upon him) once said, "Charity is obligatory on every Muslim." Asked if one has nothing to give in charity? He replied, "He should work with his hands, then enjoy the fruits of his labour and give [something out of] it in charity." Asked what if it is not possible for him to work, or if he does not work? He replied,

> "He should help a needy person in distress." Asked again what if even this he does
> not do? The Prophet replied, "He should advise others to do good." Asked what
> if he failed to do this also? The Prophet said, "He should refrain from doing harm
> to others for even this is a charity from him."[13]

It is clear in the light of the above verses from the Qur'an and the tradition from the Prophet that the charitable behaviour required of Muslim
individuals covers material support as well as spiritual and moral guidance,
both by way of promoting goodness and preventing what is harmful. In fact,
prevention of wrongdoing is specifically declared to be a duty of every
Muslim. The Prophet has said:

> Whoever sees evil should strive to eradicate it. If he can do so by force, he should
> use force. If that is not possible he should speak out against it. If that is also not
> possible for him, he should at least abhor it in his heart, and that is the least that
> faith demands.[14]

Thus, the scope of voluntary action is not confined to the supply of
economic goods and services only. It encompasses non-material needs as well.
Islam envisions a society in which individuals, while pursuing their self-interest,
also care for the interests of others and everyone helps everyone else materially
as well as morally so that all live a life that would please Allah. The redistributive and allocative roles of the voluntary sector in an Islamic society can
easily be gleaned through this vision, which incorporates new concerns of
social policy such as protection of the environment, supply of information,
and social cohesion.

**Voluntary Action**

What is the source of voluntary action in man? What motivates him to be
charitable? Though put on the sidelines by mainstream economics, a number
of economists, starting from Adam Smith, did address themselves to this question, coming up with various answers.[15] It has been argued that voluntary
action is born out of man's awareness of mutual interdependence. Self-interest
itself urges one to help others in time of need. This explanation cannot,
however, cover all observed voluntary action and is based on too narrow a
concept of the 'economic man'. Non-selfish behaviour is an integral part of
human behaviour. Altruism defined as 'behaviour directed towards the benefit
of others at some cost to the self where no extrinsic or *intrinsic* benefit is the
primary intent of the behaviour'[16] is also part of the human nature along with
self-interest, especially after one has met his basic needs. More positive attitudes
towards helping others and far-reaching voluntary action comes from love

and from a sense of duty. Other motivating forces such as reputation and urge for recognition also play a significant role in eliciting voluntary action.

There is some truth in all these explanations, none of which need be interpreted so as to exclude the others. One must also add to the above list of motives, the religious motivation. i.e. seeking the pleasure of Allah and reward in the hereafter: one helps fellow human beings because one loves God and showing compassion to mankind is a channel to express one's love of God. It is not necessary for the purpose of our study to go into the details of this matter. It is necessary, however, to point out that social concern has been a fact of life in all human societies. It is only the economics textbooks that ignore it! But the scope and strength of it varies from culture to culture. Religious cultures promote charitable behaviour and voluntary action while secular cultures undermine it, depending on the degree of emphasis on materialism and individualism. As we have seen above, Islam has extolled charitable behaviour, giving it a central place in its scheme of living. Moreover it gives it a universal orientation and secure foundation by rooting it in a Muslim's pursuit of the pleasure of Allah.

A voluntary act is one proceeding from one's own choice or consent. It follows that all action in pursuance of Islamic teachings is voluntary action. This also applies to what is obligatory in *Sharia*, such as *zakat*, as one's profession of a faith is itself a voluntary action. Hence the voluntary activities of a Muslim include what is obligatory as well as what is recommended in Islam. The voluntary sector in an Islamic economy includes charitable activities, whether obligatory or recommended.

When an Islamic society is organized into a state where the *Sharia* is sovereign, obligatory charities such as *zakat* and *ushr*[17] are managed by the state. In a country where Muslims are a minority, or in countries with a majority Muslim population where *Sharia* is not implemented, there may be voluntary organizations managing these charities. Following the conceptual point made above, we will include all charitable activities in the voluntary sector, irrespective of the way they are organized and managed. This approach suits the contemporary reality in which the state's role in managing charities is minimal. It can also accommodate those periods of Islamic history in which the state played a more active role in this regard by keeping their management always separate from the administration of other state revenues,[18] in view of the religious nature of these charities.

### Role of the Voluntary Sector: Meeting Non-Material Needs

Despite some overlap due to expected reciprocity, the voluntary sector may be distinguished from the exchange economy where all action is based on some *quid pro quo* and where everything has a price. The exchange economy has also the distinctive feature of dealing only with measurables, because only measurable things can have a price expressible in terms of money, the medium of exchange. The voluntary sector is, sometimes, free of these constraints. There may not be a *quid pro quo* involved directly and immediately. The objects of voluntary action may not be measurable. They need not have a price. Given these characteristics, the voluntary sector has an essential role in human society, as the many needs of man (psychological, aesthetic, and spiritual) depend on non-measurables for their fulfilment. Love and affection, approval and appreciation, recognition and praise, contentment and a sense of fulfilment, courtesies, etc., are some of the non-material non-measurables for which man cares so much in life, especially after one has met his biological needs. These needs are generally met by services, not by physical goods. These services, unlike the goods and services in the exchange economy, are not always characterized by scarcity. They do not necessarily involve any transfer of scarce resources. Their production is often costless, as is the case with the smile on one's face which cheers up someone else. The satisfaction of the psychological, aesthetic, and spiritual needs of man through acts of goodness is an important function of the voluntary sector, contributing in no mean way to the sum total of human felicity.[19]

Even in the case of certain scarce goods, the voluntary sector performs better than the market. Human blood is a case in point. A voluntary donor has no incentive to lie about his blood being free of disease.[20]

When the voluntary sector is dealing with goods and services which do carry a price because of scarcity (e.g. charitable giving of food) the transfer takes place more efficiently than in the exchange sector. The cost of such a transfer to the givers as well as to the society is only the cost of the resources forgone in the exchange sector. The givers do not seek a profit, hence their cost curves include neither monopoly rents nor the normal profits included in the cost curves in the exchange sector. The givers seek the pleasure of Allah, reward in the life after death, and/or love of their fellow human beings (which, in itself, derives from their love for Allah). The supply curve of resources to be transferred in charity is therefore a decreasing function of the cost of the transferred resources in the exchange sector but it is lower and flatter than it would have been if the transfer was effected in the exchange sector. The same supply curve is also an increasing function of the faith of the givers in the pleasure of Allah and the reward in the hereafter and the love for fellow human beings. The stronger this faith the greater the supply at any given cost. This further depresses and flattens the supply curve. If the total amount of resources transferred on the basis of charity was to be effected through the exchange economy, two additional costs would have to be incurred. First, sufficient revenue would have to be mobilized through taxation, and this would involve costs of administering the tax. Secondly, cash grants would have to be made to the recipients which would involve further administrative costs.

It follows, therefore, that the transfer of any amount of scarce resources to the deserving recipients through charitable giving in the voluntary sector is more efficient than the transfer of the same amount of resources through the market using the tax-subsidy mechanism. It may be noted that the social cost of transfer would increase further, if the government is obliged to resort to borrowing or to increasing the money supply in order to finance its welfare schemes.

The amount of resources actually transferred to the poor at any particular time may not, however, meet all the needs of the poor. Sound social redistributive policy is, therefore, called for so that the role of the voluntary sector is maximized, with the remaining gap being filled by fiscal measures. This is exactly what Islam seeks to do. According to this view, the role of charity is to correct the distortion effected by the working of a competitive system in the distribution of income and wealth, caused by disparities in the initial resource endowments as well as by the malfunctioning of the competitive system. A further correction effected by public policies is needed, however, because of the failure of charity to eliminate poverty and undesirable disparities.

*Need Fulfilment within the Family*
The family is the premier voluntary institution which is responsible, among other things, for the production and consumption of many goods and services outside the exchange economy. It is here that children are born, nursed, raised, and have their biological needs satisfied. While the family draws upon the exchange economy for the material goods and services it needs, services rendered by the mother, the father, and by the other members are mixed with purchased goods and services in order to satisfy the various needs.

The fact that the services rendered by the family are largely missed by economic analysts should not deter us from realizing their crucial contribution to human welfare. Such a realization is necessary in order to appreciate the true nature and scope of the voluntary sector. The crucial point is: the family is not modelled on an exchange economy. It is a part of the voluntary sector. This view deepens our understanding of the family as well as of the voluntary sector.

*Supply of Public Goods*
The voluntary sector has an edge over both the private sector and the public sector in certain other areas, e.g. conflict resolution, information supply, and environmental protection. All three are in the nature of public goods which the market fails to provide or may not provide in the optimum way, on the basis of exchange alone. Public provision of these goods is costly and inefficient. The voluntary sector is better equipped, in these cases, to supply them

by virtue of its altruistic forces and its capacity to mobilize time, energy, and skill free of cost or at minimal cost.

A major source of conflict in the free enterprise system has been the relations between organized labour and management. The exchange economy model, based on atomistic competition, has no internal mechanism for resolving this conflict. Introducing the state into this model does not help, as the forces operating in the model tend to make the state an instrument of one party to the conflict. It requires a non-selfish, non-partisan approach to ensure industrial peace. Besides basic reforms in the organization of industry, such as replacing fixed wages by sharing,[21] labour participation in management, and introduction of democratic methods of decision making, voluntary arbitration and citizens' councils can play a significant role in this respect.

Economic decisions depend on information and the acquisition and processing of information absorb considerable resources. These costs increase with the size of the market.[22] The voluntary sector may not supplant the market, but it can reduce the costs of information if individuals and organizations are willing to volunteer information. Sometimes giving away needed information does not involve any cost to the giver while it benefits the receiver. Voluntary organizations may gather and disseminate information relating to products, prices, job opportunities, markets, etc., to the benefit of consumers, labour, entrepreneurs, etc., at minimum costs.

What applies to information costs also applies to the cost of monitoring. When the implementation of an economic decision involves co-operation or compliance by others, there is a need to monitor its implementation. Monitoring has a cost. But the need to monitor, and hence the cost, will be less the more those involved are morally committed to the cause for which the decision is taken. Since voluntary action presupposes moral commitment, it can be concluded that voluntary implementation of a decision reduces the monitoring cost to society, as compared with that of the private sector.

Pollution threatens man's natural environment and the industrial civilization is destroying the ecological balance. Market failure inhibits the private sector to do the needful while the public sector is constrained by lack of information and resources. The voluntary sector may be more efficient in terms of both prevention and remedy. Preventive and remedial measures relating to pollution can be considered an Islamic duty. In the first instance, a conscious Muslim would desist from creating pollution, as he is required not to harm others. Secondly, people in the neighbourhood would protest against policies destructive of the environment. Thirdly, when some remedial measures are to be taken, a sense of Islamic duty would counteract the selfish motive to 'free ride'. In fact, Islamic motivation would mobilize voluntary services for the preservation of a healthy environment. Islamic values persuade economic agents to sacrifice private advantage for the sake of public interest. The voluntary sector may, therefore, effectively supplement the public sector in protecting the environment.

This line of reasoning can also be extended to other public and quasi-public goods such as education, health, scientific research, etc. The voluntary sector is already playing an important role in these areas in advanced countries like the United States. In fact, these are some of the areas in which the voluntary sector has been very active in Muslim societies as well, as the brief historical survey below will show. The supply of public and quasi-public goods by the voluntary sector relieves the public sector of some responsibilities which it would otherwise have to shoulder, thereby preventing the public sector from becoming too large.

**Redistributive and Allocative Role of the Voluntary Sector**

The voluntary sector can play a major redistributive role by effecting a transfer of resources from the rich to the poor more efficiently than the state, as the costs of the transfer may be less and the identification of the needy (especially among relatives, in neighbourhoods, and at local levels) may be more accurate. As the following description of the traditional categories of voluntary action in an Islamic society demonstrates, a substantial redistribution is in fact envisaged through the voluntary sector in an Islamic society.

The recipients' marginal propensity to consume being presumably higher than those of the givers, the preferences of the (poor) recipients are also likely to differ from those of the (rich) givers. Most of the resources transferred voluntarily to the poor may be used for the fulfilment of basic needs, such as food, shelter, education, health, etc. The net impact of the transfer may, therefore, be an increase in the demand for essential goods and services. This implies a significant allocative role for the voluntary sector.

Sometimes the voluntary sector itself produces goods and services allocated directly to the needy. Consider, for example, the case of the person teaching, in his spare time, free of charge, the illiterate in the neighbourhood to read and write.

*Traditional Expressions of Voluntary Action*
Thus far, we have focused on the role of the voluntary sector in a wide sense. We shall now proceed to examine voluntary economic activities in an Islamic society in terms of certain familiar categories. This should not be taken to imply that the voluntary sector in an Islamic society is confined to certain traditional activities. On the contrary, these categories provide the means and a framework for a wider role of the voluntary sector in a modern Islamic society.

For the sake of convenience, voluntary activities in an Islamic society can be studied under the following five categories:

1.   Obligatory family support
2.   *Zakat, ushr,* and *sadaqah al fitr (fitrah)*
3.   Gifts and grants in cash, kind or usufruct
4.   Voluntary social service
5.   Charitable endowments (*waqf*)

A brief description of each is in order.

*Obligatory Family Support.* The basic institution in an Islamic society is the family. The economics of the family is built around the husband's obligation to support his wife financially irrespective of her financial condition. He is also obliged to support his minor children. The jurists are also unanimously of the view that every person is obliged to support his parents and his adult offspring, including the unmarried, divorced, or widowed daughter, in case they have no means to support themselves, provided he has the means to do so. This obligation extends to some other blood relations too, but the jurists differ on the details. The predominant view, however, is that the financial support of an indigent person devolves on those who would inherit from him if he dies leaving some property, and that this reponsibility is to be shared in the same proportions in which that inheritance would be shared.[23] To complete the picture, it may also be noted that, according to *Sharia*, the financial support of a person who has no one to support him devolves on the Islamic state.[24] Thus, the doctrine of obligatory maintenance allowances (*al nafaqat al wajibah*) provides for every indigent person in an Islamic society.

The first line of defence in the Islamic scheme of providing for the needy is the family. As we shall see below, *zakat, sadaqat* (voluntary charity), etc., buttress the defences further so that no human being goes without fulfilment of basic needs. As it stands, the above rule is designed to serve the purpose regardless of whether one is living in an Islamic state or is the citizen of a Muslim-minority country. It is interesting to note that the above rule relating to obligatory family support was recently invoked in the controversy arising from the famous Shah Bano case in India, resulting in its incorporation in the Muslim Personal Laws as enforced in that country.[25] It is significant to note that the role assigned to the Islamic state, as the source of support for an indigent person in the last resort, has been assigned by that legislation to the institution of *awqaf* (charitable endowments), in so far as the support of a divorced woman is concerned.[26]

In accordance with the conceptual point noted above, namely that fulfilment of religious obligations is to be considered as voluntary action, the system of obligatory maintenance allowances outlined above is an integral part of the voluntary sector in an Islamic society, notwithstanding any legal backing provided to it. Emphasis on this system and proper education of the community on this point can go a long way in increasing solidarity and cohesion in the institution of the family which would otherwise be threatened by the pervasive individualism and materialism of modern secular culture. The shrinkage of the family to the nuclear family in modern secular societies and its frequent break-up due to divorce have been partly responsible for transferring the social security system to the state. A large part of this system was traditionally taken care of by the extended family, at a much lower cost to society than that which state systems entail.

Zakat *and* ushr. *Zakat* concretizes the obligation towards others as analysed at the outset. It gives the right orientation to a Muslim's behaviour.

Every Muslim with some means − specified in the relevant rules − has to give away a certain portion of his possessions to those mentioned in the Qur'anic verse:

> The alms are for the poor and the needy, and those who collect them, and those whose hearts are to be reconciled, and to free the captives and the debtors, and for the cause of Allah, and [for] the wayfarer; a duty imposed by Allah. Allah is Knower, Wise. (IX: 60)[27]

The coverage of *zakat* is very wide. It can be summarized as follows:

1. Capital assets: grazing animals and stock in trade, i.e., all that is meant to be traded, including machinery, real estate, and shares and common stock.
2. Savings in cash, gold, and silver.
3. Current income in the form of agricultural produce, minerals, and marine products.

Provided one's holdings are above a specified threshold (*nisab*), which is different for different categories mentioned above, one's entire holdings (and not only what is above *nisab*) are liable to *zakat*. The rates applicable to animals are detailed in the relevant sources. The *zakat* rate for cash, gold and silver holdings, and stock in trade is 2.5 per cent. The rate applicable to agricultural produce is 10 per cent or 5 per cent, depending on whether it is irrigated by rain or by man-made means. Scholars differ as to the rate for minerals and marine products.[28] Opinions also differ regarding the *zakat* rate on honey and other wealth acquired from forests.[29]

*Zakat* is to be assessed annually except in the case of agricultural produce, mineral wealth, and marine products, which is to be paid as and when they accrue.

As the Qur'anic verse quoted above lays down, *zakat* is meant mainly for the poor. Some *zakat* can be spent, however, for meeting the cost of *zakat* administration. But the expenditure of *zakat* revenue "in the cause of Allah" and "for those whose hearts are to be reconciled" to Islam stands on a different footing. Here it is the defence and promotion of Islam that is in question. No strict rules are laid down for the distribution of *zakat* revenue over the specified heads of expenditure, leaving some room for discretion. But the first charge on *zakat* revenue from any unit of population — village, town, or region — is the needs of that unit. *Zakat* collected from a region may be transferred to another region only after meeting the needs of that region.[30] This rule implies that *ushr* revenue from the rural areas should preferably be devoted to removal of rural poverty. *Zakat* may be disbursed in cash or kind. There is no prescribed limit for what a single person or family may receive out of *zakat* during a year, but most of the scholars who raised this question agree that the entire annual expenses of a recipient may be met out of *zakat* funds,[31] if funds are available.

As the Qur'anic verse (IX: 103) provides, it is the prerogative of an Islamic state to collect *zakat* and *ushr*. *Zakat* was, in fact, collected and disbursed by the state in early Islamic history. However, from the time of Caliph Othman onwards assessment and payment of the *zakat* on non-apparent wealth, i.e., cash, gold, and silver, was left to individuals. But a Muslim's duty to pay *zakat* does not devolve on the existence of an Islamic state or the summons of a *zakat* collector. Like daily prayers and fasting in the month of Ramadhan, it is a Muslim's duty to assess and give away the *zakat* due on his possessions. Throughout Islamic history, conscientious Muslims have been fulfilling this obligation on their own as well as through religious and social organizations, when the state was not administering *zakat*. Besides providing the much needed help to the poor and supporting essential Islamic activities, this practice has been instrumental in maintaining solidarity in the community, especially in countries with Muslim minorities.

*Zakat* is collected and distributed by the state only in some Muslim countries.[32] In many other Muslim countries and countries with Muslim minorities there are numerous national, regional, or local organizations administering *zakat* on a voluntary basis. But a sizeable part of *zakat* is distributed by the *zakat* payers directly to the poor in the locality. As a result of these decentralized and *ad hoc* arrangements, there is no uniform policy on a number of issues relating to *zakat* administration which arise in the modern context. Some of these are noted below:

1.   Should the *zakat* funds lie idle while awaiting disbursement or can they be invested with a view to increasing the benefit eventually accruing to the recipients?

2.   Must *zakat* be transferred to its beneficiaries in cash or kind (in case it is collected in kind), or can it be given in the form of tools of trade,

agricultural equipment, etc., to help the working poor on a more durable basis?

3.  Can *zakat* funds be used for establishing and financing institutions that generate services, e.g. education, training, medical care, with the provision that only the poor get these services free of cost?
4.  Can *zakat* funds be used to give productive loans to the poor?
5.  Can *zakat* funds be used for the defence and promotion of Islam in the form of free distribution of Islamic literature, employing paid preachers, organizing conferences, etc.?
6.  Can *zakat* funds be used for building mosques and religious schools in Muslim-minority countries?

Most of the traditional scholars would not answer these questions in the affirmative. But some contemporary scholars have convincingly argued in favour of some of these policies.[33]

A policy of helping the able-bodied poor out of poverty and enabling them to earn their living is definitely desirable and *zakat* funds can play at the least a partial role in this respect, even while avoiding the expenditure policies which fail to gain a consensus of the *Sharia* scholars. The remaining part of the expenditure can be met out of voluntary charitable donations and general revenue of the state.

It is also important, especially in the case of countries with Muslim minorities, to adopt a model of *zakat* administration which responds to the diversity in local needs. A chain of local committees knit together under regional councils and ultimately guided by a representative body at the national level seems to be an appropriate model. One can draw upon the Pakistani experience[34] as well as suggestions made by some economists.[35]

Some of the recently established Islamic financial institutions are also collecting and distributing *zakat* (from the public in general and not only from their shareholders and depositors). In the absence of any proper evaluation of this very recent practice, which is confined to a few places only, it is difficult to comment on the appropriateness of this arrangement. On the one hand, these modern institutions are better equipped to handle the accounts and follow the guide-lines laid down for them as compared to the numerous voluntary organizations that are presently doing the job. On the other hand, the job fits ill with the main profit-making activities of these institutions. Some empirical studies are needed for a proper examination of this issue.

What is beyond controversy, however, is the need for a handy *zakat* manual to guide individual as well as institutional *zakat* payers in assessing their *zakat* liabilities and identifying optimal ways of allocating *zakat* funds.

**Sadaqah Al Fitr.** This refers to charity given on the conclusion of the month-long fasting in Ramadhan to ensure that no one suffers privation during the annual Id celebrations which immediately follow the last day of Ramadhan. Every Muslim of some means should pay, for himself as well as on behalf of his dependants. The *fitr* payment thus amounts to a poll tax. It is specified in terms of some staple food, e.g. wheat, barley, dates, the quantity to be given away being a little above 2 kg.[36] It should be handed over directly to the deserving poor as far as possible. Neither a postponement of payment to some future date nor a transfer to some other locality is desirable. Three out of the four main schools of Islamic law insist on the payment of this charity in kind, but the Hanafi school allows payment in cash and a number of contemporary scholars regard cash payments as being more convenient for both the givers and the recipients.[37]

Unlike *zakat*, *sadaqah al fitr* was not collected and distributed by the early Islamic states. Person-to-person transfers were easily possible in view of the comparatively smaller population living in a town or village. The multi-million metropolis of contemporary societies may sometimes defy this solution. The practice of voluntary organizations taking up the task of collecting and distributing this charity is now fairly widespread, without inviting disapproval from scholars.

The obligatory charities discussed above have the enormous potentialities for mobilizing a sizeable fund dedicated mainly to the eradication of poverty. It has been estimated that the annual yield of *zakat* in a Muslim country would be around 3 per cent of the gross domestic product.[38] The corresponding collection from Muslims living in countries with Muslim minorities would also be substantial. Even though the charity on the eve of the Id is modest in amount, more people are obliged to pay it, for themselves and on behalf of their dependants, than those who are liable to pay *zakat*. Given proper management, these charities can go a long way in alleviating suffering and eliminating privation.

*Recommended Charities.* Recommended charities are designed to fill any gap that obligatory charities may leave, in order to complete the task of need fulfilment. They may also take care of social needs not covered by *zakat* expenditures. No rates have been prescribed for non-obligatory charities. Nevertheless, there is a general consideration of vital importance which sets a *required* minimum at the social level: enough charities should be available to ensure the fulfilment of basic individual needs and essential social needs. This is the essence of the doctrine of *fard kifaya*, or socially obligatory duties. It is advisable, therefore, to have a brief digression into the nature and scope of *fard kifaya* before reviewing the remaining forms of charity.

Socially obligatory duties are those which the Law-Giver wants carried out, irrespective of who does them. Some must perform them so that the needful is done, lest all those who are capable of performing them become sinful. In other words, these duties are directed at ensuring common interests of a community of individuals, not devolving on particular individuals, so that if some perform them and the relevant purpose is served, others will be absolved of the responsibility.

No closed list of socially obligatory duties is handed down by *Sharia* even though a number of them have found specific mention. Any activity that is necessary for safeguarding the vital interests of the people relating to survival and Islamic living is to be considered a socially obligatory duty. Those specifically mentioned include need fulfilment, *da'wah* (communicating the message of Allah to mankind), enjoining right conduct and forbidding wrong (*al amr bi'l ma'ruf wa'l nahi 'an al munkar*), and physical and ideological defence of the community of Islam. Even the institution of a ruler to govern the community in accordance with *Sharia* (i.e. establishment of an Islamic state) is a *fard kifaya*.[39] For Muslims living under Islamic rule, the state becomes the discharger of socially obligatory duties, in the last resort. In the absence of such a state, alternative arrangements are necessary to protect the vital interests of the community. The nature of the voluntary sector in a Muslim society that is deprived of Islamic rule has to be studied in this perspective. This is especially important in the case of countries with Muslim minorities where Islamic rule is not feasible. It is only the voluntary sector that can protect these interests. In other words, the Islamic voluntary sector in a society with a minority of Muslims has to discharge many religious and welfare functions which are, in normal circumstances, discharged by the Islamic state.

It is the community's awareness of this crucial fact that has led to the emergence, throughout Islamic history, of revivalist movements, institutions for religious education, and community courts for settling disputes according to *Sharia* (in particular, disputes relating to marriage, divorce, guardianship, etc.).

What is the significance of regarding all these activities as socially obligatory duties? Two points may be noted in response to this query. Firstly, the sense of a religious duty ensures that the relevant activity will take place even though neither self-interest nor coercive power of the state is there to ensure it. This point is of special importance for the Muslim minorities. Secondly, the nature of *fard kifaya* requires vigilance on the part of every individual who is capable of performing it. Even when such an individual is in no position to perform a socially obligatory duty, he must observe whether the needful is being done by some other individuals so that he is, ultimately, absolved of *his* religious obligations.

The care for social interest as distinguished from self-interest is the most significant dimension to the doctrine of *fard kifaya*. The vigilance on the part of every individual possessing the ability to perform a particular duty, and the awareness of its being a *religious* duty, raises the chances of that duty being performed, to put it mildly.

*Gifts and Grants.* Unilateral transfers in cash or kind have been the main expression of charitable behaviour throughout history. Such acts of charity may benefit a relative, a friend, a neighbour, a needy person who asks for it, or a needy person to whom the giver himself reaches out. Charity may go to a social institution like an orphanage, a school, a hospital, a rest-room for the wayfarer, or to an organization propagating religion. It may sometimes go to the state in response to an appeal for funds in an emergency caused by war, famine, flood, epidemics, etc. Greatly encouraged by Islam, charitable giving has been widely practised in Muslim societies.

Since Islam prohibits charging interest on loans, lending is also a charitable act. The Prophet (peace be upon him) has said "every loan is a charity".[40] So is lending durable articles of use, e.g. utensils, vehicles, equipment. Refusal to do so has been characterized by the Qur'an as characteristic of the un-believers (C VII: 7). The Prophet has also recommended exchange of gifts as it contributes to mutual love and affection. He has said:

> Shake hands, it will remove rancour, and make gifts to one another [as a result] you will love each other and it will remove malice.[41]

One can also give away some part of one's legacy in charity. The Islamic laws of inheritance call for a fair distribution of what a deceased person has left among his nearest relatives. Under Islamic laws, one's will cannot modify this distribution as no will can be made in favour of an heir. The permission to will away up to a third of the legacy is designed to provide for charities as well as for distant relatives not covered by the law in a particular case. This provision has been widely utilized for making bequests for charitable purposes. Every Muslim is expected to take due notice of the Prophet's remark that:

> When a man dies his [good] deeds stop, except through three [channels]: A charity which continues [giving its benefits] or knowledge that can be utilized or an off-spring with good conduct who prays for him.[42]

*Social Service.* Services rendered free of charge to meet individual needs or promote social welfare are also an important form of charity. Participating in a literary drive, planting trees, building a dam, and volunteering to defend the community against external aggression are some of the myriad forms such charity might take. Spending one's spare time in social service adds to the sum total of human welfare at little or no cost to society. Islam has urged its followers to volunteer for these services. At the same time it wants them to distribute their energies wisely between various kinds of social needs, e.g. between defence and (religious) education.

> ... it is not desirable that all of the believers take the field [in time of war]. From within every group in their midst, some shall refrain from going forth to war, and shall devote themselves [instead] to acquiring deep knowledge of the Faith, and

[thus be able to] teach their home coming brethren, so that these [too] might guard themselves against evil. (IX: 122)[43]

*Endowments.* The emphasis Islam places on contributing to the good of society has prompted wealthy Muslims to go beyond *ad hoc* charity to making permanent provisions for supporting welfare activities. Some of them have made special arrangements whereby property is dedicated to a cause so that only the income flowing from it is available for current expenditure in that cause. This is referred to as *waqf* (endowments).

> It is reported that the son of Umar — may Allah be pleased with both of them — said, "Some land in Khaybar fell to the lot of Umar." He came to the Prophet, peace be upon him, and said, "I got a land such as I never had a property better than it, so what do you advise me regarding it?" The Prophet said, "If you wish you can give it away in charity detaining its corpus." So Umar gave it away in charity providing that its corpus may neither be sold nor gifted nor could it be inherited. It would be meant for the poor, the relatives, for freeing slaves, for the cause of Allah, for guests and for the wayfarer. It would be permissible for its custodian to eat out of it according to convention or feed a friend, without making it a source of personal wealth.[44]

## The Voluntary Sector in Islamic History

The various forms of charitable giving, seen in the broad perspective of socially obligatory duties (*fard kifaya*), provide a very wide scope for the voluntary sector in an Islamic society. They reinforce the vision that an Islamic society is a co-operative affair in which every individual, once he has ensured the fulfilment of his own needs through his own labour and inherited wealth, if any, volunteers to take care of the needs of other fellow humans and of the social and collective needs according to his capacity. This is evidenced in Islamic history, especially in its early golden period. It will, therefore, be instructive to have a look at the voluntary sector through Islamic history before we proceed to examine its contemporary status.

Both voluntary services and voluntary charity in cash or kind played a big role in Medina during the time of the Prophet (peace be upon him). The Medina mosque, named after the Prophet, was costructed by voluntary labour. Muslim residents of Medina accommodated the migrants from Mecca (the *muhajirin*) and hosted them, even shared their properties with them, till they were able to find work and establish themselves.[45] Some of the earliest endowments in Islamic society were created in this period.[46] The numerous battles to ward off the attacking Meccans were all fought by volunteer forces. Thus, the entire fabric of the early Islamic society was built around voluntary services and charitable givings, till the public treasury (*Baitul Mal*) was established with permanent sources of income like *zakat*, *ushr*, and *kharaj* (land tax). The situation during the next thirty years of pious rule of the four great

Caliphs remained more or less the same although the relative prosperity during the latter half of this period might have reduced the need for private charity. Nevertheless, charitable endowments continued to be created.[47]

The role of the voluntary sector in the later periods of Islamic history has to be studied largely in terms of charitable endowments as no data are available for the other forms of voluntary activities, such as family support, *zakat*, grants, and social services. It can be safely assumed, however, that a society which produced a wide network of charitable endowments covering almost all social services and welfare activities must have responded warmly to individual needs for succour.

There are four aspects of *waqf* throughout Islamic history which call for attention: their purpose, the kinds of properties involved, their management, and the kind of supervision exercised by the courts or the government.

As regards the purposes for which charitable endowments were made (as distinguished from family endowments[48] which do not concern us in this study), almost all kinds of social services were involved. These included, to name a few, education at all levels, facilities for prayers and other religious rites, health facilities ranging from hospitals to homes for the disabled, parks, inns and rest-rooms, drinking water facilities, food distribution centres, and animal care centres.

As regards the types of properties involved, almost every kind of property capable of yielding an income flow or giving some benefits in use was endowed. Agricultural lands, residential buildings, schools, wells, baths, bakeries, godowns, etc., in various parts of the Islamic land were all dedicated by their owners to the needy. Islamic law also provides for endowing a sum of money, to be put in trust, so that its profits are given away as charity.[49]

The management of *waqf* properties was vested in a supervisor nominated by the donor and the *waqf* deed also stipulated who would succeed the supervisor.

In the early period, the state did not have a clearly defined role *vis-à-vis* the *waqf* properties and their management, but the courts did look into any complaints relating to their mismanagement. In the later period, we find increasing state interference in *waqf* management owing to a number of causes, the chief one being widespread abuse of powers by *waqf* supervisors. Another reason for increased state intervention was the fact that *waqf* properties were exempt from taxes. This resulted in substantial loss of revenue to the state as more and more properties, especially agricultural land, were converted into *waqf*. This forced the state to take over some *waqf* properties, especially in times of financial crisis caused by wars.[50]

The Ottomans formed a Ministry of Waqf in 1840, establishing a tradition that continues in almost every Muslim country, as well as in some countries with Muslim minorities, such as India and the Philippines, in modern times.

*Some Special Features of* Waqf

*Waqf* properties have some special features distinguishing them from private and public properties. While these features confer some benefits on society which cannot be derived from private or public properties, they also pose some problems that need solution.

*Waqf* takes a property out of individual ownership, vesting the ownership in Allah. A *waqf* property is not a state property just as it is not a private property. *Waqf* is permanent and irrevocable, hence the act of endowment is irreversible. With the passage of time, private properties pass into the *waqf* sector but the reverse does not and cannot take place.

Since *waqf* is made by the rich and the society in general and the poor in particular benefit from the endowment, the above features serve to mitigate the ill effects of inequality in the distribution of wealth and income. Unlike the short-term impact of government budgetary policies, the institution of *waqf* over time counteracts the tendency towards concentration of wealth.

But problems arise as more and more properties, especially agricultural land and urban real estate, are turned into *waqf.* The urge to maximize the returns — the engine of growth in the private sector — has not been a prominent feature of *waqf* management. The *waqf* sector operates largely outside the competitive market, resulting in sluggishness and stagnation. As *waqf* properties are exempt from taxes, a growing *waqf* sector would reduce the fiscal resources of the state.

Another feature of *waqf* is the supremacy of the will of the *waqif* (the *waqf* maker) with respect to its purpose, beneficiaries, and management. In addition to the macro-economic problem noted above, this feature poses a number of problems at the micro-economic level.

Historically, tough problems were posed by the family *waqf,* which we do not propose to discuss in this chapter as it has been abolished in most places.[51] Moreover, it does not fall fully in the voluntary sector category as noted above. But, even in the case of charitable endowments, problems arise because sometimes the *waqif* defines the purposes very specifically and narrowly. As circumstances change, with the passage of time, some of these purposes may become redundant or even anti-social. In such a situation there is a need to subject the will of the *waqif* to the supremacy of public purpose (*maslaha 'amma*) and objectives of *Sharia* (*maqasid al sharia*). It will be recalled that even the exercise of individual ownership rights is subject to these overriding considerations. There is no reason why properties dedicated to social welfare should not be subject to the same considerations.

A *waqf* is normally managed by a custodian (*mutawalli*) named by the *waqif.* The *waqf* deed also provides for a successor to the custodian in the event of his death or incapacity, and how to deal with mismanagement. These provisions may not, however, be satisfactory or comprehensive enough, thereby inviting intervention by the courts or the state. The circumstances justifying intervention, as well as the scope of such intervention, have been discussed in the *fiqh* (jurisprudence) literature and enshrined in the *waqf* laws of various countries. Actual experience and new exigencies continue to necessitate fresh enactments. But there is an ever-present danger of appropriation of *waqf* properties by the state under one excuse or another. This has happened throughout history in Muslim countries and countries with Muslim minorities. Such state take-overs on a large scale have dampened the people's enthusiasm to create charitable endowments.

Thus the voluntary sector, especially *waqf*, has to be guarded against misappropriation by the state as well as mismanagement by individuals or organizations which manage the endowments. It is only vigilance on the part of the people in general that can ensure this. As regards mismanagement of endowments, corrective action may come from three directions: the public (especially the beneficiaries), the courts, and the state acting through its legislative and executive branches to streamline the laws and regulations governing *waqf* properties and implementing them meticulously.

In contemporary circumstances, a more serious threat comes from the tendency to incorporate *waqf* in the public sector, especially in countries with Muslim minorities. This threat can be countered only if the people have a clear perception of the need for, and distinctive role of, the *waqf* sector, justifying its separate existence. As noted above the Prophet (peace be upon him), when asked by Umar, did not advise him to give away his property (in this case a fertile land) to the state, even though he himself was the head of state. Instead, he advised Umar to make a *waqf*. This advice implies that the Prophet visualized a useful role for *waqf* alongside the public sector.

### Future Prospects

We have already noted the trend towards an increasing role of the state in the management of *waqf*. What about the role of *waqf* itself? It is not far-fetched to surmise that the role of *waqf* is likely to increase in the countries with Muslim minorities but not in the countries where the majority of the population is Muslim. The reason for a more active role for *waqf* in the former lies in the increasing Islamic awareness in these communities coupled with the realization that, with a state which is at best indifferent to their religion and to many of their special socio-economic needs, they have to use *waqf* for the fulfilment of these needs and for the protection and promotion of Islam. For historical reasons, the legitimacy of *waqf* and its role in the religious and social life of the community is well established and accepted by the (ruling) majority. On the other hand, increasing Islamic awareness makes Muslims in countries where they form a majority press their rulers to adopt more Islamic policies. There is no pressure on *waqf* as such, unless the rulers respond to the popular pressure by activating the *waqf*.

Apart from *waqf*, however, there is a greater recourse everywhere to voluntary action for the promotion of Islam and the improvement of socio-economic conditions of the community. Government failure (due to a lack of will as well as the sluggishness of the bureaucracy) and market failure (due to lack of motivation) draw more energies towards the voluntary sector to do the needful for the betterment of the *ummah*. We can, therefore, expect some improvement in *waqf* management and a greater mobilization of charities, regular as well as *ad hoc*. One can reasonably expect better facilities for offering prayers, increased publication and distribution of Islamic literature, and more educational institutions that include Islamic courses in the curricula. This would be more true of the Muslim communities living as minorities where one also notices a greater mobilization for the protection of Muslim personal laws, crucial for the cultural identity of the communities.

The emergence of Islamic financial institutions that operate without interest is an important development in the voluntary sector. It is a product of the community's urge to avoid interest while ensuring full participation in the modern exchange economy. Once such an institution is established it may also cater to some other socio-economic needs of the community, such as investment of (temporary) surpluses in charitable funds, (interest-free) loans to social and educational institutions, even collection and disbursement of charities. Its greater role lies in mobilizing savings by providing Islamically permissible avenues of investment and supplying needed capital to small businessmen in the community. Some modest beginning of the Islamic financial movement goes back to half a century earlier, but it came to the forefront only in the 1970s. Despite some stagnation at present, it has now reached many countries, including those in which Muslims are a minority, and includes banking institutions, investment companies, credit unions, and insurance companies.[52]

We may conclude this study on an optimistic note regarding the role of the voluntary sector in contemporary Muslim societies. It is venturing into some new areas and, at the same time, showing greater vigour in traditional spheres. In view of the conceptual framework presented in this chapter, one cannot miss the direct relationship between this renewed vigour of the voluntary sector and the ongoing Islamic resurgence. Thanks to this resurgence, one can look forward to increasing 'Islamization' of the economies in countries where the Muslims are a majority and an enlargement of the Islamic voluntary sector in countries where Muslims are a minority.

## NOTES

\*   The author gratefully acknowledges the comments made by Professors M. Anas Zarqa, Mohamed Ariff, and F.R. Faridi on an earlier draft of this chapter. Some insights provided by Professor Shamsher Ali at the workshop on 'Islam and the Economic Development of Southeast Asia: The Role of the Voluntary Sector', organized by the Institute of Southeast Asian Studies in Singapore, at which this chapter was presented as a paper, were very helpful in revising the work, for which I am grateful.

1   Muhammad M. Pickthal, *The Meaning of the Glorious Quran* (Mecca: The Muslim World League, 1977). In the parentheses following the Qur'anic verses Roman numerals indicate the number of the *sura* (chapter) while Arabic numerals indicate the number of the verse in the Qur'an.

2   Ibid.

3   Ibid.

4   Muhammad Asad, *The Message of the Quran* (London: 1980).

5   Pickthal, op. cit.

6   Asad, op. cit.

7   Pickthal, op. cit.

8   Ibid.

9   Muhammad bin Ismail al Bukhari, *Kitab al Salat, Bab Tashbik al Asabi' fi'l Masjid wa Ghairih.*

10   Abu Dawud, *Kitab al Salat, Bab ma yaqul al Rajul idha sallam.*

11   al Khatib al 'Umari, *Bab al Shafqah wa'l Rahmah 'ala'l Khalq.*

12   al Tabarani, *al Mu'jam al Saghir* (Delhi: Matba'ah Ansar, 1311H), p. 179.

13   Bukhari, *Kitab al Adab, Bab Kullu ma'ruf Sadaqah.*

14   Abu Dawud, *Kitab al Salat, Bab Khutba Yawm al 'Id.*

15   For a brief history see David Collard, *Altruism and Economy: A Study in Non-Selfish Behaviour* (Oxford: Martin Robertson, 1978), pp. 51–64 and Mark A. Lutz and Lenneth Lux, *The Challenge of Humanistic Economics* (Menlo Park, California: Benjamin/Cummings Publishing Company, 1979), pp. 28–58. Some answers to the above question may be found in these two sources, and also in *Altruism and Helping Behaviour: Personality and Development Perspective*, edited by J. Philippe Rushton and Richard M. Sorrentino (Hellsdale, New Jersey: Lawrence Elbaum Associates, 1981).

16   Rushton and Sorrentino (op. cit., p. 427). For an alternative definition, see Bela Balassa and Richard Nelson, eds. *Economic Progress, Private Values and Public Policy: Essays in Honour of William Fellner* (Amsterdam: 1977), p. 181.

17   *Ushr* is a variant of *zakat*: one-tenth of the produce of rain-irrigated land payable to state.

18    This lends further credence to our inclusion of religious obligations like *zakat* in the voluntary sector. As pointed out above, this inclusion is justified by the present reality in which obligatory charities are, generally speaking, not enforced by the state. Moreover, the classification adoped by us suits this study which focuses on the role of the voluntary sector as distinguished from the public sector and the private sector.

19    Hence the precious piece of Prophetic wisdom: "Do not regard as a petty thing any act of goodness, even meeting your brother with a cheerful face. " Narrated by Abu Dharr in Muslim, *Kitab al Birr wa'l Sadaqah, Bab istihbab Talaqat al wajh 'ind al Liqa'*.

20    Peker Singer, "Freedom and Utilities in the Distribution of Health Care" in *Market and Morals*, edited by Gerald Dovorkin, Gordon Bermant, and Peter G. Brown (Washington: Hampshire Publishing Company, 1977), p. 165.

21    Martin L. Weitzman, *The Share Economy* (Cambridge, Mass.: Harvard University Press, 1984).

22    Peter G. Elkan, *The New Model Economy* (New York: Pergamon Press, 1982), p. 65.

23    Ahmad Ibrahim Ibrahim, *Nizam al Nafaqat fi'l Shariah al Islamiyah* (1349H). Abd al Rahman al Jaz'iri, *Kitab al Fiqh 'ala al Madhahib al Arba'ah*. Vol. 3, *Mabahith al Nafaqat* (Cairo: Shirkah Fann al Tiba'ah).

24    Muhammad Nejatullah Siddiqi, "Guarantee of a Minimum Level of Living in an Islamic State" in *Distributive Justice and Need Fulfilment in an Islamic Economy*, edited by Munawar Iqbal (Islamabad: International Institute of Islamic Economics, 1986), pp. 254–57.

25    The Muslim Women (Protection of Rights on Divorce) Act, 1986. For its text see *Muslim India* (Delhi) IV, no. 40 (April 1986): 154–55.

26    *Muslim India*, ibid.

27    Pickthal, op. cit.

28    Yusuf al Qaradawi, *Fiqh al Zakah* (Beirut: 1981), pp. 432–56.

29    Ibid., pp. 425–31; M. Raquibuzzaman, *Some Administrative Aspects of Collection and Disbursement of Zakah* (Jeddah: Centre for Research in Islamic Economics, 1987).

30    al Qaradawi, op. cit., pp. 809–20.

31    Ibid., pp. 563–74.

32    See Rafiq al Misri's translation (with an introduction) of *The Zakat Manual* issued by the Central Zakat Administration of Pakistan, *Kitab al Zakah* (Jeddah: Centre for Research in Islamic Economics, 1984) pp. 9–83, for a review of the *zakat* laws in Pakistan, Sudan, Saudi Arabia, and Libya. Malaysia and Bangladesh also have state agencies for the collection and disbursement of *zakat*.

33    See, for example, the relevant sections of al Qaradawi (op. cit.); Syed Abul A'la al Mawdudi, *Fatawa al Zakah*, translated by Rafiq al Misri (Jeddah: Centre for Research in Islamic Economics, 1985); Raquibuzzaman (op. cit.); and Muhammad Abdul Qadir Abu Faris, *Infaq al Zakah fi'l Masalih al 'Ammah* (Amman: Dar al Furqan, 1983).

34   Central Zakat Administration, *The Zakat Manual* (Islamabad: Ministry of Finance, Government of Pakistan, 1982).

35   Raquibuzzaman, op. cit.

36   According to the Hanafi school the quantity of wheat to be given away is only half of this, i.e. a little above 1 kg, while in the case of barley, etc., it is a little above 2 kg.

37   al Qaradawi, op. cit., pp. 948–49.

38   Muhammad Anas al Zarqa, "Islamic Distributive Schemes" in *Distributive Justice and Need Fulfilment in an Islamic Economy*, edited by Munawar Iqbal (Islamabad: International Institute of Islamic Economics, 1986), p. 178.

39   al Mawardi, *al Ahkam al Sultaniyah* (1978), p. 5.

40   al Tabarani, op. cit., p. 80.

41   Malik bin Anas, *al Mu'atta. Kitab Husn al Khulq, Bab Ma Ja'fi'l Muhajarah.*

42   Muhammad bin Isma'il al Bukhari, *al Adab al Mufrad, Bab birr al walidain* (Beirut: Dar Maktabah al Hayat, 1980), p. 15.

43   Asad, op. cit.

44   Muhammad bin Isma'il al Bukhari, *al Jami' al Sahih. Kitab al Wasaya.*

45   Ahmad bin Yahya bin Jabir al Baladhuri, *Ansab al Ashraf* vol. 1 (Cairo: Dar al Ma'arif, 1959), p. 270.

46   For details, see Mustafa al Zarqa, *Ahkam al Waqf* vol. 1 (Matba'ah al Jami'ah al Suriyah, 1947), pp. 7–11.

47   For legal rules relating to *waqf* as well as for some historical details see Muhammad Muhammad Amin, *al Awqaf Wa'l Hiyat al Ijtima'iyah fi Misr* (Cairo: Dar al Nahdhah al 'Arabi'yah, 1980); Muhammad al Habib al Tajkani, *Nizam al Tabarru'at fi'l Shari'ah al Islamiyah* (Casablanca: Dar al Nashr al Maghribiyah, 1983); al Khatib al 'Umari, *Mishkat al Masabih*; Muhammad 'Ubaid Abdullah al Kubaisi, *Ahkam al Waqf fi'l Shari'ah al Islamiyah* 2 vols. (Baghdad: Matba'ah al Irshad, 1977).

48   It may be noted, however, that the family endowments too have a clause rendering them into a charity in case none of the descendants survives (al Kubaisi, op. cit., vol. 1, p. 43).

49   al Zarqa, op. cit., p. 49.

50   al Kubaisi, op. cit., vol. 1, p. 45; Amin, op. cit., pp. 276–320.

51   al Kubaisi, op. cit., vol. 1, pp. 47–50.

52   For details see Muhammad Nejatullah Siddiqi, "Islamic Banking: Theory and Practice" in *Islam and the Economic Development of Southeast Asia: Islamic Banking in Southeast Asia* edited by Mohamed Ariff (Singapore: Institute of Southeast Asian Studies, 1988), pp. 34–66.

**REFERENCES**

Abu Dawud. *Sunan.*

Abu Faris, Muhammad Abdul Qadir. *Infaq al Zakah fi'l Masalih al 'Ammah.* Amman: Dar al Furqan, 1983.

Amin, Muhammad Muhammad. *al Awqaf Wa'l Hiyat al Ijtima'iyah fi Misr.* Cairo: Dar al Nahdhah al 'Arabi'yah, 1980.

Asad, Muhammad. *The Message of the Quran.* London: 1980.

al Baladhuri, Ahmad bin Yahya bin Jabir. *Ansab al Ashraf.* Cairo: Dar al Ma'arif, 1959.

Balassa, Bela, and Richard Nelson, eds. *Economic Progress, Private Values and Public Policy: Essays in Honour of William Fellner.* Amsterdam: 1977.

al Bukhari, Muhammad bin Isma'il. *al Jami' al Sahih.*

_____. *al Adab al Mufrad.* Beirut: Dar Maktabah al Hayat, 1980.

Central Zakat Administration. *The Zakat Manual.* Islamabad: Ministry of Finance, 1982.

Collard, David. *Altruism and Economy: A Study in Non-Selfish Behaviour.* Oxford: Martin Robertson, 1978.

Elkan, Peter G. *The New Model Economy.* New York: Pergamon Press, 1982.

Ibn Maja. *Sunan.*

Ibrahim, Ahmad Ibrahim. *Nizam al Nafaqat fi'l Shariah al Islamiyah,* 1349H.

al Jaz'iri, Abd al Rahman. *Kitab al Fiqh 'ala al Madhahib al Arba'ah.* Egypt: Shirkah Fann al Tiba'ah.

al Khatib, Ahmad Ali. *al Waqf wa'l Wasaya.* Baghdad: Matba'a Jamiah Baghdad, 1978.

al Khatib al 'Umari. *Mishkat al Masabih.*

al Kubaisi, Muhammad 'Ubaid Abdullah. *Ahkam al Waqf fi'l Shari'ah al Islamiyah.* 2 vols. Baghdad: Matba'ah al Irshad, 1977.

Lutz, Mark A., and Lenneth Lux. *The Challenge of Humanistic Economics.* Menlo Park, California: Benjamin/Cummings Publishing Company, 1979.

Malik bin Anas. *al Mu'atta.*

al Mawardi. *al Ahkam al Sultaniyah,* 1978.

al Mawdudi, Syed Abul A'la. *Fatawa al Zakah*. Translated by Rafiq al Misri. Jeddah: Centre for Research in Islamic Economics, 1985.

al Misri, Rafiq. *Kitab al Zakah*. Translation of *The Zakat Manual* issued by the Central Zakat Administration, Pakistan, with an introduction. Jeddah: Centre for Research in Islamic Economics, 1984.

Pickthal, Muhammad M. *The Meaning of the Glorious Quran*. Mecca: The Muslim World League, 1977.

al Qaradawi, Yusuf. *Fiqh al Zakah*. Beirut: 1981.

Raquibuzzaman, M. *Some Administrative Aspects of Collection and Disbursement of Zakah*. Jeddah: Centre for Research in Islamic Economics, 1987.

Rushton, J. Philippe, and Richard M. Sorrentino, eds. *Altruism and Helping Behaviour: Personality and Development Perspective*. Hellsdale, New Jersey: Lawrence Elbaum Associates, 1981.

Shahabuddin, Syed, ed. *Muslim India* IV, no. 40 (April 1986).

Siddiqi, Muhammad Nejatullah. "Guarantee of a Minimum Level of Living in an Islamic State". In *Distributive Justice and Need Fulfilment in an Islamic Economy*, edited by Munawar Iqbal. Islamabad: International Institute of Islamic Economics, 1986.

_____. "Islamic Banking: Theory and Practice". In *Islam and the Economic Development of Southeast Asia: Islamic Banking in Southeast Asia*, edited by Mohamed Ariff. Singapore: Institute of Southeast Asian Studies, 1988.

Singer, Peker. "Freedom and Utilities in the Distribution of Health Care". In *Market and Morals*, edited by Gerald Dovorkin, Gordon Bermant, and Peter G. Brown. Washington: Hampshire Publishing Company, 1977.

al Tabarani. *al Mu'jam al Saghir*. Delhi: Matba'ah Ansar, 1311H.

al Tajkani, Muhammad al Habib. *Nizam al Tabarru'at fi'l Shari'ah al Islamiyah*. Casablanca: Dar al Nashr al Maghribiyah, 1983.

Weitzman, Martin L. *The Share Economy*. Cambridge, Mass.: Harvard University Press, 1984.

al Zarqa, Muhammad Anas. "Islamic Distributive Schemes". In *Distributive Justice and Need Fulfilment in an Islamic Economy*, edited by Munawar Iqbal. Islamabad: International Institute of Islamic Economics, 1986.

al Zarqa, Mustafa. *Ahkam al Waqf* 1, Matba'ah al Jami'ah al Suriyah, 1947.

# 3 RESOURCE MOBILIZATION THROUGH THE ISLAMIC VOLUNTARY SECTOR IN SOUTHEAST ASIA

*Mohamed Ariff*

## Introduction

The Islamic voluntary sector, both in theory and in practice, plays an important role in Muslim societies. Islam, as a religion, lays considerable stress on the need for voluntary deeds, as a way of life, and spells out the basic principles governing such voluntary actions. The institutions of *zakat, fitrah, sadaqah,* and *waqf* have contributed significantly to the preservation of the religion of Islam and the economic well-being of the *ummah.*

The Islamic economic system is clearly egalitarian in the sense that the haves are urged to share their wealth with the have-nots. The primary function of the Islamic voluntary sector is, therefore, to bring about an equitable distribution of income and wealth. This role may be performed in a number of ways: it may be effected through direct unilateral transfers from the rich to the poor; it may take the form of welfare projects and community development programmes that would benefit all, especially the poor; or it may be in the form of aid schemes that would enable the poor to be economically more self-reliant.

Although there has been considerable debate with regards to the superiority of one mode of operation over another, there is little basis to be dogmatic about this, since much would depend on actual circumstances. Thus, for instance, in societies where abject poverty prevails, direct resource transfers for consumption purposes would make considerable sense. In reality, more often than not, situations call for a multi-pronged approach so that the problems of poverty and underdevelopment can be attacked from all angles. Be that as it may, there is little doubt that the presence of the voluntary sector in whatever form tends to have an ameliorating effect.

The Islamic voluntary sector is expected to assume greater responsibilities in countries where the political set-up is secular or non-Islamic, especially where Muslims constitute a minority. Certain social functions which were traditionally performed by Islamic states in the past will now have to be performed by the Islamic voluntary sector. To put it differently, the Muslims in such societies will have to fend for themselves through voluntary arrangements.

Southeast Asia represents a region of considerable diversity. In Malaysia, where Islam is the state religion, Muslims account for only a little more than one-half of the population. In Indonesia, where Muslims form about 95 per cent of the population, the political ideology is unambiguously non-Islamic. In the Philippines, Singapore, and Thailand, Muslims represent minority groups. In the oil-rich sultanate of Brunei, the Muslims live under the patronage of the Sultan, who is guided by Islamic principles although the sultanate is not, in the strict sense of the term, an Islamic state. It is in societies such as these that the Islamic voluntary sector has a vital and meaningful role to play.

The main concern of this chapter, however, revolves around the question of resource mobilization through the Islamic voluntary sector rather than the Islamic voluntary sector *per se*. This chapter draws heavily, but not exclusively, on the various country studies contained in this volume. In the following sections, an attempt is made to assess the role of Southeast Asia's Islamic voluntary sector in terms of resource mobilization, with a particular focus on the sector's scope and limitations.

## Zakat

*Zakat* is an obligatory tax on Muslims who are above the *nisab*.[1] The religious significance of *zakat* can hardly be overemphasized, as *zakat* has been equated with *salat* (worship) itself. Most Muslims are conscious of this obligation and do pay their *zakat* annually. In an Islamic state, *zakat* must represent a major fiscal instrument and it is the duty of the state to collect and distribute *zakat* as prescribed in *fiqh* (Islamic jurisprudence based on the Qur'an and the Sunnah, or Traditions). In the Southeast Asian context, the collection and the distribution of *zakat* are carried out in the voluntary sector.

Except for Malaysia, there has been scarcely any direct government involvement in the mobilization of *zakat* funds in the Southeast Asian region. Even in Malaysia, the government involvement in *zakat* administration is somewhat partial or incomplete in the sense that it is relegated to the various states under the federal structure and that it is not strictly enforced. Ironically,

Indonesia, the largest Muslim country in the world, does not have a government machinery for the collection and distribution of *zakat*. The informal nature of the *zakat* operation is even more pronounced in countries where Muslims are scattered about or constitute a minority.

The Indonesian dilemma was clearly manifested in the move by President Soeharto (who had offered his services as a Muslim private citizen but not as the Head of State) to be the provisional *amil* (collector) for *zakat* funds in the country in October 1968. It was impossible for President Soeharto, as the Head of State, to act as the *amil* for *zakat* purposes under the *Pancasila* ideology which makes a clear distinction between state and religion.

In Indonesia, and indeed elsewhere in the region, *zakat* has traditionally been treated as a personal matter between the *muzaki* (*zakat* payer) and the *mustahiq* (recipient). The former is at liberty to determine his own *zakat* and pay to whom he wills and it is up to the recipient to use the fund any way he deems fit. More often than not, it is the functionaries in mosques who receive *zakat* and who may or may not share it with others. To be sure, such practices may not be strictly in accordance with *fiqh* requirements, which stipulate not only the sources of *zakat* and the rates of *zakat* but also the legitimate uses of *zakat*. It would be wrong for the *amil* to keep all the *zakat* for himself, although the *amil* is among the eight *asnaf* (legitimate recipients).

The role of the *amil* is that of an agent who collects *zakat* and distributes it on behalf of the *muzaki*, and the *amil* is entitled to a portion of the proceeds as a fee for his services. The *amil* may be a person or an organization. In some cases, however, where the *muzaki* himself identifies the recipients and distributes his *zakat* directly to the various *asnaf*, the role of the *amil* is done away with.

A more impersonal system of *zakat* collection and distribution has surfaced in modern times, with the emergence of *zakat* organizations or institutions. These organizations act not as agents but as recipients. This, in fact, is a case of the *asnaf* organizing themselves into institutions so that they can collect and use the *zakat* in accordance with their stated objectives. Thus, in Southeast Asia, especially Indonesia, many organizations have come into existence in recent years to tap the *zakat* sources. These organizations, more often than not, represent community efforts to mobilize *zakat* funds for the common good of all. These organizations include welfare associations, educational institutions, and orphanages. It is not, therefore, surprising that in Indonesia, as indeed elsewhere, many *madrasah* or religious schools are financed out of *zakat* contributions.

Many of these local organizations are branches of national Islamic organizations such as the Muhammadiyah or the Nahdlatul Ulama. These voluntary institutions compete not only with the traditional recipients of *zakat*, i.e., the religious functionaries, but also among themselves for *zakat* funds. The competition is often on the basis of the quality of the programmes they put up or plan to launch, and on the basis of their track record. Thus, these voluntary bodies compete with one another by putting up meritorious programmes which would appeal to the *muzaki*. The projects mounted by these voluntary organizations range from missionary activities to the construction of modern hospitals. In Indonesia, the Jakarta-based At-Thahiriyah and Asy-Syafiiyah are among the major recipients of *zakat* funds. It is, however, important to mention that these organizations tap not only *zakat* but also other voluntary sources of funding.

Among the new players in the *zakat* arena in Indonesia are the semi-governmental agencies. The pioneer agency, called Badan Amil Zakat (BAZ), was established in Jakarta in 1968. It was renamed Badan Amil Zakat, Infaq dan Sadaqah (BAZIS) in 1973, when the scope of the agency was extended beyond the collection of *zakat*. In the 1970s, several provinces in Indonesia followed suit and established their own BAZIS institutions. Thus, East Kalimantan established its BAZIS in 1972, followed by several others, including West Sumatra in 1973, West Java and South Kalimantan in 1974, and North Sulawesi and South Sulawesi in 1985. The BAZIS administrative structure has the governor as the general chairman who is assisted by an executive chairman, and a board of advisers (*Badan Pembina*). Each of the provincial BAZIS has basically three tiers — at regency (*kabupaten*), district (*kecamatan*), and village (*kelurahan*) levels.

A more recent development on the *zakat* horizon in Indonesia is the emergence of corporate-sponsored *zakat* agencies. This phenomenon is directly attributable to the re-interpretation of *zakat* to encompass not only the wealth but also the incomes and salaries of Muslim employees. The pioneering effort in this direction was undertaken by the Badak LNG Company in East Kalimantan in 1987. It is of interest to note that in just two months (January and February 1987) the *zakat* committee of Badak LNG Company collected Rp 12 million from about 300 employees who accounted for over one-fourth of the Muslim work force in the company.[2]

The collection of *zakat* on salaries, now referred to as *zakat profesi* in Indonesia, is catching on, with more and more private companies forming their own *zakat* outlets. In this regard, it is interesting to observe that most of the state banks in Banjarmasin (West Kalimantan) have made independent arrangements for the collection of *zakat profesi* from their employees.

In Malaysia, the administration of *zakat* has been institutionalized at the state level. The Heads of States, i.e., the sultans, act also as the heads of Islam in their respective states. In the case of those states without sultans, such as Melaka and the Federal Territory, the national ruler acts as head of Islam. Under the Malaysian Constitution, all matters relating to Islam are within the jurisdiction of the state rulers. Accordingly, *zakat* administration is the responsibility of individual states. *Zakat* is administered by the various State Councils of Religion, except in the case of Kedah where a separate *zakat* office exists. The council in each case represents a state statutory body. Some councils are self-financing while others receive state assistance in the form of annual financing contributions to defray the administrative costs and/or secondment of manpower on the state payrolls. It is, however, pertinent to note that *zakat* is not institutionalized at the national or federal level in Malaysia. Nor has there been any inter-state co-ordination or synchronization of *zakat* administration in the country.

Nonetheless, the modalities for *zakat* collection are pretty much the same across the states, with the *muzaki* paying his *zakat* through the appointed *amil* or through the office of the Council of Religion. However, there are interesting variations. Thus, for example, in Kelantan, an *amil* can only collect certain types of *zakat*, such as *zakat* on cereals (which actually represents *ushr*), while *zakat* on wealth (*zakat al-mal*) is payable through the office of the council.

Most states have *zakat* laws covering *zakat* collection and distribution. Under these laws, it is an offence not to pay *zakat* or to pay *zakat* through unofficial means (with some exceptions), the penalty for which includes a fine and/or imprisonment. However, we must hasten to add that not all state enactments on Islamic affairs are explicit on *zakat* matters and that *zakat* laws are not enforced to the same degree in all the states. In some states, *zakat* regulations are not even gazetted, which means that no legal action can be taken against the violators. In some other states, such as Trengganu, no *zakat* regulations exist.

The main sources of *zakat* revenue are padi farming (*ushr*), wealth, and commerce. In some states, *zakat* on wealth (e.g. Negeri Sembilan) and *zakat* on livestock (e.g. Johor) are also collected. It is interesting to note in this regard that Kedah is the only state where official *zakat* collection is limited to *zakat* on padi, which seems extremely unjust in view of the fact that padi farmers are not among the well-to-do segments of Muslim society in Malaysia.

In the Philippines, the system for *zakat* collection seems to be in complete disarray. During the period of the sultanate, in the southern Philippines, *zakat* administration was under the direct jurisdiction of the chief *santili* who was a member of the sultan's council. The chief *santili* appointed the *amil* to collect *zakat* and other voluntary contributions from the Muslims. With the abolition of the sultanate, the systematic collection of *zakat* had come to an abrupt end in the Philippines. *Zakat* is now collected by the *pakil* (religious functionaries)[3] in a haphazard or *ad hoc* manner. During the height of the Mindanao conflict in the 1970s, all *zakat* and Muslim voluntary contributions were collected by the Moro National Liberation Front (MNLF) Committee on Religious Affairs. With the Moro secessionist movement losing its momentum, the collection of *zakat* has reverted largely to the religious functionaries in the mosques, although in some areas collection through the MNLF still exists.

However, there are sporadic cases of organized *zakat* collection in the southern Philippines. An outstanding example of organized *zakat* collection is provided by the Cotabato Islamic Foundation, Inc. (CIFI) which has been collecting *zakat* and donations from among the Maguindanaos[4] since 1982. Likewise, the Jamia Mindanao al-Islamie has been collecting *zakat* and other contributions in an organized manner from among the Maranaos.[5] Similar organizations which merit special mention include the Lambayung Jamiyat Al Abidin and the Kasulutan Muslimin Parhimpunan. In Jolo, however, no such formal set-ups exist.

There are no *zakat* laws in the Philippines. An attempt to institutionalize *zakat* within the framework of Muslim personal laws was aborted in 1973 by the government which suspected that *zakat* funds might be diverted to the MNLF. However, there is a provision in Article 164 of the Code of Muslim Personal Laws of the Philippines for an office of the Jurisconsult which would be under the administrative supervision of the Supreme Court of the Philippines. In addition, there are local chapters of Darul Ifta operating in Mindanao and Sulu which are run by Moro graduates from Al-Azhar University (in Egypt) and University of Medina (in Saudi Arabia). It is envisioned that these local chapters, together with the proposed office of the Jurisconsult, will be able to institutionalize *zakat* in the Philippines.

In Singapore, the institution of *zakat* is well organized, but *zakat* on wealth, or *zakat harta* as it is locally referred to, is not mandatory. Since 1968, the Majlis Ugama Islam Singapura (MUIS), which occupies the centre stage of Muslim affairs in the island republic, has been playing a key role in the mobilization of *zakat*. MUIS was set up under the Administration of Muslim Law Act (AMLA), Part IV of which deals with financial aspects pertaining to the creation of a *Baitul-Mal* or General Endowment Fund (Section 57) and the collection of religious dues, including *zakat* (Section 70).

All this, however, does not mean that the traditional channels for *zakat* payments are no longer open. It appears that sizeable amounts of *zakat* still flow directly from the *muzaki* to the *mustahiq* in Singapore, bypassing MUIS. For, legally, it is not an offence to pay *zakat* through unofficial or informal means. In Singapore, *zakat* does not include *ushr* as there is hardly any agricultural activity in the city state. The main sources of *zakat* are wealth and commerce. In recent years, the compulsory contributions to the Central Provident Fund (CPF) have become an important source of *zakat*, following a decree by the MUIS Fatwa Committee.

In Thailand, *zakat* collection has not been formally organized. There is no institution which specializes in *zakat* collection, although there are many institutions which are involved in the collection of *zakat*, among other funds.

In Thailand, the traditional system of direct *zakat* disbursement by the *muzaki* to the *mustahiq* still seems to dominate. To be sure, a centralized Zakat Fund does exist in the office of the Chularajamontri (Shaikh-ul-Islam), but most of the contributions to this fund come from foreign sources.[6] *Zakat* is absorbed by the provincial and local religious functionaries and the poor people. This means that very little *zakat* flows into the central Zakat Fund.

There are variations in the modes of *zakat* collection. The traditional avenues, referred to earlier, rely heavily on direct transfers from the *muzaki* to the *mustahiq*, often bypassing the *amil*. Where an *amil* is involved, he is entitled to a portion of the proceeds. In the traditional system, more often than not, it is the *asnaf* who seeks out the *muzaki* rather than the other way round. However, where the recipient is a religious institution like *masjid* (mosques) or *madrasah*, the *muzaki* usually takes the initiative to effect the transfer himself. This seems to be the general pattern throughout the region.

The emergence of voluntary, non-profit, welfare Muslim organizations in several Southeast Asian countries has led to the introduction of new techniques. In Indonesia, for example, voluntary organizations send blank money order forms to the potential *muzaki*, inviting them to send their contributions through money orders. Muslim welfare organizations in the voluntary sector compete with each other for *zakat* funds. This competition is often manifested in brochures or pamphlets which outline the various welfare projects that are being planned or in the pipeline. These brochures not only explain how the projects will benefit the community but also provide statements of accounts on a regular basis. Such communications through postal services are intensified particularly during the month of Ramadhan when the Muslims generally seem most willing to pay their *zakat* dues. Some organizations even go to the extent of providing manuals which will guide the *muzaki* in the estimation of *zakat* he owes.

In the case of semi-governmental efforts to mobilize *zakat* in Indonesia, it is interesting to observe some degree of specialization among the BAZIS, with the provincial BAZIS concentrating on big national corporations and central municipal offices, the district BAZIS going after medium-scale industries and businesses, and the village BAZIS focusing on petty traders. The BAZIS institutions, like the voluntary organizations, send appeal letters to the corporations or companies with forms to be filled by potential *zakat* payers who work in these outfits. It is of interest to note that the BAZIS of Jakarta charges the *hajj* pilgrims Rp 50,000–100,000 per person, on the ground that those who can afford to perform the *hajj* must be rich enough to pay *zakat*. However, in the case of the BAZIS of South Sulawesi, *zakat* collected from each pilgrim amounts to 2.5 per cent of the pilgrimage cost.

In Malaysia, as mentioned earlier, all *zakat* would be paid through the appointed *amil* and council offices, with the exception of Kedah and Kelantan.

Payment through the appointed *amil* or the *zakat* office is applicable in Kedah only in the case of *zakat* on padi, and all other forms of *zakat* are allowed to be paid through other means. By contrast, Kelantan requires only two-thirds of all *zakat* to be paid through the official channels, while the remaining one-third may be disbursed according to the *muzaki*'s own preferences. In practice, however, such legal requirements are not always adhered to, since the laws are by no means strictly enforced.

In Singapore, MUIS represents the only official channel through which *zakat* is paid, but payment is absolutely voluntary.

It is not clear how much *zakat* is collected in each country, since the bulk of it is disbursed through unofficial channels which cannot be monitored. It would also be hard for anyone to estimate the actual *zakat* flows in any of the Southeast Asian countries. For one thing, not all Muslims are required to pay *zakat*. For another, not all those who are obliged to do in fact pay *zakat*. Besides, the *zakat* paid may not cover all 'zakatable' assets. Nevertheless, it is readily obvious that official *zakat* statistics grossly understate the actual *zakat* flows in any society.

The distribution of *zakat* is confined to the eight *asnaf*, according to jurisprudence. The Qur'anic injunctions stipulate that the legitimate recipients of *zakat* are the following: the poor (*fuqra*), the indigent (*masakin*), the public agent (*amil*), new converts to Islam (*muallaf*), slaves (*riqab*), debtors (*gharimin*), the way of God (*fi-sabilillah*), and the wayfarers (*ibn-as-sabil*). The Qur'an, however, is silent on the share of each *asnaf*. The implication is that the distribution pattern should reflect local needs and circumstances.

In Indonesia, as indeed elsewhere in Southeast Asia, three categories, namely the *fuqra*, *masakin*, and *fi-sabilillah*, have accounted for the bulk of the *zakat* disbursements. This is so not only in the case of the traditional channels where the *muzaki* pays directly to the *mustahiq* but also in the case of payments through official or institutional channels. The question of the share of the *amil* does not arise in the former case since disbursement is effected directly. However, where *zakat* is paid through official or institutional channels, the share of the *amil* can be substantial. It has been reported that the *amil* category accounted for as much as 45 per cent of the *zakat* payments in the case of the BAZIS of Jakarta in 1972, although in recent times their share has fallen to just 10 per cent.[7] In Malaysia, however, the *amil* account for a much larger proportion, even exceeding the share of the poor and the indigent in some states.[8]

There has been an attempt in Indonesia to limit payments for consumption purposes. Instead, the poor have been urged to make use of *zakat* funds for productive purposes so that the problem of poverty can be effectively dealt with. The poor are given loans to help start small business ventures. But the rate of repayment has been dismally low.

The category of *fi-sabilillah* appears to be the most prominent of all *asnaf* in all Southeast Asian Muslim societies, not only because the Muslims attach a great deal of importance to expenditures in the 'way of God' (which includes allocations to mosques, *madrasah*, and missionary activities) but also because this category is broad enough to accommodate all projects which serve the *ummah* at large. Much of the allocations by MUIS in Singapore, in particular, fall under this category. Even in countries where no organized *zakat* collection takes place, such as the Philippines and Thailand, the bulk of the *zakat* through informal channels are meant for *fi-sabilillah*.

### Fitrah

*Fitrah* is a poll tax which every Muslim (except those who are absolutely destitute) is obliged to pay in the month of Ramadhan before Id celebrations. *Fitrah* is meant to be distributed to the poor. *Fitrah* is sometimes referred to as *zakat-al-fitr* or as *sadaqah-al-fitr*. But, strictly speaking, *fitrah* is neither *zakat* nor *sadaqah*. Like *zakat*, *fitrah* is obligatory, but *fitrah* is not governed by the principles of *zakat* with regard to sources, rates, and uses. The *fitrah* rate is equivalent to the money value of 1 kg of rice per person in Southeast Asian countries. Thus, it varies from place to place and from year to year. *Fitrah* resembles *sadaqah* only to the extent that it is meant for the poor, but *sadaqah* is non-obligatory or optional. *Fitrah* is specific to the month of Ramadhan and is associated with the Id celebrations, while *zakat* and *sadaqah* may be disbursed at any time of the year.

In Indonesia, there is no specialized organization or institution in charge of *fitrah* collection and distribution. The BAZIS institutions in the various provinces collect *fitrah* contributions as well. However, it appears that *fitrah* funds are not separated from the *zakat* fund by the BAZIS arrangements, since *fitrah* is regarded as another variant of *zakat*.

In Malaysia, too, *fitrah* is treated like *zakat*. In fact, the former accounts for a significant proportion of the official *zakat* fund. In Perlis, *fitrah* collections amount to about one-third of the *zakat* collected from padi farmers. *Fitrah* collection in Malaysia is more efficiently and effectively conducted than *zakat*. The reason is that *fitrah* represents an insubstantial amount per head and is paid willingly by the people through the *amil* in *masjid* and *surau* in the month of Ramadhan. It, however, appears that *fitrah* remains largely undistributed in Malaysia, apart from the share due to the *amil* for their services.

In the Philippines, the bulk of the *fitrah* (or *pitla* as it is called in the local dialect) is collected and kept by the local *masjid*. However, it is not uncommon for the religious functionaries, to whom *fitrah* is paid, to keep all of it for themselves. In Thailand, the Chularajamontri sends out appeals to the twenty-six chairmen of the Provincial Islamic Councils around the country in the month of Ramadhan, requesting them to mobilize *fitrah* in the *masjid* and to send the collection to the central Zakat Fund, but only a handful of the over 2,000 *masjid* in the country respond to the appeal because *fitrah* collections are hardly sufficient even to meet the local needs.

Singapore has one of the most efficient systems for *fitrah* collection. Prior to 1968, *fitrah* was collected in Singapore by the JAMIYAH, a Muslim missionary society founded in 1932. From 1968 onwards, *fitrah* collection has been centralized at MUIS. Since *fitrah* payments are statutory in Singapore, it is quite safe to assume that *fitrah* is paid by every Muslim in the city state year after year. However, *fitrah* is equated with *zakat* in Singapore in the sense that it is distributed like *zakat* on the *asnaf* basis. Substantial amounts are 'saved' each year.[9] There are indications that MUIS plans to use these 'savings' on the construction of a multipurpose religious centre and the building of mosques.

## Sadaqah

As alluded to earlier, *sadaqah* is a non-obligatory or optional payment that is totally at the discretion of the Muslims. *Sadaqah* thus refers to charity that is not subject to the rules governing *zakat*. In other words, the distribution of *sadaqah* is free from the *asnaf* constraints.

*Sadaqah* represents an important source of funds available to the Islamic voluntary sector, as Islam exhorts its followers to pay *sadaqah* as much as they can. Thus, theoretically, there is no absolute limit to *sadaqah* collections, unlike *zakat* or *fitrah*. Much would depend not only on the generosity and the economic capacity of the Muslims but also the ingenuity and capabilities of the voluntary organizations which mobilize *sadaqah*. The experiences of several organizations in Southeast Asia clearly show that the funds are not hard to come by, if one can only convince the public that it is meant for a worthy cause. In fact, as pointed out earlier, many voluntary organizations in Indonesia compete with each other on the basis of the quality of the programmes presented.

In Indonesia, *sadaqah* is collected by individuals, religious institutions, voluntary organizations, and semi-governmental agencies. It is impossible to know how much *sadaqah* is actually mobilized in Indonesia and elsewhere, given the nature and scope of *sadaqah* contributions. Nonetheless, it seems that *sadaqah* forms the bulk of voluntary contributions (including *zakat* and *fitrah*) in the region, in view of the fact that *zakat* is not strictly implemented and that *fitrah* represents a relatively small sum.

In the Philippines and Thailand, the *zakat* and *fitrah* channels are also used for the collection of *sadaqah*, and there are no special institutional arrangements to tap the *sadaqah* sources. Mosques have regular *sadaqah* collections during Friday congregations. However, it is exceptional to find mosques with well-organized formal charity funds in Thailand.[10] In the southern Philippines, there are some mosques which are 'patronized' by a group of local personalities who contribute a fixed sum on a regular basis, but again these are exceptions rather than the rule.[11]

Singapore has a well-organized set-up for the mobilization of *sadaqah*. A special case in point is the Mosque Building Fund (MBF) which was launched by MUIS in September 1975. Muslim employers, employees, and the self-employed make voluntary contributions to the MBF. The minimum contribution per person has been raised from S$1.00 in 1975 to S$2.00 presently. The novelty, however, lies in the special arrangement MUIS has with the Central Provident Fund (CPF) and the Post Office Savings Bank (POSB) GIRO facility for automatic monthly contributions from the members' accounts. It is of interest to note that, between 1975 and 1985, MBF collection totalled S$26 million.[12] The MBF resources are used only for the acquisition of land and the construction of new mosques, while the operational costs of new mosques are financed from other public donations. In fact, the so-called new generation mosques in Singapore are self-sufficient in the sense that the activities organized by them bring in adequate revenue.

Since its inception in August 1981 the Council for the Education of Muslim Children, popularly known as MENDAKI, also plays an active role in the mobilization of *sadaqah* in Singapore. Like the MBF, MENDAKI has called on all working Muslims to allow a small monthly deduction (S$0.50 per person) from their salaries through the CPF. Such contributions through the CPF or POSB GIRO to MENDAKI totalled S$1.9 million during 1984–86. MENDAKI provides scholarships to deserving students and conducts tuition classes which are heavily subsidized.

The Muslimin Trust Fund Association (MTFA), which represents the oldest Muslim organization in Singapore (established in 1904), has also been mobilizing *sadaqah* to finance its two orphanages.[13] In addition, there are numerous other welfare societies[14] in Singapore which depend on voluntary contributions. In addition to this, Islamic missionary work in Singapore, undertaken mainly by JAMIYAH and MUIS, is also financed largely by charity.

In Malaysia, too, there are numerous Muslim welfare organizations which depend on *sadaqah* contributions. There are many Malay and Indian Muslim associations which mobilize voluntary funds to finance their religious and welfare activities. A more systematic collection of *sadaqah* on an elaborate scale has been introduced by the Islamic Economic Development Foundation Malaysia, or the Yayasan Pembangunan Ekonomi Islam Malaysia (YPEIM), which was established in July 1984. Muslim employees with fixed incomes in the public and private sectors are invited to contribute monthly to YPEIM by authorizing deductions from their salaries. The minimum contribution is M$1.00 per person per month. Those Muslims without fixed wages are encouraged to contribute generously by buying coupons (in denominations of M$1, $2, $5, and $10) which are sold at several places, including the post offices. In the month of Ramadhan, YPEIM also appeals to Muslims through the mail.

YPEIM has successfully mobilized substantial sums since 1985. About 135,000 contributors make their regular monthly contributions through salary deductions. Of these, 120,000 belong to the public sector. YPEIM hopes to increase the number of regular contributors to 180,000. In 1987, regular contributions totalled M$2.45 million. Contributions from the sale of coupons yielded M$213,802 in 1987, and Ramadhan contributions amounted to M$55,141. All told, YPEIM's total *sadaqah* collection for 1987 stood at M$2.72 million.

It is important to note that YPEIM is not involved in *zakat* collection and that it specializes in the collection of *sadaqah* only. A significant portion of the yearly collection is invested. As at the end of 1987, YPEIM had fixed assets worth M$3.58 million and portfolio investments of M$7.12 million.

YPEIM has spent some M$3 million on several projects since its inception. This includes expenditures on books for libraries in rural schools. About 338 schools have so far benefited from this scheme. Perhaps, economically the most significant of all the activities of YPEIM is the Projek Ikhtiar which provides interest-free loans (*gard hasan*) to the poor for financing their economic ventures such as farming, fishing, and trading. Each participant in the scheme is provided an interest-free loan of M$500 without the support of any collateral or guarantor, to be repaid over two to three years. Thus far (until 1987), 336 people have benefited from this scheme. YPEIM has allocated M$550,000 for this purpose.[15]

The success behind YPEIM may be attributed in no small measure to the government support given to it, although the organization is a nongovernmental one. The Prime Minister himself is directly involved, as the power of appointing or removing a trustee is invested in the Prime Minister who also appoints the president and the deputy president of YPEIM. It is also of interest to note that, in 1987, the Prime Minister's Department provided a grant of M$250,000 to YPEIM as a management subsidy.

## Waqf

*Waqf* represents an important Islamic institution that holds in trust properties and assets which are bequeathed by Muslim philanthropists for the common good of the community. *Waqf* acts as a foundation that serves the community, using the resources provided by endowments. The essence of the institution of *waqf* (or *awqaf* as it is sometimes referred to) is that incomes from *waqf* properties are used for achieving the goals of the organization without touching the assets themselves.

As a matter of fact most of the mosques and other places of worship, including religious schools, in the Southeast Asian region belong to *waqf*. More often than not, mosques and *surau* are built on *waqf* lands with the help of public donations. However, it is by no means rare to find both the building and the land given away as *waqf* properties by philanthropists.

*Waqf* properties may be dichotomized into specific *waqf* and general *waqf*, depending on the intentions of those who had declared their properties as *waqf*. The former refers to a *waqf* property meant for a specific purpose, whereas the latter could be put to any legitimate use.

In Malaysia, as indeed elsewhere in the region, most *waqf* properties are meant for specific purposes. Incomes from such properties are used to finance activities which were approved by the donors of the properties. Most *masjid*, *surau*, *madrasah*, cemeteries, and orphanages in the country come under this category.

*Waqf* properties in Malaysia are regulated by state laws. Selangor was the first state to enact *waqf* laws in 1952, with nearly all other states following suit. According to these laws, the Council of Islamic Religion in each state is the sole trustee of *waqf* properties in the respective state. The laws thus require all *waqf* properties to be transferred to the State Religious Council.

Prior to these laws, the practice was that *waqf* properties were held by individual trustees without proper documentation. This had resulted in the loss of some *waqf* properties, due to either the heirs of the donors claiming ownership after the death of the donors or the trustees transferring the ownership grants to themselves.

In spite of the enactment of *waqf* laws, there are many *waqf* properties in Malaysia which are still held by individual trustees. In fact, there is no complete list of all *waqf* properties in any state. Any attempt to estimate the value of *waqf* properties in the country would be a futile exercise. However, it appears that the bulk of the *waqf* lands in Malaysia do not generate income. It has been estimated that only about 10 per cent of the *waqf* lands in the country are commercially productive.[16]

There is evidence which suggests that *waqf* managements have often failed to allocate the *waqf* resources efficiently so as to maximize social benefits. Many *waqf* properties remain neglected, while others are leased or rented out for nominal sums. There are, of course, important exceptions as evidenced by the project of the State Religious Council of Melaka to build a four-storey complex of shops and office space on 1,951 square metres of *waqf* land in

Melaka Town in 1979, and the M$2 million project of the Penang State Religious Council to construct a similar complex on 5,593 square metres of *waqf* land in the city centre of Pulau Pinang.

In Thailand, *waqf* properties are held by mosques and foundations. The establishment and administration of the mosques are governed by the Masjid Act of 1947, while those of the foundations are regulated by the Civil and Commercial Code. The laws require financial reports on all *waqf* properties to be submitted to the Provincial Islamic Committee (PIC) annually, while the Central Islamic Committee (CIC) is given the powers to inspect and even control *waqf* bodies in the country. In practice, however, there has been hardly any intervention by either the PIC or the CIC.

The bulk of *waqf* properties in Thailand comprise pieces of land donated to *masjid* and foundations. Other *waqf* properties include residential houses and commercial buildings. Incomes from these properties are used for the maintenance of mosques and for financing community projects. However, these organizations, more often than not, find themselves in deficit situations with expenditures exceeding incomes. The shortfalls are met mainly by *sadaqah* collection.

It is indeed unfortunate that *waqf* properties in Thailand largely remain undeveloped with no attempts made to increase the revenue-yielding capacity of these assets. They presently bring only meagre revenues for the institutions to which they belong, thus defeating the purpose for which they were set up in the first place. However, there are exceptional cases of efficient resource allocation, an outstanding example of which is provided by a *masjid* in Chiengmai which has built commercial premises yielding lucrative rental incomes.

The *pondok* school system[17] in Thailand (and also in northern Peninsular Malaysia) has long survived on *waqf* properties. The land donated by the people in the villages for this purpose in some cases has been converted into private properties by the children of the trustees. During the last three decades, the *pondok* schools have been transformed into private or public schools. It is of interest to note that a few foundations have taken over the management of some of these schools. Thus, for example, the Foundation of Islamic Education in Yala operates three Islamic schools. Another case in point is the At-Tarkiyah School in Narathivat.

The profile of *waqf* properties in Indonesia and the Philippines is not very different from that of Malaysia and Thailand. In most cases, *masjid* and *madrasah* in these countries fall under the category of *waqf*. More often than not, *waqf* endowments are associated with prominent families which had donated their properties. Well-known examples of such family endowments include those of the Abas family, the Alontos, and the Lucmans in the southern Philippines.

In Singapore, MUIS has been given the power to administer *waqf* properties. MUIS has taken charge of some 76 mosques and 30 *madrasah* as of 1986. This, however, does not exhaust all *waqf* properties in Singapore. The first-generation mosques were endowed by individuals while the second-generation mosques were built by MUIS. Many of the endowments in Singapore date back to the nineteenth century. Mosques which fall under this category have been administered by trustees under trusts created by wills or deeds. Nearly all the *waqf* properties taken over by MUIS[18] were endowed by Indian Muslims, while the Muslimin Trust Fund Association (MTFA) manages a number of mosques (many of which are Arab endowments), two orphanages, and a *madrasah*. The JAMIYAH also manages several mosques. The name of Alsagoff, a rich Arab trader, figures prominently in the context of *waqf* in Singapore, as a benefactor of the SMA Alsagoff Wakaf Fund and the MTFA.

There have been several cases of loss of *waqf* properties due to the expiry of their leases and compulsory acquisition of land by the Singapore Government in the name of urban development. However, these losses have been to some extent offset by alternative locations provided by the authorities for mosques. Despite shortcomings of sorts, it would be fair to conclude that *waqf* properties are better managed and more efficiently used in Singapore than elsewhere in the region.

## Mobilization of Savings

Strictly speaking, the mobilization of private savings should fall within the realm of the commercial sector. Nonetheless it would be appropriate to consider it in the present context not only because it relates to resource mobilization but also because the mobilization of savings referred to here had begun as a voluntary sector effort before evolving into a full-fledged commercial sector activity.

Formal and systematic mobilization of Muslims' savings along Islamic lines seems to take place only in Malaysia and Singapore. References in this section, however, will be confined to the schemes which have had some voluntary sector involvement at one stage or another. Thus, the role of Islamic banking in the mobilization of savings along Islamic lines is beyond the scope of the present analysis, as it clearly belongs to the world of commerce (*tijarah*).[19]

The Pilgrims Fund, or the Tabung Haji as it is popularly known, in Malaysia was started in 1962 to enable intending pilgrims to save sufficient amounts for the purpose of performing their *hajj*. Prior to that, pilgrims without adequate savings sold their properties to finance their *hajj*, as a result of which many faced dire economic consequences upon their return. Efforts to set up a Pilgrims Savings Fund began as a voluntary sector initiative, which subsequently received strong government support. The Malayan Muslims Pilgrims Savings Corporation (incorporated in August 1962 and launched in September 1963) evolved into the present-day Pilgrims Management and Fund Board (PMFB) which was set up by statute in August 1969.

The PMFB accepts deposits from members and invests these funds in Islamically legitimate ways. Profits from investments are distributed among the depositors in the form of a bonus after *zakat* deductions. The minimum deposit required to open an account with the Tabung Haji is M$2.00. PMFB sends statements of accounts to the depositors twice a year and pays a bonus on an annual basis.

The Tabung Haji has grown enormously in strength in terms of both the number of depositors and the volume of deposits. The number of depositors has increased from about 7,000 in 1969 to more than 126,000 in 1986, while the size of the deposits has swelled from M$7 million to M$275 million between 1969 and 1986.[20]

Deposits into the PMFB are received through monthly salary deductions authorized by the members, through post offices, and direct counter collections. Investment channels comprise the Islamic modes of *mudaraba* (profit-sharing), *musharaka* (equity participation), and *ijara* (leasing). Nearly one-half of the investments have taken the form of equity participation. Total investments stood at M$464.3 million at the end of 1985.

Reference must also be made, at least in passing, to another similar organization in Malaysia which rivals the Tabung Haji. The Islamic political party, Parti Islam Se-Malaysia (PAS), has established a savings fund akin to the Tabung Haji. This fund, called the Darul Mal, appears to have mobilized substantial sums in Kedah, Kelantan, and Trengganu where PAS has strong grassroot support. It is of interest to note that Darul Mal investments include ownership of rubber and oil palm plantations in the country.

Organizations akin to the Tabung Haji are conspicuously absent in other Southeast Asian countries. Very similar, however, is the proposed institution called DANAMIS (Dana Masyarakat Melayu-Islam Singapura) which is the brain-child of the Kongres Ekonomi Masyarakat Melayu-Islam Singapura (KEMAS) convened in 1985. The main objective of DANAMIS is to mobilize savings and to use them to fund small- and medium-sized Malay firms. The proposed *modus operandi* of DANAMIS is similar to that of the MBF and the MENDAKI funds operating in Singapore, with monthly deductions of a minimum sum from Muslim employees. It has been estimated that DANAMIS should be able to garner about S$18 million per year, at the rate of S$10 monthly contribution per person from 150,000 Muslim employees.[21] It is also envisaged that DANAMIS will be able to launch a pilgrimage fund along the lines of Malaysia's Tabung Haji.

## Conclusion

It may be inferred from the above discussion that the Islamic voluntary sector in Southeast Asia does play an important role, especially in terms of mobilization of resources among the Muslims. The Islamic voluntary sector thus helps not only to reallocate resources in a more efficient fashion but also to redistribute them in a more equitable manner. This general observation notwithstanding, the preceding analysis points to the weaknesses and shortcomings within the Islamic voluntary sector which have prevented it from playing a more meaningful and effective role in alleviating poverty and improving the economic well-being of Muslim communities in the region.

*Zakat* represents a powerful device which, if properly organized and judiciously used, can make a significant impact on the economic profile of the Muslim communities. Care must, however, be taken in modernizing the institution of *zakat* so as not to violate the *Sharia* principles governing *zakat* which is often equated with *salat* itself. One must be particularly cautious about revamping the sources, uses, and rates of *zakat*, as funds collected from 'non-*zakat*able' sources or spent on non-legitimate purposes cannot be *zakat* by definition. Funds which do not conform to the *zakat* rules may only be considered at best as *sadaqah*.

Obviously, the institution of *zakat* in Southeast Asia has been under-utilized in the sense that its potential has not been tapped fully. The amount of *zakat* resources actually mobilized seems to be no more than a fraction of its potential. However, one must hasten to add that the situation may not be as bad as official figures might suggest, since *zakat* which bypasses official or formal outlets might well be several times that which goes through such channels. The potential is considerable indeed, since 2.5 per cent of the stock of wealth and income flows of professionals and 10 per cent of the agricultural produce would amount to a hefty sum. The situation calls not only for enactment and enforcement of *zakat* laws, but also an elaborate machinery similar to that of the Department of Income Tax which would enlist all the *muzaki*, make *zakat* assessments, and collect and distribute *zakat* funds.

Evidently, *fitrah* collections are better organized than *zakat*. This is hardly surprising, since *fitrah* represents a painless, small poll tax which is collected annually in conjunction with the Id festival. There is no question of *fitrah* evasions, as the willingness and ability of the people to pay it have never been in doubt. Besides, the cost of collection is relatively low, since the *masjid* and *surau* effectively serve as collection centres. One may, therefore, safely conclude that there is very little untapped *fitrah* resources in the region.

*Sadaqah* is a different kettle of fish altogether. As charity which can be given at any time in any quantum to anyone in an absolutely discretionary fashion, its potential is almost limitless. More often than not, *sadaqah* is given in a haphazard manner. Much more *sadaqah* can be mobilized, if the voluntary sector institutions can come up with well-planned programmes and sell them in a well-organized fashion. The emergence of many such institutions in several countries and the competition among them seem to augur well because competition can ensure efficiency in terms of costs and equity in terms of benefits.

The institution of *waqf* appears to be somewhat in a shambles in some countries. Many *waqf* properties seem to suffer from total neglect, abuse, and misuse. There is a need to streamline the management of *waqf* properties. It is indeed unfortunate that *waqf* properties have not been put to good use in many cases, although there are notable exceptions. It is these exceptions which provide proof of the enormous potential of the institution of *waqf*.

It is also distressing to observe that there has been very little new addition to the stock of *waqf* properties. Nearly all the *waqf* properties found in the region represent endowments made in the nineteenth century. The explanation that there are now not as many wealthy Muslim individuals as in the distant past is hard to accept. A plausible explanation for this may well be found in the neglect, misuse, and abuse, referred to above, which could have discouraged others from donating their properties. There is a need to breathe new life into the institution of *waqf*. A revival and revitalization of the institution of *waqf* can confer real benefits on the Muslim communities in the region, now that there are quite a few Muslim multimillionaires who can afford to leave part of their wealth in the form of *waqf*.

A moot point in the preceding overview relates to the role of governments. As mentioned, there is no Islamic state in Southeast Asia, and Muslims constitute a majority only in Indonesia and Malaysia. Thus, the voluntary sector has to shoulder heavier responsibilities than it would otherwise. This, however, does not mean that the voluntary sector can function independently without government support. To be sure, the present analysis suggests that the performance of the voluntary sector reflects the extent of government support given to the sector. Indeed, behind every major success story cited in the discussion above, there has invariably been government backing of some sort. Outstanding examples include BAZIS in Indonesia, YPEIM in Malaysia, and MENDAKI in Singapore. It cannot be denied that an official stamp can add considerable clout to voluntary sector efforts.

## NOTES

1   *Nisab* represents a demarcation line, based on the concept of basic needs, between those who are needy and those who are not.

2   See the chapter by Taufik Abdullah in this volume.

3   The *imam, khatib*, and *bilal* in mosques are collectively referred to as the *pakil*.

4   The Maguindanaos are one of the thirteen Moro ethnolinguistic groups in the southern Philippines.

5   The Maranaos are another ethnolinguistic group whose homeland is the Lanao region.

6   Surin Pitsuwan, "The Islamic Banking Option in Thailand" in *Islamic Banking in Southeast Asia* edited by Mohamed Ariff (Singapore: Institute of Southeast Asian Studies, 1988).

7   See the chapter by Taufik Abdullah in this volume.

8   See the chapter by Aidit Ghazali in this volume.

9   See the chapter by Amina Tyabji in this volume.

10  See the chapter by Preeda Prapertchob in this volume.

11  See the chapter by Carmen Abubakar in this volume.

12  See the chapter by Amina Tyabji in this volume.

13  These are the Darul Ihsan (for boys), established in 1904, and the Darul Ihsan Lilbanat (for girls), established in 1980.

14  There were some eighty Muslim benevolent societies in 1985 (see the chapter by Amina Tyabji in this volume).

15  See *Risalah YPEIM*, Bilangan 6, Tahun 1988 and the Annual Report of YPEIM, 1987.

16  See the chapter by Syed Othman Alhabshi in this volume.

17  In the *pondok* system of religious education, students of all ages (both males and females) come to seek knowledge from a religious teacher (*guru*) and reside in huts built around the teacher's residence. In this system of education one may take many years before one 'graduates'.

18  MUIS inherited ten *waqf* endowments, two of which were subsequently dissolved.

19  Mohamed Ariff, "Islamic Banking: A Southeast Asian Perspective" in *Islam and the Economic Development of Southeast Asia: Islamic Banking in Southeast Asia* edited by Mohamed Ariff (Singapore: Institute of Southeast Asian Studies, 1988).

20  See the chapter by Radiah Abdul Kader in this volume.

21  See the chapter by Amina Tyabji in this volume.

# 4 ZAKAT COLLECTION AND DISTRIBUTION IN INDONESIA

*Taufik Abdullah*

## Introduction

For various reasons 1968 was an important year for contemporary Indonesia. It was the year the Acting President Soeharto was confirmed by the Provisional People's Consultative Assembly (MPRS) as the new President. This meant that the New Order government had already secured its legitimate position. Now that the communist threat had been practically eliminated and the remnants of Soekarno's followers had been tamed, the New Order government was ready to embark on the new phase of Indonesia's political history.

The search for a proper political structure, which would guarantee the success of economic reconstruction and development and secure political stability and pave the way toward the manifestation of *Pancasila* ideas, began to take its full course. The year 1968 was, indeed, a year of high expectations. Indonesia was about to enter into its First Five Years' Development Plan. No less important was the fact that, in 1968, the so-called religious conflict — the first and the only conflict on a national scale — had largely subsided. But, in the meantime, the newly established Islamic political party, the Parmusi, was undergoing a near-fatal internal crisis.

It was on 24 September 1968 that eleven influential *ulama* of Jakarta made a historic appeal to the newly confirmed President. They reminded the President of the importance of *zakat*, both as a religious obligation and as a way to social amelioration. Mindful of the prevailing unhealthy economic situation and aware of the real spirit of '*Pancasila* and the 1945 Constitution' the eleven *ulama* concluded that the institution of *zakat* could help hasten the process of development. The fulfilment of *zakat* obligation by the Muslims would not only be beneficial to the Islamic community, but also to the nation and the state as a whole. Therefore, they asked President Soeharto, as "the Head of the State" to urge the Islamic adherents, "particularly [those who live] in the capital city of the Republic of Indonesia" to comply with this religious obligation. They asked the President to advise the governors of all provinces to take the initiatives in co-ordinating the collection and distribution of *zakat*, "in accordance with the principles of *zakat* law". The eleven *ulama* also hoped that the President would be willing to set an example by paying his *zakat* obligation, "as a Muslim, who is faithful to his Islamic religious precepts".[1]

The President responded to this appeal in his official *Isra' Mi'raj* (Prophet's Ascension Celebration) speech, at the Merdeka Palace, on 26 October 1968. He stressed the religious and social importance of *zakat* and urged the Muslims to comply with this noble religious duty. It would be ideal if the collection and distribution of *zakat* were nationally co-ordinated. As the first step he, as "a private citizen", was willing to take charge of the "massive national effort of *zakat* collection" and to submit annual reports on the collection and distribution of *zakat*.[2]

Until 1974, the President repeated this message in his speeches in conjunction with Islamic celebrations. Meanwhile, on 31 October 1968, he officially instructed three high military officers to make all necessary preparations for a nation-wide *zakat* collection drive.[3]

The first governor to respond to the President's speech was Ali Sadikin, the governor of Jakarta. In December 1968 he established a semi-autonomous *zakat* agency. Securing the co-operation of *ulama* and Muslim intellectuals in Jakarta, the governor not only managed to find a suitable organizational structure of *zakat* collection and distribution for Jakarta, but also introduced new approaches in *zakat* distribution. The successes and failures of the government-sponsored *zakat* organization of Jakarta was carefully monitored by other provinces. It was an example to be followed, if not copied.

Since the early 1970s, *zakat* has become a subject of many seminars or workshops, both at the national and local levels. Methods of *zakat* propagation, jurisprudence (*fiqh*) governing *zakat*, structural arrangement of *zakat* organization, patterns of *zakat* distribution, and potential role of *zakat* in community development have been some of the central themes of these various scholarly meetings. In the meantime several experiments in *zakat* management were undertaken. An equally significant development was the direct participation of private organizations in the mobilization of *zakat* funds.

This chapter attempts to describe the various modes of *zakat* collection and distribution in Indonesia. Since it is not possible to scrutinize the experiences of *zakat* collection all over Indonesia, we shall focus on the Jakarta experiment. By way of comparison, experiments in the provinces of South

Sulawesi and West Java are also discussed. Several experiments at lower levels of administrative regions and small-scale programmes in *zakat* management are also investigated. The chapter concludes with a general overview of *zakat* situation in Indonesia.

### *Zakat*: *Fiqh* Problems and Social Strategy

No one ever questions the fact that *zakat* is one of the pillars of Islam. It is the third *Rukun Islam* (Islamic Pillars). *Zakat* is mentioned in the Qur'an no less than thirty times. It is mentioned in twenty-seven verses along with *salat* (worship), the second pillar.[4] From Islamic legal perspectives, *zakat* belongs to the category of *ta'abuddi* obligation — a dogmatic regulation, which is clearly stated in the *nash* (Qur'anic text). As such, its existence as part of religious obligation should be simply followed, without any questioning. *Zakat* has to be paid as a way "to purify" one's wealth over and above the *nisab* (minimum), as stated in Sura at-Taubah (Qur'an 9:103).[5] And, *zakat* could only be given to eight categories of *asnaf* — the right *zakat* recipients.[6] Islamic legal tradition has also determined the types of wealth or properties on which *zakat* should be collected and the correct *nisab* and *haul*, or time of payment, for each category of '*zakat*able' wealth and property.

But there are still many aspects which remain unclear. What is the real essence of *zakat*? How should *zakat* be collected? How should one proceed with the management of *zakat*? Should all the eight *asnaf* be treated equally? And how should existing *fiqh* precepts on *zakat* be understood in changing circumstances?

The Indonesian *ulama* who began to look at the legal aspects of *zakat* management more closely seem to agree that *zakat* should be seen as a dogmatic regulation which should be rationally deliberated (*ma'qul al ma'na*). Like any other legal problem derived from *nash*, *zakat* should be viewed from the perspective of the Islamic system of jurisprudence. One of the basic principles of the Islamic law is that it should be directed toward "the creation of wellbeing and the avoidance of disharmony" (*jalb al mashalik wa dar'al mafasid*). To plug loopholes in the execution of the law, another principle could be invoked: "the avoidance of disharmony should precede the creation of wellbeing" (*dar'al mafasid muqaddam a la jalb al mashalik*).[7]

Does this mean that the *ulama* can ignore legal traditions and rely exclusively on their understanding on what is good and bad for society? On this particular point, despite differences in doctrinal or ideological orientations, most of the Indonesian *ulama* seem to adopt a moderate stance. On the basis of an opinion survey of *ulama* and intellectuals on *zakat* conducted in Jakarta, a workshop underscored the need for legal interpretations (*ijtihad*) on something that is not clearly stated in the *nash*. However, it did not favour the *instimbath* procedure, which tries to find new legal precepts the way the *mujtahid* (reformers) had done in the past or that of *tarjieh*, which compares all existing legal opinions before selecting the strongest one. Instead the workshop favoured a *tahqiequl manath* procedure, which tries to find *illat* or reasoning to something that is still not very clear.[8]

From this stance it appears that most *ulama* and Muslim intellectuals begin their opinions on *zakat* by first of all stressing the individual religious obligation of *zakat*. The identification of *zakat* with tax, as suggested by some influential Muslim intellectuals, because of their similar social objectives, is therefore unacceptable. The social significance and objectives of *zakat* are only derivative of God's command to individual believers. It is also from this standpoint on *zakat* that many *ulama* would define it as the obligation of the rich toward the poor and the needy. A seminar, held by a *pesantren-co-ordinative* body (in 1986), concluded that "the most urgent task of the *ulama* is to formulate a *zakat*-system, taking into consideration changing social realities, without abandoning the spiritual value of *zakat* as a religious act".[9] However, the goal of *zakat*, as a traditionalist-oriented *ulama* put it, is to transform a *mustahiq* (*zakat* recipient) into a *muzakki* (*zakat* payer).

Most *ulama* and Muslim intellectuals in Indonesia tend to look at *zakat* as a socially significant individual religious act. *Zakat* helps create a social structure based on economic justice which is blessed by God. Since *zakat* can help to eradicate poverty, the old tradition of using *zakat* for consumption purposes should be reviewed. In order to secure the ultimate social objectives of *zakat*, its use should be more productive-oriented. *Zakat* should also be seen as an integral part of the development programmes. Therefore, as will be seen later, several programmes have been designed so that *zakat* not only helps solve problems of individual poverty — as an expression of Islamic concern for social justice — but also facilitates the establishment of a righteous society.[10]

But who should be responsible for the collection and the distribution of *zakat*? An opinion survey of *ulama* and Muslim intellectuals on *zakat* (conducted in 1974–75) shows some general consensus. The majority of the *ulama* saw the government as the key factor in *zakat* management. Although a minority (about 7 per cent) thought that the government should be the only body responsible for it, an overwhelming majority (59 per cent) was of the opinion that *zakat* ideally be collected by a semi-autonomous *amil* — that is, by a government-sponsored agency. The majority (this time only 46 per cent) thought the same semi-autonomous body should also be responsible for the distribution of *zakat*. Not surprisingly, a large majority of the respondents of the survey thought that the distribution of *zakat* should be in accordance with social needs. Only a minority suggested that *zakat* should go directly to the *mustahiq.* The majority of the *ulama* respondents of Jakarta in 1975 agreed that *zakat* should be better used for productive rather than consumptive purposes. In other words, most of the *ulama* respondents preferred to look at *zakat* as *ibadah ijtima'iyah* — a religious social obligation — instead of as *ibadah mahdkah* — a purely religious obligation, which is an end in itself. Many non-*ulama* intellectuals, whose opinions were also solicited by this survey, underscored the need for an efficient organizational set-up of a national *Baitul Maal* (treasury) or *amil* agency.[11]

Similar findings were also reported by *TEMPO* in its special issue on *zakat.* An overwhelming majority of the respondents of the *TEMPO*'s opinion poll thought that the government should be involved in *zakat* management. Since *zakat* is seen as a means of eradicating poverty, the majority (about 43 per cent) thought that *zakat* ought to be used for productive purposes. About 25 per cent thought that *zakat* should be distributed to the mosques, orphans, etc., for consumptive purposes. The rest preferred to combine the two approaches.[12]

The opinion that *zakat* is a religious obligation with definite social significance has become a general consensus, regardless of the continued divergent doctrinal orientations. But to what extent can a secular state get itself involved in this society's religious activities? The President's willingness to act as a kind of provisional *amil* reflects the central government's attitude — it was Soeharto, as a Muslim private citizen, not as the Head of State, who would be responsible for *zakat* management. But who could deny the fact that either way he is the same person? In other words, that Indonesia is not an Islamic state does not mean that it has no role in facilitating or securing the performance of religious obligations of the vast majority of the population. On this particular point, there is no major disagreement between the President's attitude and the opinion of the majority of *ulama* and Muslim intellectuals, disclosed by the survey of 1975. But how essential is the role of the state in *zakat* management? An influential traditionalist-oriented *ulama*, who has been very much involved in community development programmes, stated that although social organizations could establish *zakat* collecting and distributing agencies, only those that were sponsored or established by the state could legally be considered as *amil.* The non-governmental *zakat* agencies, in other words, could consider themselves one of the eight *asnaf.*[13] In other words, according to this opinion, they could only function as the intermediary between the *muzakki* and the *mustahiq*, without the sanction of *fiqh.*

This is one of the controversies which surround the *zakat* issue in Indonesia. The essentiality of the state's role would gradually take one to the problem of the legitimacy of the state according to *fiqh* and Islamic ideology. The second controversy centres on the relationship between *zakat* and tax. If the ultimate objective of *zakat* is the creation of a society based on economic justice, what is, then, the objective of tax?[14] If *zakat* should first of all be seen as a way to purify one's wealth, the 2.5 per cent *zakat* is, of course, understandable. However, it would seem pointless to talk about social justice or poverty as being the social objective of *zakat* if the *zakat* rate is only 2.5 per cent. It has been argued that the *zakat* rate should have been 20 per cent of the income.[15]

These three controversies (the first is mostly legalistic in nature; the second ideological-political; and the third, sociological) do not manifest themselves in the real activities of *zakat* collection. They are merely part of the on-going discussions in the wake of Islamic resurgence in Indonesia. They reflect the continuing search for an ideal *zakat* management in a changing social order.

## Organization of *Zakat* Collection and Distribution

Traditionally *zakat* is largely a matter between the *muzakki* and the *mustahiq*, i.e., the obliged *zakat* payer and the lawful recipient. It has also been a purely local affair. A *muzakki* would simply go to his chosen *mustahiq* (e.g., religious teachers, *ulama*, or orphans) and give his *zakat* in accordance with his own calculations. Rarely, if ever, is *zakat* used for communal purposes. For these latter purposes the most important religious devices are *sadaqah*, *infaq*, and *waqf*. In other words *zakat maal* (*zakat* on wealth) is usually treated as if it is a *zakat fitrah* (poll *zakat*) which is largely consumptive and very personal in nature. *Zakat fitrah* is given to enable the *mustahiq* to celebrate the *Idul Fitri*. The use of *zakat* or *zakat maal* is entirely dependent on the *mustahiq*. A religious teacher, if he wants to, might use a portion of the *zakat* he receives for the enlargements of his school (*surau*, *pesantren*, or *dayah*).

A new style of this traditionalist approach to *zakat* distribution seems to be gaining popularity among the Muslim *nouveau riche* in Indonesia. The rich *muzakki* would distribute coupons to prospective *mustahiq*, who in turn would cash the coupons at the former's office.

Although this traditional system of *zakat* collection and distribution still continues, a new type of *zakat* organization with a new system of collection — which is more impersonal, relatively inter-local in character, and also more communally oriented in its use — emerged. The beginning of this type of *zakat* organization can be traced back to the early years of Islamic social and educational organizations when the Muslims migrating to urban areas launched programmes for the modernization of religious schools and social welfare. Today, it is not an exaggeration to state that these urban-based organizations have been receiving the biggest share of *zakat* collection. A common practice these days is for social-religious organizations to send blank money order forms in the month of Ramadhan to Muslims whose names are registered in telephone books. They are 'invited' to send their *zakat maal* to these organizations which are still, as stated in the invitations, in the process of establishing, enlarging, or renovating hospitals, orphanages, mosques, schools, etc.

Although many of these organizations are in fact branches of national Islamic organizations, such as the Muhammadiyah or the Nahdlatul Ulama, their entire activities are often locally initiated. These local-based organizations raise funds for their activities from all over the country. It is not unusual for a *muzakki*, say, in Medan (North Sumatera) to receive an invitation to send a portion of his *zakat* or *sadaqah* (or whatever category of religious contribution the sender or *muzakki* has in his *niyah* or intention) to a small village in Bali. It is also not uncommon for a *muzakki* to send as many as fifty or more money orders to organizations all over the country.

These local-based organizations have to compete with not only the continuing traditional system of *zakat* collection, but also national organizations, which mount fund mobilization for big projects such as university campuses, modern hospitals, and centres of Islamic studies. Ambitious projects of the local-based organizations can be taken as signs of the growing importance of *zakat* as a source of funds for social projects. The Dewan Dakwah (Council of Dakwah), a modernist organization in Jakarta, for example, is now erecting a modern mosque (Al Furqan), at an estimated cost of about Rp. 550 million. One day a *muzakki* simply dropped in at the office and wrote a cheque for Rp. 25 million.[16] At-Thahiriyah, one of the two biggest traditionalist educational organizations in Jakarta (the other one is Asy-Syafiiyah), is also in the process of completing a mosque complex, which is to include a library and an Islamic study centre, at an estimated cost of around Rp. 1.3 billion. Within eight months, it managed to collect more than Rp. 230 million. In addition to *zakat maal* At-Thahiriyah, unlike other organizations, also receives *waqf*, *infaq*, and *sadaqah*. Besides its formal school networks, which range from kindergarten to university, At-Thahiriyah, like its competitor Asy-Syafiiyah, also has its own *majlis taqlim* and radio station, which is used to 'invite' people to contribute to the project. The organization receives about Rp. 2 to 3 million every month from *majlis taqlim*.[17]

In spite of the relative success of these organizations in administering *zakat*, the need for direct government involvement has been felt. There are several reasons for this. In the first place, *zakat* represents a test case in the intricate relationship between religious social duties of the Muslim citizens and the non-religious character of the *Pancasila* state. Where is the boundary between social obligations of the Islamic *ummah* and the political duties of the state? Secondly, the possible nation-wide collection of *zakat* also promises, as the President stated in his famous speech, a more beneficial and strategic use of the institution for the betterment of the Islamic community as a whole. Thirdly, it is hoped that government involvement would result in better management and control of *zakat*. The government would also be able, as some *ulama* emphasize, to put pressure on the potential *muzakki* to 'purify' their wealth, when the *nisab* has been reached.

The genesis of central government's interest in *zakat* collection and distribution can be traced back to the nineteenth century, when the then Netherlands Indies government realized that the misuse of *zakat* by its own appointed officials might, in the end, be detrimental to its authority. In the nineteenth century Banten (West Java), according to Snouck Hurgronje, *zakat fitrah* was mostly received by religious teachers, either *kiai* (teachers of classical texts or *kitab*) or simple village Qur'an teachers. In East Java, unlike most parts of West Java, *zakat maal* fell under the jurisdiction of the *kiai* and other *ulama*. *Zakat fitrah*, on the other hand, was presented to village religious functionaries, such as *khatib* (preachers), and other mosque officials. Since both *zakat maal* and *zakat fitrah* in East Java were not channelled through any *amil* agency, as was the case in West Java (particularly in Chirebon and Prianger regencies), the misuse of these religious contributions was very rare. In West Java, on the other hand, the *amil* was mostly under the jurisdiction of appointed religious functionaries, who were directly under the supervision of the so-called native chiefs in their respective administrative divisions. It was in these regions that the government received reports of misuse of *zakat* funds.[18]

It is not surprising that the government of the Netherlands Indies, which always claimed to be neutral in religious affairs, issued a regulation (in 1893) to prevent misuse of *zakat* by appointed religious officials (*penghulu, naib,* etc.)[19] and their supervisors-cum-partners, the native officials. In 1905, the government issued another regulation (Bijblad 6200), which specifically forbid native officials (the *priyayi* and members of the *binnenlands bestuur*) to intervene in *zakat* management. At the same time, as any student of Dutch Islamic policy would remember, the government issued the notorious Guru Ordinance which put religious teachers under the direct supervision of the native officials, particularly the Regents.[20] Thus, the Dutch government policy toward *zakat* management did attempt to make a clear distinction between the state and the society's affairs in religious matters.

It was during the Japanese occupation that an attempt was made to get a more direct involvement of the government in *zakat* collection. The Majlis Islam A-la Indonesia (MIAI), the pre-war federation of Islamic political parties and mass organizations revived by the Japanese, took the initiative of establishing a Java-wide *Baitul Maal* in 1943. The MIAI hoped that by establishing the *Baitul Maal*, it could regain its influence after the Japanese occupation administration had changed its Islamic policy. Despite the rather lukewarm attitude of the Japanese, the MIAI managed to establish several branches of

*Baitul Maal* all over Java. But soon after that the MIAI itself was dissolved in late 1943. The attempt to involve the government for *zakat* management thus ended in failure.[21]

A more promising attempt was made in Aceh (Sumatera) when the Japanese occupation administration established the *Mahkamah Syariah* (*Syu Kyo Hoin* — the Syariah Court). The court was part of the Japanese-sponsored Islamic Council for the Support of Great East Asia (*Majlis Agama Islam Untuk Bantuan Asia Timur Raya*), founded in 1943. In its statute, issued in 1944, it was stated the *Syu Kyo Hoin* was entrusted to manage, among other things, *zakat, zakat fitrah,* and *waqaf.* With the membership consisting of most of the influential *ulama* in Aceh, it was hoped that the *Majlis Syariah* would be able to establish the long-awaited All-Aceh *Baitul Maal.* But whatever the real intention of the Japanese might be, the end of the Japanese occupation and the outbreak of Indonesian national revolution made the *Majlis Syariah* no longer operative.[22]

After Indonesia won its independence, Aceh was the first provincial administration to manage *zakat* collection and distribution. Recognized by the central government as a Special Region (1959), which gave Aceh the special right in the fields of religion, education, and custom (after some years of rebellion against the central government), the local government directly undertook the management of *zakat*.[23] At the provincial level the governor, with the support of the Council of Ulama (*Majlis Ulama*), was the highest authority in the semi-governmental *zakat* organization. In every level of administrative divisions — *kabupaten* (regency), *kecamatan* (district), and *kampong* (village) — the administrative heads were appointed as the chairmen of their respective local *Baitul Maal.* The main target of these government-sponsored *Baitul Maal*, however, was *zakat fitrah*, which was also mostly spent for the renovations of mosques, *dayah* (boarding religious schools), and *madrasah.*

In 1967, immediately after Indonesia had overcome the communist attempted *coup d'état*, the central government showed interest in the promotion of *zakat* collection. When the Minister of Religious Affairs presented a draft of *zakat* law to the provincial parliament (officially called Mutual Help People's House of Representatives — DPRGR), the Minister of Finance thought that *zakat* management would be better regulated by ministerial instruction instead of by law. Accordingly, the Minister of Religious Affairs suspended the instruction he had issued in 1968, which suggested every governor take the initiative in establishing the *Baitul Maal*.[24] By the time the Minister of Religious Affairs suspended his 1968 instruction, the President had already delivered his important speech on *zakat* in which, as already noted earlier, he stressed his willingness to manage *zakat* collection and distribution — as a private citizen.

However, the voluntary nature of *zakat* collection, which was under-scored by the President, was seen by the officials of *zakat* agencies as one of the stumbling blocks in the management of *zakat*.[25] This led the governor of Jakarta (Ali Sadikin) to take the first action. He established a semi-governmental *zakat* agency, called Badan Amil Zakat (BAZ) in December 1968. For various reasons (among others, the very limited scope of activities of the agency, the competition with traditional *zakat* collection, and the activities of Islamic social religious organizations), the governor changed the structure and the scope of activities of BAZ in December 1973 . It was re-named BAZIS (Badan Amil Zakat, Infaq dan Sadaqah), because it would also collect *infaq* and *sadaqah*. In *fiqh* terms *zakat* is the obligatory, while *sadaqah* and *infaq* represent recommended contributions.[26] The scope of the newly organized BAZIS would then include both the obligatory *zakat* and the recommended religious contributions. If *zakat* should be based on the *nisab* of one's wealth and collected at its *haul* (time-span) and its use should be determined by the proper understanding of the eight *asnaf*, *sadaqah* and *infaq* can be collected any time and used in accordance with local social needs. Many provinces would later follow the steps of Jakarta.

On 5 February 1976, on the basis of recommendations made by the workshop on the findings of the research team of *zakat* (held in July 1975) the governor of Jakarta improved the structure of the BAZIS, which is still operative. The BAZIS, according to its new statute, "is an executive agency of the Administration of the Capital Special Region of Jakarta", to help the governor "in the collection and distribution of *zakat*, *infaq* and *sadaqah*". The governor himself is the general chairman of the BAZIS; but, for day-to-day operations, he appoints an executive chairman who is directly responsible to the governor. Given the main functions to undertake the collection of *zakat*, *infaq*, and *sadaqah* (from now on simply abbreviated as ZIS), to arrange and to supervise their use, and to ensure that funds are used productively and for the general well-being of the *ummah* and Islam, the BAZIS is organized in accordance with the administrative divisions of Jakarta. In each administrative level — section, district (*kecamatan*), village (*kelurahan*) — the heads of the respective levels — the mayor, the *camat*, and the *lurah* — are the general chairmen of the local BAZIS. In short, the structural arrangement of the BAZIS in each administrative level is similar to that of the centre. In case the mayor, the *camat*, or the *lurah* is not a Muslim, the general chairmanship should be entrusted to one of his deputies who is a Muslim. The mayor, the *camat*, or the *lurah* would also appoint the local executive chairmen. At all levels, from the centre to the *kelurahan*, there are executive bodies and advisory boards. (At the governor level the board is called *Badan Pembina* or board of advisers, at the mayor level it is called *Badan Musyawarah* or consultative body, and at the *kelurahan* level, it is referred to as *Penasehat Teknis* or technical advisers.) The members of the advisory boards comprise the representatives of *ulama*, indigenous entrepreneurs, youths, government officials, and (only at the governor level) "prominent members of the society" (*tokoh-tokoh terkemuka*).[27] In addition to its formal functions, the political function of these advisory bodies is clear enough — it serves as the bridge between the *ummah* and the government, which has made itself one of the *amil*.

All executive officers of the BAZIS are civil servants, and it is entirely financed by the government. Therefore, although the BAZIS, according to *fiqh*, can be regarded as the legitimate *amil*, it only treats itself as one the *asnaf* on paper. The deep involvement of the heads of local administration in the affairs of the BAZIS is indicated, among others, by the fact that since its inception (in late 1968) the three successive governors of Jakarta have issued more than thirty decrees on the various aspects of ZIS management.[28]

Since 1970, several provinces have followed the example set by Jakarta. Several provincial administrations have taken direct or indirect responsibilities in the management of *zakat*. In 1972, East Kalimantan established its BAZIS. It was soon followed by West Sumatera (1973), West Java (1974), South Kalimantan (1974), South Sumatera (1975), Lampung (1975), Irian Jaya (1978), North Sulawesi (1985), and South Sulawesi (1985), among others.

By the time the governor of South Sulawesi took the initiative of establishing the provincial *zakat* agency (1985), there were already 141 *kecamatan amil* or agencies scattered all over the province. Out of the 1,006 villages in the 21 regencies, 986 had already had their respective *amil*.[29] The province had infrastructural bases at its disposal, and it could learn from the experiences of its regencies, or *kabupaten*. The province could have learned of, for example, the dismal failure of the *kabupaten* of Gowa, the nearest *kabupaten* to the capital city of the province (Ujung Pandang, formerly called Makassar), which finally forced the *bupati*, or the regency head, to relinquish *zakat* authority to the *camat* (district heads).[30] The Panitia Pengumpul dan Panyalur Zakat (Committee for the Collection and Distribution of Zakat — P3Z) was established in 1975. It began to operate in 1976 and was dissolved in 1980. According to the head of the Social Affairs Bureau of the *kabupaten*, the P3Z had to be dissolved because the distribution of *zakat* was not carried out in accordance with the *Shariah*. It meant, of course, that *zakat* was misused. The province was presumably aware of the relative success of several regencies, such as Majene, Pangkajene, and Kapulauan (Pangkep). If the failure of Gowa can be attributed to the fact that the administration-sponsored *amil* was made entirely the business of the local bureaucrats (not even the officers of the Office of Religious Affairs were invited to participate), the relative success of the other regencies can be seen as proof of the workable relationship between the bureaucrats and the *ulama.* From its inception the *amil* of Pangkep regency seems to have copied the style of the BAZIS of Jakarta.[31]

If the experiences of several regencies in the province of South Sulawesi are anything to go by, it appears that the personal style of the *bupati* could determine the continuation of the participation or leadership of the local administration in *zakat* management. And not least important is the attitude of the *ulama.* The *ulama,* who thought that their interests were threatened by the government participation in *zakat* management, could emerge as the most potent stumbling block in the early stage of the government-sponsored *amil.*[32]

In less than a year since its establishment, the government-sponsored *amil* of South Sulawesi (in February 1986) changed its status into an autonomous foundation, called Yayasan Badan Amil Zakat dan Shadaqah and known by its acronym, BAZIS. As a private, autonomous organization it is, in accordance with the law, based on *Pancasila* and the Constitution of 1945. The general chairman of the foundation is the governor, who serves as a Muslim private citizen. Not unlike the BAZIS of Jakarta, the BAZIS of South Sulawesi also has a two-layer structure — the council and the executive board. As a policy-making body, the council is assisted by a board of advisers, consisting of government officials, *ulama,* intellectuals, and opinion makers.[33]

In addition to (1) the traditional system of *zakat* collection and distribution, (2) religious educational organizations, and (3) government-sponsored or semi-governmental *zakat* management apparatus, a new type of *zakat* organization has recently made its appearance — i.e., organizations directly sponsored and supervised by private companies. This new type of organization is the direct outcome of the general acceptance of a new interpretation of *zakat* obligation, according to which professional income or salary that has reached its *nisab* — determined by a comparative method — should also be subject to *zakat.*[34]

Shortly after it held a national seminar in August 1986 on the management of *zakat,* which was attended by several Islamic scholars and prominent Muslim intellectuals, and highly endorsed by the Majlis Ulama Indonesia (MUI), the Badak LNG Company (Bontang, East Kalimantan) encouraged the formation of a *zakat* organization among its Muslim employees.[35] In two months (January and February 1987), the *zakat* committee collected Rp. 12 million, paid by about 300 employees, who accounted for more than a quarter of the Muslims working in the company.[36]

The Badak LNG is only an example of the growing popularity of this voluntary company-sponsored *zakat* collection. On Banjarmasin (West Kalimantan) most of the state banks, since 1986, have also sponsored the *zakat profesi* among their respective employees.[37]

## Toward the Enlargement of the *Muzakki* Group

Just as war is too important to be left entirely in the hands of the generals, *zakat*, so it seems, is too important to be simply entrusted to the persuasive capability and the managerial ability of the *ulama*. At least, this is one of the conclusions that never fails to appear in any seminar or workshop on *zakat*. "Finally", as one of the latest seminars emphasized in its recommendations, "the problems of *zakat* are not the monopoly of experts of Islamic law (*fuqaha*), they should also be tackled by the economists and experts in other disciplines".[38]

Naturally one of the most pressing problems felt by both the semi-governmental and private *zakat* collecting and distributing organizations is the relative slow growth in the number of *muzakki*, or *zakat* payers. After about ten years in operation, the BAZIS of Jakarta estimated that it could only reach about 3 per cent of the potential *muzakki*. An official of the BAZIS of South Sulawesi optimistically remarked that his organization has reached about 25 per cent of the *muzakki*. But he was actually referring to the persons who paid *zakat fitrah*, not *zakat maal*, which formed the basis of the estimate by the BAZIS of Jakarta.

There are many explanations for the low level of *zakat* collection. The most readily available scapegoat is the weak economic position of the *ummah*. There is evidence that at least in some villages (e.g. Pekalongan and Ngablak in central Java), the number of people who paid *zakat maal* had decreased while the number of people who paid *zakat fitrah* had increased. The statistics also show that the level of people's welfare had somewhat worsened. In other words, although religious commitment was not weaker (as shown by the increases in the number of people who paid *fitrah*), *zakat* payment did not improve.[39]

The validity of the above explanation is, however, limited. Improvements in the economic conditions of the Muslims do not immediately lead to any increase in the number of *muzakki*. Most of the *ulama* and government officials ascribe the low number of *muzakki* mainly to the low levels of religious consciousness and knowledge of the Muslims and to the institutional weaknesses of existing *amil*. The persistent traditional practices, which simply look at *zakat* as a direct relationship between the *muzakki* and *mustahiq*, represent a major stumbling block. Furthermore, officials of the Department of Religious Affairs suspect that many potential *muzakki* are still not convinced that their *zakat* would be properly distributed, if *zakat* is entrusted to the *amil*.

The strategy for increasing the number of *muzakki* is accordingly geared toward removing the stumbling blocks. The basic idea behind the notion of transforming the *mustahiq* into *muzakki* means nothing less than the eradication of poverty or, to put it more concretely, to make *zakat* a vehicle for income-generating projects. Be that as it may, *zakat* strategy should first address problems of (1) raising the consciousness and knowledge of the Muslims about their religious obligations, and (2) improving the *zakat* machinery. Most religious organizations use both individual and public appeals. Individual appeals take the form of letters of appeal to the people whose addresses are already registered in their ever expanding mailing lists. Public appeals take a variety of forms, including distribution of pamphlets, holding of religious public gatherings (*tabligh, majlis taqlim*), and radio lectures. In this regard, Asy-Syafiiyah and At-Thahiriyah intelligently use their highly popular *majlis taqlim* and their radio programmes. The Dewan Dakwah sometimes uses its widely circulated *Bulletin Dakwah* for *zakat* purposes.[40]

These organizations also publicize their *zakat* (as well as *waqaf, infaq,* and *sadaqah*) inflows and their uses of these religious contributions. These annual reports serve as a means to show their credibilities as well-managed *zakat* collecting and distributing organizations. They are also intended to inform the *muzakki* and other donors that their contributions have been spent in accordance with their wishes.

As a result of a series of seminars and workshops on *zakat* (which also serve as a method of *zakat* promotion), the Department of Religious Affairs has designed an elaborate programme for the propagation of *zakat*, which includes face-to-face communication, printed media, audio-visual communication (radio, TV, etc.), and *zakat* management training and pilot projects.[41]

However, the competition among *zakat* collecting organizations and among systems of *zakat* management, the fragmentary nature of *zakat* information, and inadequate information through electronic mass media which could reach potential *muzakki* easily, have resulted in the slow growth of *zakat* payers or contributors. Substantial increases have been registered only in the case of *zakat fitrah*.

From 1979/80 to 1985/86, the average increase of the ZIS intake of the BAZIS of Jakarta was less than 9 per cent per year.[42] This figure, however, does not really reflect the real growth of payment. In 1980/81 of Rp. 437.1 million received by the BAZIS of Jakarta, only 10 per cent belonged to the category of *zakat*.[43] The BAZ of West Java, on the other hand, provides a more optimistic picture. From 1979 to 1985, the average annual growth of *muzakki* was 24.6 per cent (1980 was the highest with 37.5 per cent increase compared to the previous year). In money terms, the annual increase was 19.1 per cent. At the same time there was also a decline in the number of *mustahiq*. The *mustahiq-muzakki* ratio declined from 31.9 per cent in 1983 to 24.1 per cent in 1984. The relative decline of the *mustahiq*, however, was most probably due to the intensification of the collection of *zakat fitrah* rather than the decrease in the number of lawful *zakat* recipients.[44]

Realizing the low turnover of *zakat*, the governor of Jakarta made an appeal in November 1981 to all principals of elementary schools and *madrasah* that they should begin to educate their pupils on the principles and practices of ZIS in their respective schools.[45] The impact of this appeal, however, is yet to be felt.

Finally, the Minister of Finance, in his ministerial decree (number 650/MK/11/5/1976), stated that *zakat* was tax-deductable. By this decree the Minister of Finance not only tried to encourage the potential *muzakki* to pay their *zakat* (thus, in a way he also deepened government involvement in *zakat* collection) but also, and more importantly, helped promote semi-autonomous *zakat* agencies. For tax can be deducted after one could prove that one had properly paid one's *zakat*.

## Patterns of *Zakat* Collection

If the traditional system of *zakat* collection is a purely personal relationship between the *muzakki* and the *mustahiq*, the company-sponsored *zakat* committee is entirely based on the voluntary approval of the employees to have their salaries cut in accordance with *zakat* regulation. Quantitative and qualitative changes, however, take place in the second type of *zakat* agencies, that is, the Islamic social and educational organizations. In the first place, the fields of operations of these organizations have become largely nation-wide, regardless of their basically local character. These organizations have very strong tendencies to maintain permanent *muzakki*, through postal services. Not only do these organizations regularly send blank money orders to their potential *muzakki*, they also usually send them annual financial reports. They usually ask for their share in *zakat* of the potential *muzakki* on the basis of their on-going projects (e.g. hospitals, orphanages, schools) which, more often than not, are officially endorsed by local administration and the local council of *ulama*. Sometimes they also send their representatives to big cities and personally approach potential contributors. Hence, the importance of primordial and collegial networks.

The trends in *zakat* collection show that the changing concept of boundary (as determined by *fiqh*), from a local to a national (such as recommended by the seminar held by the IAIN of Jakarta in September 1972),[46] has immensely widened the scope and magnitude of the activities of Islamic social organizations. However, the local roots and local autonomy of Islamic national social organizations remain largely unchanged.

The government-sponsored or semi-autonomous *zakat* agencies have to operate against these backgrounds. The traditional system of *zakat* collection might even hinder or slow down the establishment of such organizations. The province of East Java, where most of the biggest *pesantren* are located, is still in the process of establishing a provincial *Baitul Maal*. Apparently, the strength of the traditional system of *zakat* collection is still too strong to overcome.[47]

In 1976, the governor of Jakarta issued a statement identifying five categories of '*zakat*able' properties and income, viz. domestic animals, food crops, gold and silver, enterprises (commerce, industries, services), and "unexpected income, which is received without much effort". In the first four categories the governor's decision simply followed the general agreement of *ulama* — such as 2.5 per cent to any type of income and property which has reached its *nisab*. In the last category the governor was daring enough to endorse a rather radical proposal put forward by several younger Muslim intellectuals and scholars. The "unexpected income" is identified by the governor as *rikaz* (hidden treasure), warranting a 20 per cent *zakat* on its value without *nisab*. The *muzakki* is expected to calculate his *zakat* in accordance with the guide provided; those who are not obliged to pay *zakat* are encouraged to pay *infaq/sadaqah*; and employees are encouraged to pay monthly as soon as they receive their salaries.[48]

The governor's stance has encouraged the BAZIS of Jakarta to design various approaches in its efforts to reach its annual target of ZIS collection. Several provinces with Islamic majority and relatively strong *kabupaten zakat* organizations, particularly South Sulawesi, closely watch the steps taken by Jakarta.

However, the methods of *zakat* collection in Jakarta differ from those of many other provinces in some respects. Firstly, Jakarta is a city-province which has no autonomous sub-regions. The line of command from the governor to all layers of administrative divisions is direct, without any intermediary, unlike other provinces (except Yogyakarta) with the respective *kabupaten* DPRDs (Local People's Representatives). Secondly, since Jakarta, unlike other provinces, is largely based on the service economy, the BAZIS of Jakarta does not put too much emphasis on the *zakat fitrah*. Only recently did it begin to pay some attention to this source of ZIS. This is certainly not the case with most other provinces. The BAZ of West Java, for example, from the beginning has regarded *zakat fitrah* as one of its most important resources of ZIS.

The ZIS collection of the BAZIS of Jakarta is based on both the territorial arrangement (in accordance with the administrative hierarchies) and the social categories of the potential *muzakki*. Each administrative hierarchy is responsible for certain *muzakki* categories. The provincial BAZIS is responsible for the collection of ZIS from big national corporations and central municipal offices; the *kelurahan* branch of BAZIS would tap the general populace; the mayoral branch is entitled to approach middle-sized industries

and other business ventures; and the *kecamatan*, the second lowest administrative hierarchy, would focus on petty traders as their targets.[49]

At the early stage of its development, the BAZIS of Jakarta identified
three major social categories as its potential *muzakki*, namely the national
and local entrepreneurs, employees of the municipal offices, and the general
populace. Beginning with the fiscal year of 1981/82, a new category was
added, namely the *haj*-pilgrims. Based on the belief that any *haj*-pilgrim can
economically be considered as a potential *muzakki*, each pilgrim is charged
Rp. 50,000 to 100,000. Finally, starting from the fiscal year of 1985/86,
military personnel (ABRI) have become the newest social category of potential *muzakki*.

Since the BAZIS began its operation in 1969, its ZIS collection has been
increasing almost consistently. The collection in 1981/82, for example, was
seventy-three times higher than that in 1969.[50] With improved *zakat* mechanism, new ways of ZIS collection,[51] and enlargement of the *muzakki* group,
the intake of the BAZIS continues to grow (see Table 1). Except in 1984/85,
when the ZIS intake fell by about 4.7 per cent, the average growth of ZIS
intake from 1980 to 1985/86 was about 12.41 per cent per year.

TABLE 1
**The BAZIS of Jakarta: Collection of ZIS, 1980/81–1986/87**
(Rp. million)

| Year | Entrepreneurs | DKI Employees | Community | *Haj*-pilgrims | Military | Total |
|------|---------------|---------------|-----------|----------------|----------|-------|
| 1980/81 | 67.2 | 49.8 | 316.7 | – | – | 433.7 |
| 1981/82 | 59.6 | 37.3 | 207.7 | 133.0 | – | 437.6 |
| 1982/83 | 80.1 | 41.4 | 371.7 | 41.5 | – | 534.7 |
| 1983/84 | 76.0 | 45.3 | 365.7 | 144.0 | – | 631.0 |
| 1984/85 | 60.1 | 50.7 | 347.4 | 143.2 | – | 601.4 |
| 1985/86 | 62.6 | 94.5 | 343.1 | 169.4 | 3.8 | 673.4 |
| 1986/87 | 58.6 | 128.6 | 410.9 | 187.8 | 10.0 | 795.9 |

SOURCE: BAZIS of Jakarta, 3 April 1987.

Understandably, the easiest ZIS to tap are the contributions of municipal
employees and, to a lesser extent, *haj*-pilgrims. The figures for these two
groups (except for *haj*-pilgrims in 1982/83 and for municipal employees for
1981/82) have been continuously growing. A potentially easy target are
the military personnel, but it is very much dependent on the co-operation
of the military commander in charge. Although the ZIS intake from the
national/local entrepreneurs is greatly influenced by economic fluctuations,
this category of *muzakki* has always been a reliable source of funds to the

BAZIS. At present, there are about sixty corporations registered as permanent *muzakki*. Every Ramadhan, the BAZIS would send these corporations its appeals, invoking the religious importance of *zakat* and the social benefits that can be expected from the performance of this religious duty. To these rather routine appeals the BAZIS would attach forms to be filled by individual *muzakki* in the company. This form is printed in such a way that it enables the employees to calculate their *zakat* for the year. This method, however, does not by any means make the BAZIS the monopoly holder of *zakat* from company personnel. Nonetheless, being an apparatus of the municipal administration, the BAZIS could have an upper hand in dealing with the companies, particularly those that have direct business interest in the administration. Especially when licences for new business ventures have to be issued or company supplies to the needs of the government have to be made, forms of ZIS sent by BAZIS would receive better attention.

The BAZIS has a more tricky business in its dealing with the general populace, especially those who are petty traders in the market places or those who need government services in the *kelurahan* offices. Since the competition with other *zakat* collecting organizations is stiffer in this category of potential *muzakki*, and the economic position and/or religious awareness are also somewhat lower, the BAZIS could not hope to collect substantial amount of ZIS in general and *zakat* in particular. Furthermore, if the BAZIS were to tap this category properly, it would need not only a large personnel but also a strong legal rational for its existence. In order to overcome these difficulties, the BAZIS has been issuing the GAS (*Gerakan Amal Sadaqah*) coupons with face values ranging from Rp. 100 to 500. These coupons should only be presented to the Muslims who need the services of the *kelurahan* office and who, according to the judgement of the *kelurahan* civil servants, are in a position to contribute. But since the *kelurahan* offices would usually like to meet the target set by the *camat* as the chairman of the *kecamatan* BAZIS, it is not rare for the coupons to be presented to anybody, regardless of religion or economic position. Understandably enough, this type of deviation usually takes place in the Chinese sections of Jakarta.[52]

The BAZIS of South Sulawesi, which is very much dependent on the activities of the existing government-sponsored *zakat* agencies in the *kabupaten*, has identified five categories of potential *muzakki*, namely civil servants, *haj*-pilgrims, military personnel, Muslim entrepreneurs, and general populace. After two years of existence, it could still scarcely touch the last three categories. But unlike the BAZIS of Jakarta, which only 'charged' the *haj*-pilgrims at the rate of Rp. 50,000 to 100,000 per person, the BAZIS of South Sulawesi uses the official cost of *haj*-pilgrimage as the *nisab*. In other words, on top of the official cost (the amount of which is annually decided by the Department of Religious Affairs) the *haj* candidate has to add 2.5 per cent.

This is his *zakat* for the year and it goes directly to the BAZIS.[53] In a way, religious obligation has become state requirement by putting *fiqh*-reasoning aside. But regardless of the legal or moral rationale behind this policy, the main bulk of ZIS of this *zakat* foundation is still the *zakat fitrah*, collected in the *kabupaten*. It is significant to note that ZIS collection of the BAZIS of South Sulawesi jumped from Rp. 156.3 million in 1985 to Rp. 270.6 million in 1986, an increase of about 40 per cent.

There is no way to ascertain whether the direct participation of local administration in the collection of ZIS has had any direct impact on the collections of private social religious organizations. Since the target groups of the government-sponsored *zakat* agencies are largely the untapped resources, there is a strong possibility that they do not really pose any threat to existing *zakat* collecting system. The ZIS promotion campaign conducted by the government-sponsored organizations is likely to increase *zakat* awareness among the Muslims. The activities of the Muhammadiyah, Dewan Dakwah, At-Thahiriyah, and Asy-Syafiiyah in Jakarta, for example, reinforce this assumption.

Taking the case of Ngunut, a small village in East Java, as an example, there is empirical support for the above assumption.[54] The BAZIS of Ngunut was established in 1978. Although it was founded by alumni of the Gontor *pesantren*, the BAZIS was strongly endorsed by *kecamatan* and village authorities. At the time of its establishment (1978) two existing *zakat* collecting agencies, the PKU Muhammadiyah and the Mabarot Nahdlatul Ulama, received respectively 1,980 kg and 4,015 kg of paddy as *zakat maal*. In 1979, the year the village BAZIS began to collect *zakat maal*, both organizations received even higher contributions (see Table 2).

TABLE 2
ZIS Ngunut, 1979–82

| Year | PKU Muhammadiyah | Mabarot NU | BAZIS |
|---|---|---|---|
| 1979/80 | 2,000 kg | 4,128 kg | 3,800 kg |
| 1980/81 | 3,050 kg | 6,500 kg | 11,526 kg |
| 1981/82 | 3,259 kg | 10,100 kg | 17,290 kg |

SOURCE: BAZIS Desa Ngunut.

Friendly competition in a small village and the clever use of *zakat* funds might contribute positively to the general improvement of *zakat* collection. But the need for an enlargement of the *muzakki* group should not be lost sight of.

## Patterns of *Zakat* Distribution

In his *Idul Fitri* speech at the Istiqlal Mosque on 30 November 1970, President Soeharto reported that since 1968, when he made himself available as a provisional national *amil*, he had collected Rp. 39.5 million (US$2,473).

> After receiving advices from *ulama* and Islamic leaders I have returned the amount [of money] to the Islamic *ummat*. In the middle of last year I returned Rp. 17,200,000, which has since been used all over the country. This year I have returned Rp. 18,200,000, which has been spent on 265 mosques and *mushalla*, 241 *madrasah*, and *pesantren* and [subsidies] to 222 Islamic foundations — they are scattered all over Indonesia. To those who have received these *zakat* contributions, I must again emphasize that the money is not the government's money, and certainly not my money; it is the contribution and the efforts of the Muslims themselves.[55]

This was the last report of the President on *zakat*. By that time, as has been noted earlier, several provinces had taken over the provisional nature of the President's role as the *amil*.

Practically all the items mentioned by the President can easily fall into one of the eight *asnaf* categories, clearly identified in *At-Taubah*/9:60. In the early years of the BAZIS of Jakarta and, for that matter, of most of the other government-sponsored *amil*, this conservative interpretation of the Qur'anic precepts was adhered to. Since the share of each legal *asnaf* is not clearly stipulated in the Qur'an or the Hadith, local needs were usually given serious consideration. The biggest share was most likely spent on the *fakir-miskin* (the poor, including village religious teachers) for consumption purposes. The second largest would usually go the *sabilillah* category under which religious buildings are listed. In 1973, for example, the BAZIS of Jakarta received Rp. 148 million and spent about Rp. 58 million on religious buildings (including the expansion of *haj* dormitory). From 1972 to 1974, it consistently set aside a certain amount of money for itself as the *amil* so that it could develop its apparatus and start productive projects.[56]

TABLE 3

*Amil*'s Share in *Zakat* Distribution by the BAZIS of Jakarta

(Rp. million)

| Year | Received | *Amil* Purposes |
|------|----------|-----------------|
| 1972 | 73.3 | 35.1 |
| 1973 | 148.0 | 39.7 |
| 1974 | 151.0 | 38.1 |

SOURCE: *Pedoman Zakat*, p. 75.

Compared to the shares of other categories, the amount received by the *amil* from 1972 to 1974 was quite substantial. In 1972, it received about as much as 45 per cent of *zakat* collection. The relative decrease of the share of the *amil* in 1974 and the increase of the BAZIS receipts can be simply explained by the fact in that year the BAZIS began to collect *infaq* and *sadaqah* which were sometimes clearly earmarked for certain purposes by the contributors.

A series of seminars and a survey on the opinions of the *ulama* and experts on *zakat* collection and distribution, as stated earlier, not only changed the structure of the BAZIS but also altered its basic strategy. A workshop under the auspices of BAZIS, held after the completion of the survey on *zakat*, finally recommended that the distribution of *zakat* should follow some basic policies, namely:

1.    It should be educational, productive, and economical, so that in the end the recipients of *zakat* would no longer need *zakat*; they should be the *zakat* payers.
2.    In the cases of *fakir miskin* (the poor), *riqab* (slaves to be liberated), *muallaf* (new converts), and *ibnu sabil* (travellers in search of knowledge) emphasis should be on the individuals, while the legal institutions that take care of them should receive a smaller share.
3.    In the cases of *sabilillah* (in the path of God) and *al-gharimin* (men in debt), the *amil* should be the main legal institution to carry out Islamic activities.
4.    The undistributed *zakat* can be used as funds for development purposes (deposit in the state banks).

These basic policies or principles were adopted by the governor of Jakarta and the BAZIS. They were later endorsed by the Department of Religious Affairs.[57]

Naturally some of the eight *asnaf* categories have become meaningless or much less significant in the present times. Who could now be considered as the *riqab*? In a time when the transportation system has become so advanced who could now be classified as the *ibnu sabil*? "Nowadays many small traders", the recommendation states, "have to borrow money at high interest". These *al-gharimin* could be given *zakat* so that they could pay off their debts and start new ventures. "The amount [of money] given to them can be assessed in accordance with their needs to start new business ventures." How about the *ibnu sabil*? The concept of stranded traveller can at present mean scientific expedition, scholarship, inexpensive boarding house for students, etc.

With the support of *fiqh* interpretation on *At-Taubah*/9:60 the BAZIS of Jakarta distributes its ZIS into four sectors, namely:

1.    35 per cent for the *fakir miskin* sector (25 per cent for productive funds and 10 per cent for consumption funds);

2.  10 per cent for the *amil* sector (but since the BAZIS is entirely funded by the local annual budget its share is divided into two parts: 5 per cent goes to the first sector and 5 per cent to the fourth);
3.  10 per cent for the *muallaf, al-gharimin,* and *ibnu sabil* sector; and
4.  45 per cent for the *sabilillah* sector (25 per cent for physical buildings, 15 per cent for institutional supports, and 5 per cent for social supports).[58]

On paper at least, the *sabilillah* sector would receive 50 per cent and the *fakir miskin* sector 40 per cent of the proceeds. In practice, however, the BAZIS is flexible about the ratio, depending on the needs of the year. Thus, in three consecutive years (1982–85) the *sabilillah* sector received much more than 50 per cent of the proceeds.

A similar pattern of distribution was also seen in 1985/86, when the *sabilillah* sector received Rp. 431.4 million while the *fakir miskin* sector received Rp. 129.2 million and the *muallaf, al-gharimin,* etc., sector was allocated Rp. 69.5 million.[59]

TABLE 4
**Distribution of ZIS by the BAZIS of Jakarta**
(Rp. million)

| Sector | 1982/83 | 1983/84 | 1984/85 |
|---|---|---|---|
| *Fakir miskin* | 119.9 | 113.0 | 98.8 |
| *Muallaf, al-gharimin*, etc. | 5.6 | 4.7 | 4.5 |
| *Sabilillah* | 382.5 | 383.9 | 465.8 |
| Total | 508.0 | 501.6 | 569.1 |

SOURCE: BAZIS DKI Jakarta.

A closer look at the *sabilillah* sector of the 1985/86 fiscal year reveals that a large amount of money (Rp. 260.6 million) was spent on building facilities, including the construction, expansion, or renovation of 595 mosques/*mushallah*, 7 kindergartens, and maternity hospitals. The rest was used for institutional supports, *dakwah* organizations, scholarships (120 high school students, 55 university students, 5 doctoral supports), and religious teachers without regular incomes.

The distribution of *zakat* in the *fakir miskin* sector in the 1985/86 fiscal year is quite revealing. According to the basic policy of *zakat* distribution, about 30 per cent of the 40 per cent allocated for this sector (after 5 per cent from the *amil* sector is added) should be used for productive funds. But not more than Rp. 33,950,000 was allocated in 1985/86 for productive funds (i.e., capital support for the economically weak entrepreneurs) while the consumption funds received not less than Rp. 96,280,000, which was almost three times higher than the former.[60]

The share of the so-called productive funds has been consistently decreasing since 1980/81 when the BAZIS provided capital supports for no less than 1,777 *mustahiq*. Subsequently, the number of recipients has been declining.

TABLE 5
**Productive Funds for Small-Scale Entrepreneurs**

| Year | Number of *Mustahiq* | Funds Provided (Rp. million) |
|------|------|------|
| 1980/81 | 1,777 | 90.4 |
| 1981/82 | 1,583 | 78.4 |
| 1982/83 | 1,262 | 74.9 |
| 1983/84 | 490 | 70.0 |
| 1984/85 | 174 | 54.2 |
| Total | 5,286 | 367.9 |

The major reason for this continuing decline is easy to find. As a matter of policy, the BAZIS only gave capital support in the form of loans to the small-scale or needy entrepreneurs. It was intended to be a self-generating fund that was expected to grow, and it was hoped that the *mustahiq* could transform themselves into new *muzakki*. But only a very small percentage of the *mustahiq* paid back the capital they had borrowed. In the period between 1977 and 1985, there were 9,656 *mustahiq* but only 1,164 of them made regular repayments on an instalment basis. Out of the Rp. 569 million lent out, only Rp. 143.4 million was repaid to the BAZIS.

In its evaluation of the above scheme, the BAZIS identified several problems. One of these related to the weakness of apparatus and the mechanism of the BAZIS itself. BAZIS is still not well equipped to manage the programme properly. It could neither establish a well-planned control mechanism nor could it give much-needed guidance to the *mustahiq*. The Regional Development Bank (BPD), which channelled the funds, was either too far away from the domiciles of the borrowers, who mostly lived at the outskirts of Jakarta or in the *kampong* sectors of the city, or simply too busy to provide any control or guidance. Furthermore, as the executive chairman of the BAZIS has put it, "the executives and staff of the BAZIS are rather reluctant to recruit new *mustahiq* candidates, because most of the old ones did not fulfil their duties and nor have they returned as *infaq* the productive funds they received".[61]

But why did the *mustahiq* fail to fulfil their obligations? They reason that since the funds come from ZIS and since there is no religious regulation requiring the *mustahiq* to return the ZIS they have received, they are not obliged to repay. Moreover, the officials of BAZIS suspect that the lifestyle of the *mustahiq* is still largely consumption-oriented. Be that as it may, the BAZIS officials do admit that the amount of capital allocated to each individual is too small to start new business ventures. In other words, regardless of the good intention, the BAZIS was not able to uplift the *mustahiq* from their subsistence level.

The major beneficiary of this abortive experiment has been the *sabilillah* sector. Beginning with the fiscal year 1985/86, however, the BAZIS has designed a new approach to the productive funds projects, giving top priorities to the successful *mustahiq* and being selective in recruiting new *mustahiq* or borrowers. The BAZIS would naturally write off the official debts of the non-paying *mustahiq*. More importantly it would channel the funds collectively through legal institutions which have programmes for developing cottage industries or other business ventures suitable for the economically weak entrepreneurs. In other words, the BAZIS is returning to its original idea of having close working relationship with the various NGOs (Non-Governmental Organizations) or Lembaga Swadaya Masyarakat (Social Institutes for Self-reliance).

Jakarta is, of course, not representative of Indonesia. The lack of success in Jakarta does not have to be repeated in other provinces. Despite the near debacle in Jakarta, in the first year of its existence the BAZIS of South Sulawesi allocated Rp. 24 million of its Rp. 156.3 million ZIS proceeds to support 974 poor and small entrepreneurs (Rp. 25,000 per person). In 1986, the number of these poor and weak entrepreneurs was down to 664, each individual receiving Rp. 50,000. The BAZIS of South Sulawesi allocated Rp. 33.2 million of its Rp. 270.6 million proceeds to help these small entrepreneurs. But, unlike in 1985, these funds were not directly distributed by the provincial BAZIS; instead, these funds have become the responsibilities of *kabupaten* BAZIS.

The small amount allocated for such a programme relative to that of the BAZIS of Jakarta can be attributed to the fact that the major source of funds for the BAZIS of South Sulawesi has been *zakat fitrah*, the use of which, according to prevailing *fiqh* interpretation, cannot be as flexible as that of *zakat maal*. The BAZIS of South Sulawesi did not expect the *mustahiq* to repay the money they received.

On the whole, the BAZIS of South Sulawesi distributed its ZIS rather conservatively. In 1985 the largest share was used for the renovation and expansion of 169 mosques (Rp. 54.1 million) and to support 85 religious schools and 761 religious teachers (Rp. 41,675,000). As the legal *amil*, the BAZIS (both the centre and the *kabupaten* branches) allocated to itself about Rp. 25.5 million.

A new pattern of distribution was introduced in 1986, whereby the *kabupaten* branches would deal directly with the *mustahiq*, while the provincial BAZIS would mostly be responsible for the improvement of organizational capabilities of the *amil* and the propagation of *zakat* (including the training of the BAZIS personnel). For these purposes the BAZIS has allocated to itself about 30 per cent of its ZIS collection. Unlike the BAZIS of Jakarta, which is fully funded by the government, the BAZIS of South Sulawesi has to rely exclusively on its generated resources. On the basis of the proposals of its branches in the *kabupaten*, the BAZIS would return its ZIS to the *kabupaten*, from where the ZIS actually originates. The *kabupaten* would spend most of the returned ZIS on mosques, religious schools, religious teachers, and *fakir miskin*. In 1986, the BAZIS of South Sulawesi financed the publication *tafsir al Qur'an* in Buginese and the construction of a small model mosque. It also gave scholarships to students, including a research grant for a doctoral candidate in Islamic law.[62]

The most important innovation in *zakat* distribution has been the institutionalization of revolving funds for productive purposes. In spite of its dismal performance, the attempt of the BAZIS of Jakarta has, nevertheless, shown some positive signs. It is encouraging to note that about 15 per cent of the *mustahiq* did repay the funds they officially borrowed; and about 25 per cent of the funds were actually returned to the BAZIS. This brave approach of the BAZIS of Jakarta was not imitated by South Sulawesi. The latter simply gave away the capital, hoping that the *mustahiq* would be successful in their new ventures. It is of interest to note in this regard that the Yayasan Dana Sosial Islam (Foundation of Islamic Social Funds) of West Sumatera, established in 1984, is trying to apply the Jakarta approach, with one major modification: instead of looking for poor *mustahiq*, it provides working capital to promising and enterprising young school drop-outs or high school graduates. It is still too early to evaluate the success of this programme.

### *Zakat* and Experiments in Community Development

A few years ago a professor of economics, who was known as an influential *ulama* on campus, started an experiment. It was really an individual experiment. After contacting several close friends whom he could consider as *muzakki* he simply appointed himself as the *amil*, without any right to the share of *zakat*. From the collection of his and other friends' *zakat*, he provided additional capital to some selected fishermen. He hoped that with the additional capital, which was officially a borrowed capital, the fishermen could increase their incomes and contribute to the establishment of a new co-operative which was also to be supported by *zakat*. In short, he started a small-scale income-generating programme for the fishermen, who were sometimes the prey of the money lenders' avarice. But, to his dismay, after two or three experiments the initial capital simply dried up.

In the meantime he tried another venture. Applying the same approach (the *mustahiq* were given capital as loan and they were expected to repay in instalment) he provided capital to street vendors. After a year or two he could boast that he was quite successful. Not only was the capital repaid, without interest, but he could also recruit new *mustahiq*. His success in the second attempt may be attributed to the fact that he was more familiar with the community of street vendors than that of the fishermen.[63]

The experiment of this professor is only an example of many individual attempts to make *zakat* something more than just a matter of religious obligation. Such experiments show that the familiarity of the *muzakki* with the life situation of the *mustahiq* is a crucial factor in ensuring the success of the programme. The case of the Pesantren of Gontor (Ponorogo Regency, East Java) also shows the importance of this very elementary lesson in community development, as will be seen.

The Pesantren of Gontor is a modernist-oriented *pesantren*. Established by Kiai H. Zarkasi, who had received his religious training at the pre-war Islamic Normal School in Padang (West Sumatera), the *pesantren* is known for the language abilities (Arabic and English) of its students.[64] In each of the last few years the number of students living in the *pesantren* compound is about 3,000. According to the estimate of the *pesantren* board, each student normally spends about Rp. 25,000 per month. This means that the students spend about Rp. 75 million per month. Since most of the money is spent for consumption purposes, presumably the major beneficiary of this student-economy are the communities around the *pesantren*.

The Pesantren of Gontor has thousands of graduates. Quite a number of them have become respectable members of their respective communities. And a handful of the successful graduates regularly send their *zakat* to the *pesantren*. In compliance with the wishes of the *muzakki*, the *pesantren* spent the *zakat* on the *sabilillah* sector, if the term used by the BAZIS of Jakarta can be used, that is, on school buildings. Subsequently, a decision was taken that some portions of the *zakat* should be used for social welfare — to help needy students and, more important, to help finance the establishment of women co-operatives on the *pesantren*. Later *zakat* was also distributed to the surrounding communities.

This was the beginning. At the initiative of the alumni, several communication centres were established. The main function of these centres was to serve as a channel between the *pesantren* and the society. At the present time there are already several communication centres in the *kabupaten* of Ponorogo. Through these channels the *pesantren* is expected to design community development projects. Under this arrangement several cottage industries have been supported. These industries, small as they are, have provided jobs to unemployed youths in the villages around the *pesantren*.

One of the most successful uses of *zakat* for community development programmes undertaken by the alumni of Gontor is the BAZIS of Ngunut in the *kecamatan* Babakan, Ponorogo (East Java).[65] Established in 1978, the BAZIS collects agricultural *zakat* (or paddy) from the peasants of the village and ZIS from civil servants who live in the village. The collection of ZIS from the civil servants has been from the beginning very successful, because it is carried out with the co-operation and strong approval of the *Bupati*, the local office of Religious Affairs, and that of Education and Culture. Its regular *infaq* collection amounts to about Rp. 20,000 per month.

The first achievement of the BAZIS of Ngunut lies in the fact that it could establish itself without any resistance from two competing Islamic organizations which had dominated the social religious lives of the village until 1978, viz: reformist or modernist oriented PKU Muhammadiyah and the bigger traditionalist Mabarot Nahdlatul Ulama. In a relatively short time, the BAZIS of Ngunut was able to make itself the main force behind the ZIS movement. The BAZIS carefully avoided encroachment into the 'territories' of the two existing organizations. It is interesting to note that the ZIS campaign of the BAZIS helped these two organizations to increase their *zakat* collections. In 1978, a year before the BAZIS began to operate, the PKU Muhammadiyah received 1,980 kg of paddy and the Mabarot 4,128 kg; in the third year of the BAZIS (1981) they received 3,259 kg and 10,000 kg of paddy respectively, while the BAZIS itself managed to collect 17,290 kg of paddy as *zakat*.

The experience of the BAZIS of Ngunut demonstrated the importance not only of mutual respect with existing organizations and the need to win people's confidence, but also of the co-operation of both officials and opinion leaders. Furthermore, the early success of this BAZIS as reflected in its ZIS collections can be seen as proof of its ability to establish a proper working mechanism. The decision-making body of the BAZIS consisted of three important boards, namely, the supervisory (with the village head as the supervisor), advisory (comprising the *ulama* and village intellectuals and officials), and the executive. Like any modern NGO, the BAZIS also has its own research and development, information and public relations, and collection sections. The BAZIS tries not only to relate itself to the community as a whole but also to learn from the experience of others. Of the thirty-five officials of the BAZIS elected for fiscal year 1981/82, three were holders of *doctorandus* degrees, and six had bachelor degrees. In other words, among the officers of the BAZIS are the better-educated members of the small community.

The BAZIS began its operation by introducing new methods. The first step was to acquire data on land holding and land use from the office of the *kecamatan*. On the basis of these data, the BAZIS would send letters to the peasants, informing them of (1) its estimate of the year's yields which the peasants could expect and (2) the estimated amount of *zakat* the peasants are expected to pay. After the harvest, the officers of the BAZIS would visit the peasants to collect their obligatory agricultural (paddy) *zakat*. In co-operation with the other two organizations the BAZIS also collects *zakat fitrah*.

To collect *infaq* from the civil servants, the BAZIS employs school children who visit the houses of civil servants outside their school hours. As a token of gratitude they would receive 10 per cent of the receipts. At present, the BAZIS is also planning to tap other social categories, subject to the consent of the *ulama* and *umara* (government officials) in the village.

On the basis of the recommendations made by the *ulama* and government officials, the BAZIS divides its ZIS into two sectors: 70 per cent for *fakir miskin* and 30 per cent for *sabilillah*. It has been decided that 50 per cent of the *fakir miskin* should be given during Eid celebrations or during bad harvests. The other half should be used as productive funds, i.e., as initial capital for the poor peasants. From 1979 to the beginning of 1981, the BAZIS managed to distribute eighty-two goats, and at the end of 1981 the BAZIS distributed forty goats plus a capital subsidy of Rp. 150,000 to street vendors (Rp. 5,000 each).

The *sabilillah* funds have been used for village road reconstructions, renovation of dilapidated buildings, water pipes, and, of course, mosques and *mushallah*.

The *infaq* from civil servants has been mainly used to provide scholarships for the village children. In 1980/81 it could give monthly scholarships to 24 elementary school children and 6 junior and 3 senior high school students. In addition, the BAZIS also subsidized Qur'an classes and gave financial support to poor families in despair (death or sickness). Ngunut is an example of a relatively poor village which tries to help itself without any outside financial support.

Unlike the early attempts of the Jakarta BAZIS and the various individual efforts cited earlier which focused on the individual *mustahiq* as their immediate target group, the BAZIS of Ngunut has been aiming at the community as a whole. The main interest of Ngunut is not only the eradication of poverty or the transformation of *mustahiq* into *muzakki*, but also the attainment of social harmony.

A more ambitious programme is being attempted in Klaten (Central Java). Under the guidance of a Jakarta-based NGO (LP3ES) a community-based development programme (which is expected to be completed in six years) was started in 1984. The programme began with an imaginary *zakat* collection — as if the financial resources came from *zakat* — which is to be used in accordance with the jurisprudence (*fiqh*). However, the seed money for the programme came not from *zakat* proceeds but from foreign aid. In other words, it can only be considered as a pilot project in productive use of *zakat*. For the moment, this experiment can only be seen as one of the several designs for the productive use of *zakat* that are now being written in many Islamic journals and discussed in various seminars and workshops.

**Conclusion**

In a seminar held recently, a participant presented a paper entitled "How to Estimate One's Own *Zakat*". Held at a university campus, the main objective of the seminar was to provide management training to the so-called *zakat* motivators. This seminar, important as it might be from local perspective, is far from being a unique event at the national scene. Similar seminars or workshops have been held in several places in recent years. The theme of this particular seminar, however, clearly reflects the development of thinking on *zakat*. In the earlier stage, the major concern of the *ulama* and Muslim intellectuals was *zakat* as a *fiqh* problem and its significance in social life; now it is the management of *zakat* collection and distribution that has been receiving the widest attention.

   Seminars, workshops, and trainings on *zakat* (or ZIS) management would continue to be held; but the ever-growing interest in *zakat* could not be separated from related aspects. Firstly, the contemporary *zakat* movement, i.e., the drive for *zakat* collection and productive use of *zakat*, has from the beginning been a manifestation of the renewed interest in Islam. To put it more specifically, it is a part of the process of the so-called Islamic revivalism in Indonesia. It is around this undercurrent that theological and political debates have been conducted. Secondly, the changing forms and character of the *zakat* movement reflect the somewhat ambiguous position of Islam, the religion of the majority, in the *Pancasila* state of Indonesia. Finally, the *zakat* movement also shows the shift in emphasis of Islamic social movement in the country — from the attempt to make Islam the foundation of the state to the struggle for "the creation of a just and prosperous society, which is blessed by Allah", if the jargon of the battle-cry can be quoted. The *zakat* movement, in other words, is also an integrated part of "the return to the *ummah*" tendencies that are now becoming more prevalent among the *ulama* and Muslim intellectuals in Indonesia. The *zakat* drive and the new strategy for the use of *zakat* have been taken as an example of the *dakwah bil hal* (missionary activity through exemplary deeds) approach in dealing with the poverty and backwardness of the *ummah*.[66]

After twenty years in operation — that is, if we take the President's speech in 1968 as the milestone — the most important achievement of the *zakat* drive in Indonesia is the growing awareness of the Muslims about their *zakat* obligations. According to a nation-wide opinion poll, conducted by the newsmagazine *TEMPO* (May 1988), about 84 per cent of the 930 respondents knew that *zakat* was obligatory or *wajib*.[67] But it is hard to estimate from their answers how many do pay *zakat*. However, the chairman of the BAZIS of Jakarta has made a rough estimate. By comparing the number of the Muslim population in Jakarta with the annual proceeds of BAZIS, he has estimated that, on the average, the population of Jakarta pays only Rp. 150 or not more than US9 cents (1988) per person annually. In other words, only a handful of relatively devout Muslims do pay their *zakat*.

According to the opinion poll of *TEMPO*, 41 per cent of the *zakat* payers channelled their *zakat* to the official *amil* and only 38 per cent of the respondents preferred to pay *zakat* directly to their chosen *asnaf*, while the rest (21 per cent) use all available channels. These figures clearly demonstrate that the role of the *amil*, either BAZIS or BAZ, is still not very predominant. It thus appears that the possibility of *zakat* being used for productive purposes is constrained. To eradicate poverty or to transform the *mustahiq*, the *zakat* recipient, into the *muzakki*, the *zakat* payer, *zakat* (and other forms of religious alms, *infaq* and *sadaqah*), should be organized and strategically distributed. The irony is that a substantial part of the *TEMPO* respondents stated that *zakat* ought to be used for the eradication of poverty and the attainment of distributive justice.

The significance of this opinion poll lies in the fact that its findings seem to confirm the fragmentary accounts on *zakat* drive and management in several localities discussed in this chapter. In spite of the growing awareness of the Muslims about their *zakat* obligation and their interest in the institution of *zakat*, the role of the *amil* is far from adequate, and the institutionalization of *zakat* is still in its embryo stage. The story of trials and errors of the BAZIS of Jakarta, despite the full participation of the local administration, and the continuing story of success of the small village Ngunut, in East Java, are cases in point. Both types of experience seem to suggest that the closer the *zakat* organization is to the capitalistic economy, the lesser the possibility for *zakat* to achieve its objective of transforming the *mustahiq* into *muzakki*. In other words, in economic terms, the social impact of *zakat* is very much dependent on the degree of social solidarity of the community in which it operates. The relative success of several *pesantren* in the collection and distribution of *zakat*, particularly those which have established their own community development programmes, can be attributed mainly to the managerial capacity of the *kiai*, the central figure of the *pesantren*, and the respect and loyalty which the *kiai* could command in his community.

Needless to say, poverty is not the only social disease of the *ummah*. Backwardness represents yet another illness. Since the concrete meanings of backwardness are manifested in the lack of educational, health, religious, and other social facilities, it is understandable why most of the semi-autonomous BAZIS in the provinces are addressing these problems.

Given the variety of experiments and the varying degrees of success of the *zakat* drive in Indonesia, it is manifest that *zakat*, as a religiously based social institution, is in the process of finding its proper place in a changing modern society. Many new methods of *zakat* collection and distribution will have to be attempted and many failures may have to be endured in the future, but a note of optimism is still in order. *Zakat* drive is, after all, an integral part of Islamic revivalist movement. Equally important is the recognition of the role that the institution of *zakat* can play in the economic development of the *ummah*.

## NOTES

1   *Saran Alim Ulama Kepada Bapak Presiden Soeharto tentang Zakat*, issued in Jakarta on 24 September 1968. Document reproduced by BAZ Secretariat of Jakarta.

2   Reprinted in *Pedoman Zakat: 9 Seri* (Jakarta: Proyek Pembinaan Zakat dan Wakaf [Department of Religious Affairs]), pp. 403–9.

3   For presidential addresses on *zakat*, see *Pedoman Zakat*, ibid., pp. 403–39. With the Presidential Decree No. 07/PRIN/10/1968, 31 October 1968, Major-General Alamsyah, Colonel Azwar Hamid, and Colonel Ali Afandi were instructed to establish an organizational apparatus for the nation-wide *zakat* collection.

4   M. Hasby Ash-Shiddieqy, *Beberapa Permasalahan Zakat* (Jakarta: Tintamas, 1976).

5   "Take alms, of their wealth, wherewith thou mayst purify them and mayst make them grow, and pray for them. Lo! thy prayer is an assuagement for them. Allah is Hearer, Knowee." (Surah IX-Repentance: 103). Mohammed Marmaduke Pickthal, *The Meaning of Glorious Koran* (New York: Mentor Book, 1954), p. 154.

6   "The alms are only for the poor and the needy, and thore who collect them, and thore whose hearts are to be reconciled and to free captives and the debtors, and for the cause of Allah, and [for] the wayfarers; a duty imposed by Allah. Allah is Knower, Wiser." Ibid., p. 150.

7   Brief discussions on this are given in Syaichul Hadi Pernomo, "Pola Pemikiran Zakat. Badan Amil Zakat, Infaq/Shadaqah (BAZIS) DKI Jakarta". Unpublished *magister* thesis. (Jakarta: IAIN Syarif Hidayatullah, 1984).

8   *Rekomendasi dan Pedoman Pelaksanaan Zakat,* Hasil Penelitian dan Seminar Zakat DKI Jakarta (Jakarta: BAZIS DKI Jakarta, 1981), pp. 37–55. Hereafter referred to as *Rekomendasi.*

9   *Laporan Hasil Seminar-Lokakarya: Mencari Model Sistem Pengelolaan Zakat* (Jakarta: P3M, 1986), p. 13. Hereafter referred to as *Laporan.*

10   See, for example, Ali Yafie, "Islam dan Problema Kemiskinan", *Pesantren* 2, III (1986): 3–11. Kiai Ali Yafie is an influential traditionalist orthodox *ulama.* He is a vice-chairman of the Council of Syuriah of the Nahdlatul Ulama and concurrently also a vice-chairman of the Indonesian Council of Ulama.

11   Reprinted in *Rekomendasi,* pp. 24–33.

12   *TEMPO* 12, 21 Mei 1988.

13   An interview with Kiai H. Sahal Mahfudz, "Perlu Pengembangan Konsep", *Pesantren* 2, III (1986): 61–64.

14   A leading Muslim intellectual and former leader of the Masyumi political party, Syafruddin Prawiranegara, who is a lawyer by training, has been a major proponent of this opinion. Those who have paid tax (usually in the range of 10 to 40 per cent of income), according to him, are no longer obliged to pay *zakat.* A middle-way attempt to solve this problem is given by, among others, Amir Syarifuddin in "Zakat dan Pajak, Alternatif Memadukannya", *Pesantren* 2, III (1986): 21–28.

15   A popularized version of the controversy between 20 per cent and 2.5 per cent *zakat* is given in *TEMPO* 12, XVIII, 21 Mei 1988. The major proponent of the 20 per cent *zakat* is Dr M. Amien Rais, a young leader of the Muhammadiyah and a lecturer of political science at the Gadjah Mada University. A Ph.D. degree holder from the University of Chicago, Rais is one of the influential Muslim intellectuals.

16   Interview with M. Yunan Nasution, a leader of the Dewan Dakwah, 4 May 1987.

17   Interview with S. Ahmad of the At-Thahiriyah, 6 May 1987.

18   E. Gobeé and C. Adriannse, *Ambtelijk Adviezen van C. Snouck Hurgronje 1889–1939,* Vol. II ('s-Gravenhage: Martinus Nijhoff, 1957), pp. 1245–46, 1282–85.

19   On religious officials see, for example, G.F. Pijper, *Studien over de Geschiedenis van de Islam in Indonesie 1900–1950* (Leiden: Brill, 1977), pp. 63–96.

20   On controversies surrounding the Guru Ordinance see, for example, Deliar Noer, *The Modernist Muslim Movement in Indonesia* (Kuala Lumpur: Oxford University Press, 1973).

21   See H.J. Benda, *The Crescent and the Rising Sun: Indonesia Under the Japanese Occupation (1942–1945)* (The Hague/Bandung: Van Hoeve, 1958).

22  H. Nourrouzzaman As-Shidiqi, "Muhammad Hasbi Ash-Shiddieqy dalam Perspektif Sejarah Pemikiran Islam di Indonesia" (Unpublished Ph.D. thesis, IAIN Sunan Kalijaga, Yogyakarta, 1987), pp. 183–87. On Aceh during the Japanese occupation, see A.J. Piekaar, *Atjeh en de Oorlog met Japan* ('s-Gravenhage/Bandung: Van Hoeve, 1949).

23  Nazaruddin Syamsuddin, *Republican Revolt: A Study of the Acehnese Rebellion* (Singapore: Institute of Southeast Asian Studies, 1985).

24  M. Dawam Rahardjo, "Zakat dan Perspektif Sosial-Ekonomi", *Pesantren* 2, III (1986): 36–50. One informant recalled that in 1966 Dr Moh. Hatta, the former first Vice President of the Republic of Indonesia, suggested that the state promulgate "Legislation of Compulsory Zakat", but to no effect (*TEMPO* 12, XVIII, 21 Mei 1988). Perhaps time was not ripe for it.

25  K.H. Muchtar Natsir, "Pengalaman Pengelolaan Zakat BAZIS Jakarta" in *Laporan*. The author is the chairman of the BAZIS and concurrently the *imam* of the Istiqlal Mosque in Jakarta.

26  Pernomo, "Pola Pemikiran": 8–9.

27  On the structural arrangement of the BAZIS, see *Rekomendasi*, pp. 69–121.

28  Marzani Anwar, "BAZIS DKI Jakarta: Sosok Keamilan Modern", *Pesantren* 2, III (1986): 69–79. Some of the more important and revised decrees and instructions are reprinted in *Pedoman Pengkelolaan Zakat dan Infaq/Shadaqah* (Jakarta: BAZIS DKI Jakarta, 1980).

29  *Laporan Tahunan: Bidang Urusan Agama Islam, Kantor Wilayah Departemen Agama Propinsi Sulawesi Selatan,* 1984/1985.

30  Abdul Samad Satuhang, "Konsepsi Dalam Pendayagunaan Zakat Sebagai Sjaran Sosial Menurut Syariat Islam di Kabupaten Gowa" (Unpublished *doctorandus* thesis, IAIN Alauddin, Ujung Pandang 1984/1985).

31  Ummi Salam, "Zakat Sebagai Modal Usaha Keluarga Kecil" (Unpublished *doctorandus* thesis, IAIN Alauddin, Ujung Pandang, 1982).

32  Muh. Djunaidi, "Suatu Analisa Tentang Intensifikasi Zakat Sebagai Sumber Dana Peningkatan Pendidikan Islam di Kabupaten Sidenreng-Rappang" (Unpublished *doctorandus* thesis, IAIN Alauddin, Ujung Pandang, 1982).

33  H. Abdul Malik Hambali, "Yayasan Badan Amil Zakat, Infaq dan Shadaqah, Propinsi Dati I Sulawesi Selatan" (A lecture, reproduced by BAZIS, Ujung Pandang, 1987).

34  See the statistics on the *zakat* collection of the BAZIS of DKI Jakarta. *Laporan Tahunan BAZIS DKI Jakarta*, 1985/1986.

35  "Pengelolaan Zakat Ditinjau dari Aspek Hukum Islam, Sosial, Ekonomi". (Seminar tanggal 2–3 Agustus 1986). Bontang (Kalimantan Timur): Badan Dakwah Islamiyah LNG Badak, p. 14.

36  Data collected by Dr Analiansyah, one of the participants of the above-mentioned seminar.

37 Dr H. Aspar Djarman, *Zakat Profesi* (Banjarmasin: Bagian Proyek Penerangan Bimbingan dan Dakwah/Khotbah Agama Islam, Propinsi Kalimantan Selatan, 1986/1987).

38 *Laporan* (1985/86). p. 12.

39 D.H. Burger, "Desa Ngablak (Kabupaten Pati) dalam tahun 1869 dan 1924" (translation), in *Sejarah Lokal di Indonesia*, edited by Taufik Abdullah (Yogyakarta: Gadjah Mada University Press, 1985), pp. 177-98. And D.H. Burger, *Desa Pekalongan* (translation) (Jakarta: Penerbit Bhratara, 1971).

40 The *Bulletin Dakwah* is a four-page weekly publication which publishes a Friday sermon per issue. Most of the big mosques subscribe to this bulletin and distribute them free of charge to the congregation.

41 *Pedoman Zakat*, pp. 31-64.

42 *Rekapitulasi Pengumpulan BAZIS DKI Jakarta*, 1986.

43 *Pedoman Zakat*, p. 37.

44 See the table on *zakat* collection of the BAZ of West Java, as quoted in M. Dawam Rahardjo, "Zakat dalam Perspektif Sosial-Ekonomi", *Pesantren* 2, III (1986): 42. For a short discussion on the experience of *zakat* collection and distribution in West Java, see Sudjangi, "Badan Amil Zakat: Sebuah Studi Permulaan Tentang Pelaksanaan Zakat di Jawa Barat", *Dialog* VIII (16 Maret 1984): 65-75.

45 Governor's Instruction *Surat Edaran Gubernur DKI Jakarta* No. 1346/088.437, 3 November 1981.

46 *Rekomendasi*, pp. 63-64.

47 Interview with K.H. Misbach, Chairman of the Council of Ulama of East Java, April 1987.

48 Governorial Decree, *Gubernur/KDKI Jakarta*, 12 Juli 1976, No. D III 5401/f/5/76.

49 BAZIS DKI Jakarta (Annual Report), pp. 485-88.

50 *Pedoman Zakat*, p. 75.

51 Anwar, op. cit.

52 Interview with a former BAZIS official, May 1987.

53 Dr H. Halide, "Pengalaman Pengelolaan Zakat di Ujung Pandang", in *Laporan* (1984/85).

54 K.H. Abdullah Syukri Zarkasyi, MA, "BAZIS Desa Ngunut, Kecamatan Babadan, Kabupaten Ponorogo", in *Laporan*. Cf. Imam Tholchah, "Studi Lembaga Amil Zakat, Infaq dan Shadaqah", in *Laporan Hasil Studi Lembaga Amil Zakat, Infaq dan Shadaqah di Wilayah: DKI Jakarta, Jawa Barat, Jawa Tengah, Daerah Istimewa Yogyakarta, Jawa Timur dan Nusa Tenggara Barat* (Jakarta: Departemen Agama R.I., 1982/1983).

55 Reprinted in *Pedoman Zakat*, p. 421.

56 *Pedoman Zakat*, p. 75.

57   *Rekomendasi*, ch. XIII.

58   *Rekomendasi*, pp. 61–67. *Pedoman Zakat*, pp. 89–91.

59   K.H.M. Natsir, *Laporan Ketua Harian BAZIS DKI Jakarta*, 1984/1985.

60   Ibid.

61   *Laporan Kerja BAZIS DKI Jakarta Periode Tahun 1986/1987* (Disampaikan pada Rapat Paripurna Badan Pembina BAZIS DKI Jakarta, 26 Maret 1987).

62   Data collected from the field by Dr M. Saleh Putuhena, of the IAIN Ujung Pandang (reports of the chairman and series of decisions made by the several chairmen/the governor).

63   Prof. Dr H. Halide, "Pengalaman Pengelolaan Zakat di Ujung Pandang", in *Laporan*, Appendix (1984/85).

64   On the Pesantren of Gontor, see Lance Castles, "Notes on the Islamic School at Gontor", *Indonesia* 1 (1 April 1966): 30–45. On the history of the Islamic Normal School in Padang, see Taufik Abdullah, *Schools and Politics: The Kaum Movement in West Sumatra* (Ithaca, New York: Cornell Modern Indonesia Project, 1971).

65   This part is based on K.H. Abdullah Syukri Zarkasyi, MA, "BAZIS Desa Ngunut, Kecamatan Babadan, Kabupaten Ponorogo", in *Laporan* (1984/85), and Imam Tholchah, "Studi Lembaga Amil Zakat, Infaq dan Shadaqah di Wilayah Jawa Timur", in *Laporan Amil Zakat*.

66   See Taufik Abdullah, "Pandangan Hidup Ulama Indonesia: Ikhtisar Laporan Umum Sebuah Penelitian", *Masyarakat Indonesia* XIV, no. 3 (1987): 181–221.

67   *TEMPO* 12, 21 Mei 1988.

# 5 *ZAKAT* ADMINISTRATION IN MALAYSIA

*Aidit bin Ghazali*

## Introduction

*Zakat* is an obligatory payment, made compulsory upon all Muslims who satisfy the necessary conditions. Being one of the five pillars of Islam, it is an important feature of any Muslim community everywhere since the coming of Islam itself. Indeed, this is true for Malaysia where the emergence of Islam in the thirteenth century established, among others, the tradition of *zakat* payment.

Historically, the issue of *zakat* and its concomitant aspects may be traced to and identified with specific periods of the Malaysian history. Briefly, *zakat* payment in the pre-colonial era was not administered through any formal framework. Rather, it was guided more by the village tradition of contributing *zakat* proceeds to religious teachers who might have spent it either for their own needs or on the needs of the *asnaf* (those entitled to receive *zakat* payments). This is not certain. What is clear is that such forms of *zakat* payments arose from a show of appreciation by the peasants towards their religious teachers. Not surprisingly, this tradition still continues in some states today. What may be said in addition is that much of the *zakat* paid during those days came from the yields of padi cultivation, a common profession at the time.

During the colonial times, a dichotomy was established by the British over the administration of (1) matters related to Islam and Malay customs and (2) other aspects of state and national administration which were governed by the British civil and criminal legal systems. The former was administered by the establishment in each state of a central organization eventually known as the Council of Religion and Malay Customs. It was this council which governed all aspects pertaining to Islam and Malay customs, including *zakat* administration. Kelantan was the first state in Malaysia to establish such a council, which became a model for other states. Under this model, *zakat* administration for each village was under the respective village *imam*. Eventually, part of the *zakat* collected at the village level was given to the state as a means of financing the administration of Islamic matters. Indeed, a lot of developments have taken place since then, but all these will not be deliberated at length in this chapter, as its focus is on the current situation. However, it is fair to state that the current situation bears the imprint of the legacy of the colonial times.

An attempt is made in this chapter to analyse the various pertinent aspects of *zakat* administration in the states of Malaysia. Inadequacy of the data presented in the tables has limited the depth of the analysis. Nonetheless, whatever has been gathered thus far should be able to provide a fair view of the current state of *zakat* administration in Malaysia.

### Organizational and Administrative Framework

Although the administration of *zakat* in Malaysia has been institutionalized, its administration in the various states is not systematically synchronized or co-ordinated. *Zakat* administration for each state is still an independent state matter.

To understand this state of affairs, one needs to understand the Malaysian constitution. The constitution has clearly stipulated the areas which fall under the governance of the federal and state governments by laying the division of power under the federal, state, and concurrent lists. The federal list comprises matters such as foreign affairs, defence and security, administration of justice, citizenship and naturalization, finance, trade and industry, communications, education, health, labour, and social security. The state list covers Muslim laws and Malay customs, land, agriculture, forestry, state government machinery, state works and water, and local government. Finally, the concurrent list includes social welfare, town and country planning, public health, and drainage and irrigation.

Every state has its own written constitution and Head of State. The Head of State is also the head of Islam in each state. In the case of Pulau Pinang and Melaka (both of which do not have a Head of State), and the Federal Territory, the national ruler acts as the head of Islam for Islamic affairs in these states.

Since Islamic affairs fall under the jurisdiction of these Heads of State (or state rulers), all aspects relating to *zakat* administration are also handled by the individual states. The main policy-making and administrative body is the respective state Council of Religion. The only exception is Kedah, which has an independent board named the Zakat Committee, operating under a separate *zakat* office directly responsible to the state ruler.

With the respective Heads of State being the heads of Islam, the passing of statutes and regulations pertaining to state *zakat* administration is a state matter. The federal government can only recommend proposals which it may deem desirable and it is up to the respective states to adopt the proposals or reject them. This being the case, one cannot really say that the administration of *zakat* in Malaysia is at the moment institutionalized at the federal level. This has been, as will be seen later, a major obstacle towards a more systematic and effective administration of *zakat* in Malaysia as a whole.

While the relationship between the federal government and the respective state Councils of Religion is clear, the relationship between the councils and the respective state governments is not uniform throughout Malaysia. Each state government also has what is known as State Department of Islamic Affairs which is part of the state government machinery. The functional scope of this department *vis-à-vis* State Islamic Affairs and the role of the Councils of Religion depends on several factors:

1. who sits as the head of the State Council of Religion; and
2. whether the council is self-financing and if the council is state-assisted either financially or administratively.

Where *zakat* administration in involved, additional relevant questions include:

1. What is the position of the *zakat* division in the whole set-up of the council's organizational chart?
2. Is the *zakat* administration merely restricted to be a unit of the whole council set-up? Or is its administration given greater autonomy and a more significant role to play to enhance Muslim community welfare?
3. Is the *zakat* administration an independent body or is it still being tied to the council within the latter's organizational framework?

Indeed, more questions can be posed in the form of factors which affect (1) the relationship between the State Department of Religion and the State Council of Religion, and (2) the manner in which *zakat* is being administered in the various states.

However, to portray a simplified picture, it is correct to state that the State Department of Religion is more concerned over matters such as the administration of religious schools, official *dakwah* (missionary) activities, arrangement of religious courses, enforcement of Islamic laws, bearing of administrative expenditure pertaining to Islamic affairs conducted by the state government, and the administration of the *Sharia* (Islamic law) courts. The

State Council of Religion, on the other hand, focuses on the administration of *zakat*, *Baitul-Mal* (treasury) funds, *waqf* (endowments), etc.

The independence of each state to administer Islamic affairs (including *zakat*) is evident from the quite different organizational framework that each adopts. Each state organizes its administration somewhat differently although there are areas common to all. For example, each council has a unit or committee for the administration of *zakat*. However, the difference perhaps lies in the role that *zakat* is allowed to play within the organizational set-up. The study reveals that the *zakat* divisions in the Federal Territory and Perak, for instance, are more effective in their planning and use of funds, mainly owing to the fact that the role of *zakat* has been allowed to develop. This will be more apparent when we analyse the uses of *zakat* funds. What is evident is that where the role of *zakat* has not been fully appreciated, the development of its administration has been pathetic, resulting in dormant *zakat* funds, which are used more for investment purposes than for meeting the needs of the *asnaf*, and the lack of creative and positive endeavours to create an awareness among the Muslim community to pay *zakat*.

Earlier, the writer has raised questions as to whether the State Councils of Religion are self-financed or state assisted. The question of who sits as the head of the State Council of Religion was also raised. Except for Kedah, the main *zakat* governing body for each state and the Federal Territory is the council (Table 1). In all cases, the council is a state statutory body. However, some are fully self-financed, while others receive some form of state assistance which is normally given in the form of annual financial assistance to meet administrative costs or/and seconded staff from the State Department of Religion to meet staff inadequacy in the council.

To be self-financed or state-assisted has its advantages and disadvantages, depending on how the administration of the council reacts to the situation. In some cases, the self-financed status has helped to develop a spirit of self-dependence, thus generating efforts towards more productive work (especially in *zakat* administration). Hence, the effect here is positive. However, it is also true to say that, in some cases, the extent of this positive effect is retarded by the fact that the head of the council does not offer his utmost commitment to the administration, particularly if he is already holding other offices.

State assistance is a good thing, since it spells extra help. However, it should be supervised in order that it does not result in negative attitudes towards commitment needed in the administration of significant Islamic matters such as *zakat*, *waqf*, and other *Baitul-Mal* funds. These are matters of trust that should not be betrayed, for betrayal here is betrayal of the trust given by Allah.

Table 1 confirms our earlier observation that the administration of *zakat* and other Islamic affairs still remains a state matter. This study, however, has

TABLE 1

**Administrative Status of Main *Zakat*-Governing Body in Each State**

| State | Council of Religion | | | Head of State Council of Religion |
|---|---|---|---|---|
| | State Statutory Body | Self-Financed | State-Assisted (Financial/Administrative) | |
| Perlis | ✓ | ✓ | | State Regent |
| Pulau Pinang | ✓ | ✓ | ✓ | Head of Religious Dept. |
| Kedah | *Zakat* administration is under an independent board named the Zakat Committee under the permanent chairmanship of the State Secretary. | | | |
| Perak | ✓ | ✓ | | Head of Religious Dept. |
| Trengganu | ✓ | ✓ | | Head of Religious Dept. |
| Pahang | ✓ | ✓ | ✓ | State Regent |
| Negeri Sembilan | ✓ | ✓ | ✓ | Chief Minister |
| Melaka | ✓ | ✓ | | State Exco |
| Johor | ✓ | ✓ | | State Exco |

discovered that the appointment of high-ranking figures as the heads of the state councils has not been as significant a factor as expected in generating efficiency in the administration of *zakat*. Many implications may accrue from this observation, most of which revolve around the question of whether some of these heads could have instilled greater accountability and commitment in *zakat* administration. The greater the authority that one has in the administration of Islamic affairs, the greater the trust that one is entrusted with.

Shifting to the issue of the system of *zakat* collection, the writer finds that there exists much in common among the states. Basically, there are two channels through which the Muslim community can pay their *zakat* — firstly, through the appointed *amilin* (collectors), and secondly, through the offices of the Councils of Religion. Other than these, district *qadi* and *zakat* supervisors assist in the collection of certain types of *zakat* in some states. Table 2 illustrates that in some states, for example in Kelantan, the *amilin* are empowered to collect only certain types of *zakat*, namely *zakatul-fitr* (poll tax) and *zakat* on cereals, mainly padi. *Zakat* on wealth and commerce are payable through the offices of the council. The simple rationale behind this is to prevent the *amilin* from receiving a large portion of the *zakat* paid (if they were to be responsible for the collection of *zakat* on wealth and commerce). However, this question would not have arisen had the council been following the principle of allocating *zakat* funds according to needs and priorities of the *asnaf* rather than adopting the principle of allocating to the *amilin* ⅛ or more of the *zakat* collected by the *amilin*.

TABLE 2
**Types of *Zakat* Collected by the Various Formal Channels**

| State | Channels | |
| --- | --- | --- |
| | Council Office | *Amilin* |
| Perlis | All | *Fitr* |
| | | Cereals |
| Pulau Pinang | All | *Fitr* |
| Kelantan | All | *Fitr* |
| | (especially for wealth and commerce) | Cereals |
| Perak | All | All |
| Trengganu | All | All |
| Pahang | All | *Fitr* |
| | | Cereals |
| Melaka | All | All |
| Johor | All | All |

The appointments of the *amilin* and their assistants are made according to the state Islamic laws and the gazetted *zakat* regulations of the council. There are basically two types of appointment:

1.  Fixed appointment: Under this appointment, the *amilin* and their assistants are appointed for their districts or villages for an unspecified period of time. They will remain in this appointment for as long as they are approved by the respective state councils. Normally, such appointments are given to officers of the mosques, that is, the *imam* and other representatives of the mosque committee.
2.  Timed appointment: Those who are selected under this appointment are normally empowered to collect *zakat* in a certain area for a specified period of time, for example a year or a season. Such appointments occur annually and the *amilin* need not necessarily be the same person for every year.

Whichever term of appointment is applicable, the appointed *amilin* and their assistants will hand over the *zakat* proceeds to the council. In most cases, the share of the *amilin* will be given before the *zakat* proceeds are passed on to the council. In fact, of all the eight *asnaf*, it is the *amilin* who receive their share first.

## Legal Framework

The power to administer *zakat* in each state in Malaysia is subjected to the respective state constitution and laws. Each state has its own enactment on the administration of Islamic affairs, which includes general clauses on *zakat* administration. Subjects covered in these clauses include, among others, (1) the basic system of *zakat* collection, that is, through the appointed *amilin*, (2) the distribution of the *zakat* proceeds, and (3) the liability of prosecution of those who prevent others from paying *zakat*, do not themselves pay *zakat*, or pay *zakat* through unofficial means, except where stated otherwise. The amount of fine imposed or the prison sentences for such offences are also stated.

However, not all state enactments on Islamic affairs are explicit on these matters. There is, thus, a need for *zakat* regulations to spell out the procedures of *zakat* administration in each state. The problem of enforcement, however, arises when these regulations are still not gazetted as part of state laws. Enforcement is only possible if violations of gazetted regulations are made. Regulations which are not gazetted are only guiding in nature. In some states, such as Trengganu, no *zakat* regulations exist since it is felt that the state enactment on the administration of Islamic affairs is sufficient to enforce the administration of *zakat*.

An interesting observation is that, in reality, there does not exist maximum enforcement of the *zakat* laws, especially with regards to the non-payment of *zakat* or the payment of *zakat* through unofficial means. (There will be a separate discussion later on the second matter.) Many constraints give rise to this situation. The more conspicuous constraints are the following:

1.  The inadequacy of *zakat* laws in empowering *zakat* administrators to check on one's bank accounts. Here, banks are able to deny access to their customers' accounts based on the confidentiality privilege enjoyed by bank customers.
2.  Unwillingness or hesitancy of some *zakat* administrators themselves. In some states, the council administrators do not seem to take the issue of non-payment of *zakat* as seriously as they would take the non-payment of income taxes. *Zakat* evasion is not considered a serious offence, quite unlike income tax evasion. This, unfortunately, is another manifestation of the colonial legacy inherent in the mentality of much of the Muslim community, especially in the urban areas.
3.  Apathy on the part of some council administrators to take up the issue on a more rigorous scale. Even though there had been some small efforts on behalf of the federal government to improve the *zakat* administration, these have not been adopted swiftly by some states which are still languid in their commitment to improvements in the administration.

Are the penalties covered by the *zakat* laws so severe that it causes some council administrators to be hesitant in carrying out prosecutions in clear cases of violations? To answer this, we may refer to Table 3 where the penalties for violations of *zakat* laws are listed. As expected, it varies between states. However, these are maximum fines or periods of imprisonment. In other words, a lesser penalty can be meted out. In spite of this, the records of some states do not reflect a rigorous imposition of these penalties for cases of non-payment of *zakat*, even though there seems to be no problem in the collection of *zakatul-fitr* (*fitrah*). Generally, most *zakat* administrators admit that there is still much that can be collected by way of *zakat* on wealth and commerce.

One final but disturbing observation is that there seem to exist a substantial number of Muslims who can only be coerced into payment of *zakat* on wealth and commerce. To these Muslims, the Holy Qur'an and its inherent injunctions on *zakat* are apparently insufficient to generate a sense of accountability towards *zakat* payment. Besides, there is no concerted and comprehensive implementation of the *Sharia* in Malaysia. Whatever existing *Sharia* laws in Malaysia are still open for increased jurisdictional role. As a final comment in this section, the effectiveness of *zakat* administration should never be viewed in isolation, segregated from the total overview of the existing state of the *Sharia* in the country.

TABLE 3
**Penalties for Violations of** *Zakat* **Laws**

| State | Penalty | |
|---|---|---|
| | Maximum Fine M$ | Maximum Period of Imprisonment |
| Perlis | In the process of passing a new set of regulations | |
| Pulau Pinang | 100 | 7 days |
| Kedah | 500 (applicable for *zakat* on padi only) | 6 months (applicable for *zakat* on padi only) |
| Kelantan | 300 | 1 month |
| Perak | 500 | 6 months |
| Trengganu | 100 | 7 days |
| Pahang | 100 | 1 month |
| Selangor | 100 | 7 days |
| Federal Territory | 100 | 7 days |
| Negeri Sembilan | 500 | 6 months |
| Johor | 10 | n.a. |
| Sarawak | 200 (applicable for other than *zakatul-fitr*) 25 (applicable for *zakatul-fitr* only) | n.a. |

n.a. − not applicable.

## Sources of *Zakat* Funds

The provisions of *zakat* laws and regulations in Malaysian states generally cover the collection of *fitrah* and *zakat* on cereals (mainly padi), wealth, and commerce. In some states, *zakat* accounts contain proceeds from *zakat* on livestock and in Negeri Sembilan there is record of some collections of *zakat* on gold. Other types of *zakat* are also collected but they are often in insignificant amounts. However, one must remember that this observation covers only those which are officially recorded as *zakat* collections by the councils (Table 4). In other words, one cannot rule out the possibility that other types of *zakat* may have been paid but not through the councils or their appointed *amilin*. As a corollary to this, one cannot conclude that *zakat* on livestock, for example, is collected in states such as Negeri Sembilan and Johor because raising livestock is a major feature of these states. Rather, it could be that Muslim communities in these states are made aware of this type of *zakat* by the councils.

TABLE 4

**Amount Collected from Each Type of Zakat by State in 1986**

(In M$)

| State | Type of Zakat | | | | | | Total Collected | Total Expenditure on the Asnaf |
| --- | --- | --- | --- | --- | --- | --- | --- | --- |
| | Fitr | On Wealth | On Cereals | On Livestock | On Commerce | Others | | |
| Perlis | 216,047 | 149,536 | 759,607 | — | — | 10,159 | 1,135,349 | 848,777 |
| Pulau Pinang | 576,129 | 182,222 | — | — | 135,377 | — | 893,728 | 781,502 |
| Kelantan | 1,256,848 | 233,996 | 167,654 | — | 151,766 | — | 1,810,264 | 2,636,090 |
| Perak | 1,837,943 | 956,694 | 219,765 | — | — | — | 3,014,402 | 1,728,175 |
| Selangor | 1,730,930 | 1,116,693 | 42,000 | — | Partly included under wealth | — | 2,889,623 | 2,228,914 |
| Federal Territory | 682,761 | 938,151 | — | — | 490,860 | — | 2,111,772 | 163,205 |
| Negeri Sembilan | 741,161 | 345,493 | 16,102 | 1,400 | 235,858 | 514 | 1,340,528 | 630,012 |
| Melaka | 628,498 | 321,433 | 14,555 | — | — | — | 964,486 | 265,381 |
| Johor | 2,608,086 | 944,070 | 1,765 | 6,451 | 490,469 | — | 4,050,841 | 1,172,783 |

SOURCES: Various annual reports, annual budgets, and state gazettes.

Some of the possible factors as to why only certain types of *zakat* are collected by each state are:

1. the uniqueness of *zakat* laws of each state;
   (The most illustrative example is that of Kedah. Kedah is the only state in Malaysia which provides only for the collection of *zakat* on padi. Payment of other types of *zakat* may be made individually and not through the *zakat* office. The argument here is that the collection of *zakat* on padi is substantial enough.)
2. lack of publicity and information on the types of *zakat* that should be paid;
   (This will be detailed later under the section of problems and shortcomings of *zakat* administrators.)
3. inadequacy of *zakat* laws.
   (This has already been elaborated on in the preceding section.)

With the exception of Kedah, all other states focus their efforts on the collection of *zakatul-fitr* (*fitrah*). Several reasons may be advanced as to why this is the case:

1. *Fitrah* is collected only once a year in the holy month of Ramadhan. The Muslim community regards the payment of this *fitrah* as an undying and unquestionable feature of Ramadhan. In the holy month of Ramadhan, Muslims tend to exhibit their commitment to Islam through not only ritualistic worship and prayers but also good, charitable acts. The payment of *fitrah* thus becomes a traditional feature of Ramadhan.
2. The amount of *fitrah* payable is almost insignificant for an average Muslim. It varies between states and normally stays within the range of M$2.30–M$2.50 per individual. This amount is indeed minimal compared to the amount that may be collected for other types of *zakat*.
3. The calculation of the *fitrah* is not as complex as how the Muslim community views the calculation of other types of *zakat* to be. This may not be a valid reason for not paying other types of *zakat* but this constraint arises from one's own ignorance.
4. Owing to its once-a-year basis, *zakat* administrators find *fitrah* administratively easier to manage as compared to the varied periods of payment for other types of *zakat* because of the *haul* requirement. Again this may not be a valid reason and one should not make any generalization, in any case.

Although *zakatul-fitr* is the most efficiently collected form of *zakat* in Malaysia, it does not necessarily mean that *fitrah* forms the major proportion of *zakat* collected in all the states. Perlis is a case in point where the collection of *zakat* on cereals (that is, padi) exceeds the collection of *fitrah* two to three times during the period 1980 to 1987 (till 30 June 1987 only). This implies that the potential of *zakat* does not lie solely in the collection of *fitrah*.

The efforts to exploit the *zakat* potential should not be focused on cereals only. As cereal in Malaysian *zakat* terminology is normally taken to be padi, such a narrow focus would mean that padi farmers will be the major source of *zakat* funds in the country. This, however, is not just, in view of the fact that padi farmers form the major portion of the poor in Malaysia. Hence, the call for greater mobilization of *zakat* funds from other sources such as wealth, commerce, livestock, and the more lucrative crops of agricultural farmers such as cocoa, palm oil, peppers and the like, should result in a more balanced *zakat* structure. A promising development is that an increasing proportion of share capital is owned by Malays (who are Muslims by definition, according to the Malaysian Constitution) in limited companies. It will be hard to believe that this does not accrue in increased '*zakat*able' sources that can further enhance the redistribution and development efforts of the Muslim community. This expectation is clearly manifest in the case of the Federal Territory where the amounts of *zakat* collected on wealth and on commerce individually have been surpassing the amount collected from *zakatul-fitr* in recent years (Table 5).

TABLE 5
**Contributions of Various Forms of *Zakat* — Federal Territory (1974–85)**
(In percentages)

| Year | *Zakatul-Fitr* | *Zakat* on Wealth | *Zakat* on Commerce |
|------|------------|---------------|-----------------|
| 1974 | 3.23  | 0.02  | 0.06  |
| 1975 | 5.13  | 0.31  | 0.02  |
| 1976 | 5.72  | 0.32  | 0.23  |
| 1977 | 6.20  | 0.44  | 0.16  |
| 1978 | 6.43  | 1.23  | 0.48  |
| 1979 | 7.09  | 3.71  | 0.77  |
| 1980 | 8.81  | 5.56  | 0.94  |
| 1981 | 9.60  | 6.11  | 7.93  |
| 1982 | 10.32 | 18.49 | 12.27 |
| 1983 | 10.7  | 23.95 | 7.58  |
| 1984 | 12.2  | 9.70  | 41.75 |
| 1985 | 14.57 | 30.14 | 17.81 |

Tables 6–13 give the percentage contributions of various forms of *zakat* in some Malaysian states. What is revealing for Perak, Selangor, Federal Territory, and Negeri Sembilan is that the *zakat* potential exists, especially for *zakat* on wealth. If the emphasis laid on the collection of *zakatul-fitr* is also given to other forms of *zakat*, there is little doubt that total *zakat* proceeds will increase substantially.

TABLE 6
**Contributions of Various Forms of *Zakat* — Perlis (1980–86)**
(In percentages)

| Year | *Zakatul-Fitr* | *Zakat* on Wealth | *Zakat* on Commerce | *Zakat* on Livestock | *Zakat* on Cereals | Other Forms of *Zakat* | |
|------|------|------|------|------|------|------|------|
| 1980 | 26 | | | | 71 | 3 | 100 |
| 1981 | 20 | | | | 74 | 6 | 100 |
| 1982 | 26 | | | | 62 | 12 | 100 |
| 1983 | 28 | | | | 62 | 10 | 100 |
| 1984 | 25 | | | | 66 | 9 | 100 |
| 1985 | 18 | 5 | | | 64 | 13 | 100 |
| 1986 | 19 | 13 | | | 67 | 1 | 100 |

TABLE 7
**Contributions of Various Forms of *Zakat* — Pulau Pinang (1980–86)**
(In percentages)

| Year | *Zakatul-Fitr* | *Zakat* on Wealth | *Zakat* on Commerce | *Zakat* on Livestock | *Zakat* on Cereals | Other Forms of *Zakat* | |
|------|------|------|------|------|------|------|------|
| 1980 | 83 | 17 | | | | | 100 |
| 1981 | 85 | 15 | | | | | 100 |
| 1982 | 78 | 22 | | | | | 100 |
| 1983 | 90 | 10 | | | | | 100 |
| 1984 | 63 | 23 | 14 | | | | 100 |
| 1985 | 75 | 14 | 11 | | | | 100 |
| 1986 | 64 | 20 | 16 | | | | 100 |

TABLE 8
**Contributions of Various Forms of *Zakat* — Kedah (1980–86)***
(In percentages)

| Year | *Zakatul-Fitr* | *Zakat* on Wealth | *Zakat* on Commerce | *Zakat* on Livestock | *Zakat* on Cereals | Other Forms of *Zakat* | |
|------|------|------|------|------|------|------|------|
| 1980 | | | | | 100 | | 100 |
| 1981 | | | | | 100 | | 100 |
| 1982 | | | | | 100 | | 100 |
| 1983 | | | | | 100 | | 100 |
| 1984 | | | | | 100 | | 100 |
| 1985 | | | | | 100 | | 100 |
| 1986 | | | | | 100 | | 100 |

* Note that only *zakat* on cereals (padi) is collected by the State Council of Religion.

TABLE 9
**Contributions of Various Forms of** *Zakat* **— Kelantan (1980–86)\***
(In percentages)

| Year | Zakatul-Fitr | Zakat on Wealth | Zakat on Commerce | Zakat on Livestock | Zakat on Cereals | Other Forms of Zakat |
|---|---|---|---|---|---|---|
| 1980 | 79.2 | 2.9 | 0.3 | | 17.6 | 100 |
| 1981 | 43 | 9 | 41 | | 7 | 100 |
| 1982 | 43 | 10 | 42 | | 5 | 100 |
| 1983 | 43 | 11 | 39 | | 7 | 100 |
| 1984 | 41 | 13 | 40 | | 6 | 100 |
| 1985 | 57 | 8 | 27 | | 8 | 100 |
| 1986 | 69 | 13 | 9 | | 9 | 100 |

\* Note that the Kelantan Council of Religion requires that only ⅔ of total *zakat* payable per individual be paid through the council.

TABLE 10
**Contributions of Various Forms of** *Zakat* **— Perak (1982–86)**
(In percentages)

| Year | Zakatul-Fitr | Zakat on Wealth | Zakat on Commerce | Zakat on Livestock | Zakat on Cereals | Other Forms of Zakat |
|---|---|---|---|---|---|---|
| 1982 | 73 | 18 | | | 9 | 100 |
| 1983 | 71 | 22 | | | 7 | 100 |
| 1984 | 63 | 33 | | | 4 | 100 |
| 1985 | 72 | 22 | | | 6 | 100 |
| 1986 | 61 | 32 | | | 7 | 100 |

TABLE 11
**Contributions of Various Forms of** *Zakat* **— Selangor (1980–86)\***
(In percentages)

| Year | Zakatul-Fitr | Zakat on Wealth and Commerce | Zakat on Livestock | Zakat on Cereals | Other Forms of Zakat |
|---|---|---|---|---|---|
| 1980 | 84 | 13 | | 3 | 100 |
| 1981 | 74 | 23 | | 3 | 100 |
| 1982 | 71 | 28 | | 1 | 100 |
| 1983 | 66 | 33 | | 1 | 100 |
| 1984 | 59 | 38 | | 3 | 100 |
| 1985 | 63 | 35 | | 2 | 100 |
| 1986 | 60 | 39 | | 1 | 100 |

\* Note that the *zakat* on wealth and commerce are accounted together and not separated.

TABLE 12
**Contributions of Various Forms of** *Zakat* — **Federal Territory (1980–86)**
(In percentages)

| Year | *Zakatul-Fitr* | *Zakat* on Wealth | *Zakat* on Commerce | *Zakat* on Livestock | *Zakat* on Cereals | Other Forms of *Zakat* |
|------|------|------|------|------|------|------|
| 1980 | 62 | 35 | 3 | | | 100 |
| 1981 | 51 | 29 | 20 | | | 100 |
| 1982 | 32 | 50 | 18 | | | 100 |
| 1983 | 27 | 53 | 20 | | | 100 |
| 1984 | 20 | 47 | 33 | | | 100 |
| 1985 | 28 | 54 | 18 | | | 100 |
| 1986 | 32 | 44 | 24 | | | 100 |

TABLE 13
**Contributions of Various Forms of** *Zakat* — **Negeri Sembilan (1980–86)**
(In percentages)

| Year | *Zakatul-Fitr* | *Zakat* on Wealth | *Zakat* on Commerce | *Zakat* on Livestock | *Zakat* on Cereals | Other Forms of *Zakat* |
|------|------|------|------|------|------|------|
| 1980 | 80 | 16 | 2 | | 2 | 100 |
| 1981 | 71 | 12 | 14 | | 2 | 1 | 100 |
| 1982 | 68 | 17 | 13 | | 2 | 100 |
| 1983 | 64 | 17 | 17 | | 2 | 100 |
| 1984 | 58 | 18 | 23 | | 1 | 100 |
| 1985 | 69 | 26 | 4 | | 1 | 100 |
| 1986 | 55 | 26 | 18 | | 1 | 100 |

## Uses of *Zakat* Funds

Uses of *zakat* funds in Malaysia depend on three major factors:

1. interpretation of the *asnaf*;
2. allocation for *asnaf* considered as existing in each state; and
3. priorities over *asnaf* considered existing in each state.

The interpretation of the eight *asnaf* in the Malaysian context is as follows:

1. *Faqir* refers to a person who has no property or vocation or receives income from other sources not amounting to 50 per cent of the cost of living of an average person and/or his dependants.

2. *Miskin* refers to any person who has property or income from vocation which is insufficient to meet his daily needs and those of his dependants.
3. *Amilin* refers to the official appointed by the council at the village, district, and state levels, responsible for the collection and, where required, the disbursement of *zakat* proceeds.
4. *Muallaf* refers to a person who has newly embraced Islam and is in need of financial assistance.
5. *Ibnus-sabil* refers to any person from any state, who undertakes a journey with Islamic purposes and is in need of assistance even though he may have property in his own state.
6. *Fisabilillah* refers to any activity to uphold and defend Islam and its welfare.
7. *Gharimin* refers to a person who is in debt for purposes acceptable to the *Sharia*.
8. *Riqab* refers to a person held in slavery or bondage who needs assistance to free himself from such obligation imposed on him.

Table 14 gives the amount spent on each of the *asnaf* in various states. Among the revealing facts from this table are the following:

1. The *asnaf* which form the major portion of expenditure from *zakat* funds are the *fuqara* (*faqir*), the *masakin* (*miskin*), the *amilin* (*amil*), and *fisabilillah*. High expenditure on the *fuqara* and the *masakin* reflects the unsolved problem of poverty in most states, while that on the *amilin* reflects the relatively high administrative costs related to *zakat* collection and distribution. High expenditures under *fisabilillah* reflects the wide scope of this *asnaf* for financing Islamic activities aimed at enhancing the level of welfare and *dakwah* in each state.
2. The expenditure on each of the *asnaf* varies, some more substantially than others. This invalidates the view that the *asnaf* in Malaysia are given equal allocations. Rather, allocations and expenditures are based on priorities attached to each *asnaf*.
3. In some states, such as Perlis, Kelantan, and Negeri Sembilan, expenditure for the *amilin* exceeds that for the *fuqara* and the *masakin*. In some ways, it does tickle one's mind to question the rationale behind this, as the nature of *zakat* mobilization should be geared towards alleviating poverty.
4. The *asnaf al-gharimin* and *ar-riqab* are not believed to exist in the states of Perlis, Kelantan, Negeri Sembilan, and Melaka. Johor, Perak, and Kedah do not reckon the existence of *ar-riqab* in their states. Only Selangor and the Federal Territory report any expenditure for these two *asnaf*. The writer opines that this difference arises from the interpretation accorded to the *asnaf*. Unnecessarily rigid or over-orthodox

TABLE 14

**Expenditure for Each *Asnaf* by Selected State in 1986**

(In M$)

| State | Asnaf | | | | | | | |
|---|---|---|---|---|---|---|---|---|
| | Al-Fuqara | Al-Masakin | Al-Amilin | Muallaf | Ibnus-Sabil | Fisabilillah | Al-Gharimin | Ar-Riqab |
| Perlis | 129,895 | | 268,115 | 10,265 | 279 | 440,223 | – | – |
| Kelantan | 505,774 | | 362,486 | 26,776 | 2,857 | 1,738,197 | – | – |
| Perak | 758,500 | | 262,635 | 126,002 | 3,475 | 577,563 | – | – |
| Selangor | 416,245 | 388,113 | 252,000 | 305,500 | 160,363 | 263,594 | 287,280 | 155,819 |
| Federal Territory | 20,008 | 56,966 | 11,436 | 17,948 | 285 | 52,722 | 3,840 | – |
| Negeri Sembilan | 150,345 | | 127,095 | 5,868 | 964 | 435,740 | – | – |
| Melaka | 77,897 | 78,012 | 85,192 | 2,560 | 810 | 20,910 | – | 1,925 |
| Johor | 312,198 | 331,345 | 429,271 | 92,796 | 5,248 | – | – | – |

SOURCES: Various annual reports, annual budgets, and state gazettes.

interpretation of the *asnaf* will inevitably lead to the exclusion of some *asnaf*.

A common list of detailed particulars on the expenditure for each *asnaf* may appear as follows:

1.  *Al-fuqara*:
    (a)  monthly financial or household provisions assistance;
    (b)  medical assistance;
    (c)  Id contributions;
    (d)  funeral finances for those without immediate kins;
    (e)  contributions for orphanages.
2.  *Al-masakin*:
    (a)  Id contributions;
    (b)  initial capital for small business;
    (c)  scholarships for the poor;
    (d)  monthly financial or household provisions assistance;
    (e)  funeral finances.
3.  *Al-amilin*:
    (a)  share of council-appointed *amilin*;
    (b)  costs arising from *zakat* administration;
    (c)  financing courses pertaining to *zakat* assessment and administration in general.
4.  *Muallaf*:
    (a)  financing poor new converts in meeting their needs, including studies;
    (b)  financial assistance to organizations which manage the affairs of *muallaf*;
    (c)  financing Islamic development programmes for the *muallaf*;
    (d)  managing lodgings specially bought/constructed for the *muallaf*;
    (e)  financing the publication of literature for the *muallaf*.
5.  *Ibnus-sabil*:
    (a)  assisting those who face financial difficulties to return to their own states;
    (b)  financing travelling expenses of those wishing to pursue Islamic studies abroad;
    (c)  financing travelling expenses of needy students in their respective states.
6.  *Fisabilillah*:
    (a)  study grants/contributions for needy students both at home and abroad;
    (b)  financial contributions for Islamic welfare and *dakwah* organizations;

(c)   conducting of religious classes;
(d)   financing of *dakwah* activities such as sponsoring talks and research activities on matters relevant to Islam;
(e)   maintenance of mosques and cemeteries;
(f)   purchase and maintenance of funeral facilities, for example, the purchase of a hearse;
(g)   financing the publication of Islamic literature.

7.   *Al-gharimin*:
(a)   assisting in the payment of debts out of actions acceptable to Islam.

8.   *Ar-riqab*:
(a)   financial contributions to Muslim minorities facing difficulties in non-Muslim dominated countries;
(b)   supplementary financial assistance for *dakwah* and information dissemination activities of the council.

The extent to which these programmes will have a real impact on the community's welfare will depend on several factors:

1.   the amount of careful planning so as to avoid unwise decisions and wastage of funds;
2.   the priorities accorded to each programme so that a more important programme will not be superseded in terms of emphasis by a less significant one;
3.   the follow-up programmes to the initial programmes in terms of maintaining continuity and ensuring proper supervision of programme effectiveness;
4.   commitment of *zakat* administrators to formulation of programmes and implementation of the programmes; and
5.   response of the community to such *zakat* efforts.

Indeed, other factors may be listed as equally important in contributing to the community welfare. However, purposeful neglect over any of the above factors will only be to the deteriment of the programmes.

## Problems and Shortcomings

In conducting the administration of *zakat*, several problems and shortcomings faced by the administrators became evident. Most of the problems discussed below are representative of the majority of the *zakat* administrators interviewed. Where a problem or shortcoming is unique for a particular state, specific references will be made.

First of all, administrative problems were associated with inadequacy, in the forms of both physical manpower and expertise. The possible causes for this problem include, among others, the lack of training in the field of *zakat* administration, the insufficiency of senior *zakat* officers to plan and co-ordinate the administration and in some cases, for example Negeri Sembilan, the lack of funds to finance the employment of more senior *zakat* officers. The last reason accrues from the fact that the Negeri Sembilan Council of Religion, being self-financed, obtains most of its finances from *zakat* collections without any state assistance. The problem here is not so much of there not being enough funds, since the total collection from *zakat* far exceeds the total expenditure. Rather, the writer's observation is that the lack of finance, if it exists in a severe form, arises from the fact that the other assets, such as *waqf*, have not been mobilized effectively. For instance, there is no senior officer supervising the administration of *waqf* in Negeri Sembilan. This is indeed unfortunate, considering the enormous potential inherent in *waqf* assets. However, it is only fair to say that Negeri Sembilan is not the only state with this predicament.

As regards expertise, it is not merely a question of having an officer from a religious background, e.g. a *Sharia* graduate. As an imperative complement, *zakat* administration should also be augmented by those with trained administrative acumen and economic perspectives. This observation is not meant to be prejudicial to any party. Rather, it is an observation based on the conviction that *zakat* administration is also an economic-oriented profession. Indeed, failure to realize this has in some states caused lack not only of creative thoughts in the planning, publicity campaigns, and mobilization of potential *zakat* funds but also of proper data filing. Existing *zakat* funds are, more often than not, invested, but such investment is justified only if one is satisfied that the destitutes, poor, and other needy and rightful recipients of *zakat* have been satisfactorily attended to.

Shortage of manpower has caused a lack of publicity campaigns regarding *zakat*. Often, there is only one *zakat* officer with a handful of clerks and typists under him. Often, these clerks and typists also do service functions for the other departments. In some states, the *zakat* officer is also the officer in charge of *waqf* and some other departments which should justifiably have their own respective officers. Hence, it is not surprising that publicity of *zakat* suffers in frequency, intensity, and scope.

Another consequence of manpower shortage is the inadequacy of organized survey or census data that could facilitate *zakat* administrators in their planning. Such surveys, usually conducted on an annual basis by the respective district and village *amilin*, are however aimed at the collection and disbursement of *zakatul-fitr* rather than other types of *zakat*. Among the pertinent aspects which have not been covered in these surveys are progress reports over the assistance provided by *zakat* funds to individuals and the assessment of the impact of *zakat* mobilization on the community welfare at the village, district, and state levels.

Second, there are legal constraints about which much has already been said in the earlier sections of this chapter. What should be reiterated, however, is that the effectiveness of *zakat* administration lies in the strength and scope of the laws and the accompanying *zakat* regulations. *Zakat* administrators should have access to confidential but necessary information on the assets of Muslims, with built-in safeguards to avoid any abuse of this right.

It is particularly disappointing to note that even the existing laws are not fully implemented. This is evident from the admission of some *zakat* administrators themselves. To blame *zakat* administrators would not be fair, since the ultimate responsibility to ensure that *zakat* is paid lies with the respective councils.

Third, there are problems arising from the absence of co-ordination among states over matters such as the fixing of the *nisab* for padi. It is 480 gantang in Perlis, 375 gantang in Kelantan and Trengganu, 363 gantang in Selangor, and 358⅓ gantang in Johor. Such variations only prove to be a source of confusion for the Muslim community. This, however, is not as serious as the problems and shortcomings discussed earlier.

Fourth, there are problems related to the discrepancy arising from the fact that *zakat* administration is state-assisted in some states but not in others. The salaries and other benefits for the latter group are dependent on the state of *zakat* funds. In view of the limited funds, this group could not be accorded the same benefits enjoyed by their counterparts under state government finance. Perhaps a more motivating approach can be adopted with fairer incentives accorded to *zakat* administrators, irrespective of their status either as state-government servants or as employees of the financially independent council.

Finally, there are problems associated with *zakat* payment not being made through the appointed *amilin* and council offices, but rather through unofficial channels. The majority of the *zakat* administrators interviewed, however, think that the problem is not significant. However, the writer thinks otherwise, as there is no evidence to substantiate their claims. This phenomenon will be discussed in the following section based on a survey conducted in the month of Ramadhan (1987).

## Issue of *Zakat* Payment through Unofficial Channels

Except for Kedah and Kelantan, all forms of *zakat* are required by state Islamic laws to be paid through appointed *amilin* and council offices. Any other way would violate the laws and *zakat* regulations and cause one to be liable for prosecution.

Kedah only requires the payment of *zakat* on padi to be paid through the appointed *amilin* and its *zakat* office. All other types of *zakat* can be paid out of individual initiatives. The recipients of these other types of *zakat*, including *zakatul-fitr*, are for the donors to determine. The explanation given for this is that the *zakat* on padi is sufficient to meet state needs. Hence, the burden of *zakat* payment in Kedah is officially borne by the padi farmers who represent the poorest group of households in Malaysia.

Kelantan, on the other hand, requires only two-thirds of each type of *zakat* payable by each individual to be handed to the council. The remaining one-third may be disbursed according to the individual's own choice and initiative.

All other states require that payment of all types of *zakat* must be through the officially determined channels. *Zakat* administrators were interviewed over this matter and the results are reported in Table 15.

When asked about the proportion of *zakat* payers who pay *zakat* through unofficial channels, most respondents claimed that it is not more than 3 per cent. The survey results in Table 15 provide a broad-brush picture of the situation as seen by those who are directly involved in *zakat* administration. The top three frequently quoted reasons for *zakat* payments through unofficial channels are as follows:

1.   political factor, which has led *zakat* payers from the opposition political party, Parti Islam Se-Malaysia (PAS), to circumvent official channels;
2.   individual inclination to pay to personal acquaintances, including one's religious teacher, village midwives, and the destitute and poor known to oneself; and
3.   lack of confidence in the council's efforts to distribute the *zakat* proceeds. The third reason is closely related to the second explanation. Perhaps it is an indication of the community's concern over the undistributed *zakat* funds, especially in those states where poverty still remains an unresolved problem.

To supplement these official views, a survey covering rural districts in eight states of West Malaysia was conducted. Appendix Tables A–G contain the results of the survey. Again, this survey is meant to provide an impressionist view.

Among the more interesting findings of this survey is that the top three possible reasons for this phenomenon concur with the top three possible reasons given by the *zakat* administrators interviewed. About 17 per cent of the respondents claimed lack of confidence in the council's method of distributing *zakat*, 13 per cent admitted that it was the political factor which

TABLE 15

**Reasons for Payment of *Zakat* through Non-Formal Channels: Perspectives of *Zakat* Administrators**

| State | | Reasons | | | | | | |
|---|---|---|---|---|---|---|---|
| | Lazy to Visit Council Office | Lack of Confidence in Council's Distribution | Inefficiency of Council in Collecting *Zakat* | Political Factor | Inclination to Pay to Personal Acquaintances | Lack of Publicity | Society's Ignorance |
| Perlis | ✓ | ✓ | ✓ | ✓ | ✓ | | |
| Perak | | ✓ | | ✓ | ✓ | | ✓ |
| Trengganu | | | ✓ | ✓ | ✓ | | ✓ |
| Pahang | | ✓ | | ✓ | | | |
| Negeri Sembilan | | | ✓ | | | ✓ | |
| Melaka | ✓ | ✓ | | ✓ | ✓ | | |
| Johor | ✓ | | | ✓ | ✓ | | |

motivated them to pay individually, and 60 per cent attributed their actions to self-confidence in their individual efforts to distribute *zakat* (Appendix Table F). That many respondents in this survey are themselves paying *zakat* on a person-to-person basis lends some support to the earlier claims of the *zakat* administrators. However, the claim by the latter that this phenomenon does not exceed 3 per cent of the *zakat*-paying population in the respective states is still open to question. According to the survey, 17 per cent of the respondents pay through informal channels while 18 per cent utilize both formal and informal channels.

However, even if we know the correct percentage of those who pay *zakat* as such, this would still not indicate the *zakat* potential inherent in the Malaysian Muslim community. Indeed, it would be more interesting, albeit difficult, to survey those who do not pay *zakat* of one kind or another. To the writer, as long as Muslims are paying *zakat*, whether through official or unofficial channels, some improvement in community welfare will occur. But if *zakat* is not paid when it should be paid, it will mean that the community is deprived of the material benefit of Islam.

### Some Observations

Some fundamental observations may be made as to why the state of *zakat* administration is what it is today. No doubt, some improvements have been made. However, it would be a gross mistake to attempt to rectify the present-day *zakat* situation within a system which itself needs rectification.

One does not need to look far for these fundamental observations. The first observation concerns the concept of *Baitul-Mal*. With the exception of the Federal Territory and Perak, the department of *zakat* administration is separated from the department of *Baitul-Mal* within each council. Islamic history has shown that the administration of *zakat* falls under the administration of the *Baitul-Mal*. What was different was the separation of the accounts that were kept for *zakat* and the other non-*zakat* funds of the *Baitul-Mal*. Hence, to separate the *zakat* division from the *Baitul-Mal* division in the council indirectly denies co-ordinated planning in the utilization of funds collected in a particular state.

The role of *zakat* is further confused with the segregation between *zakat* and *fitrah*. In some ways they may be different. However, the writer opines that the perception that one gets when one views the organizational chart of the council tends to blur the true role of *zakat*. It is perhaps because of this that MAMPU (Modernization and Administration of the Manpower Planning Unit in the Prime Minister's Department) has recently completed a proposal for a more realistic organizational structure of *Baitul-Mal* administration in Malaysia. This proposal has been adopted by the Federal Territory and is in the process of being adopted by Perak and some other states.

Our second observation relates to the existence of the two conservative groups hampering the effective mobilization and utilization of *zakat* funds: (1) those adhering to a rigid and orthodox interpretation of the *asnaf* and (2) those contented with the existing limited role and scope of the *Baitul-Mal* and *zakat*.

One may query why this is so. The answer to this lies mainly in issues ranging from the education system to the need for greater interaction between *Sharia* scholars and Muslim intellectuals.

Our third observation concerns the lack of co-ordination and co-operation between states. There is a need for greater co-ordination and co-operation between states in matters of common interests pertaining to the administration of *zakat*. At present, efforts towards this end represent individual initiatives by some *zakat* administrators. Individual initiatives such as these must be realized within a concerted national effort towards more effective and sound planning of *zakat* administration.

Through such efforts at the national level, mistakes, problems, and short-comings can be shared and minimized. Although *zakat* administrators and council heads have conducted meetings together on a national scale, useful views and proposals voiced in such meetings are not uniformly implemented. This problem can possibly be resolved by making the agreements collectively made at these meetings binding on all states. Indeed, such attempts will initially require the agreement of all the Heads of State who are also the heads of Islam.

Our fourth and final observation relates to legal considerations. The effects of prolonged periods of lack of legal leeway for *zakat* administrators have worked to the detriment of the Muslim community. It can be argued that there is a need for *zakat* laws to carry the same force as income tax laws. Again, it is with such realisation that MAMPU is in its final stages of com-pleting a proposal on the Zakat Act to be implemented, if approved, for the Federal Territory as a trial ground.

## Efforts towards Improving *Zakat* Administration

Recent years have witnessed some efforts involving MAMPU towards formu-lating proposals for the improvement of state *Baitul-Mal* (1986) and the drawing up of the Federal Territory Zakat Act which was referred to above. Each project involved scholars and experts on the subject, with MAMPU acting as a member on behalf of the Prime Minister's Department.

As a result of the first project, a proposal was made to streamline *zakat* administration along a more organized framework. This framework encompasses the three main functions of *zakat* administration, i.e., assessment, collection, and distribution. The Federal Territory adopted this model and its success can be observed from the more organized data and working system evident at its office. Perak has also adopted the proposal while other states are gradually adopting aspects of the proposal. This 1986 project may not have been a major step of any kind. However, the fact that some viable proposals have been formulated and gradually adopted augurs well for the future developments in *zakat* administration in Malaysia.

The proposed Federal Territory Zakat Act is the more significant project of the two. This proposed Act covers aspects relating to improvements in *zakat* organization and administration, such as power to check on income returns, *zakat* assessments, distribution of *zakat*, *zakat* violations and penalties, recovery of *zakat*, etc. Several provisions which were previously non-existent or insufficient are included or clarified in greater detail. If passed as law, this Act will be enforced in the Federal Territory initially. Since the proposed Act is regarded as classified information, the writer will not deal with it in greater detail. On a final note, the success of the Act will depend on the commitment of the authorities to implementing it and the responsiveness of the Muslim community.

**Some Proposals**

The state of *zakat* administration in Malaysia clearly reveals that there is much room for improvement. The situation calls for a comprehensive approach which would take into consideration a wider spectrum of factors instead of focusing merely on the *zakat* administration. In other words, improvement in *zakat* administration at all levels cannot be considered in isolation independent of other considerations such as legal constraints, public attitude, political will, and co-ordination and co-operation between states and their respective heads of Islam. *Zakat* administration is not merely a religious issue but also an administrative and economic one. Based on this perspective, the following proposals should be considered seriously:

1.  The administrative problems highlighted earlier should be solved immediately. This necessitates proper planning by the councils themselves, which should be sensitive to the needs of the *zakat* administration. The issue of inadequate manpower has prevailed long enough. In every state, except perhaps the Federal Territory, there is a glaring need for additional *zakat* officers. However, quantity is not the major issue here as the

quality of the administrators does matter a lot. They should not only be well-versed in all aspects of *zakat*, but also possess sharp administrative and planning skills. This can be fulfilled by adequate training and, more importantly, careful selection of potential administrators. Commitment to the cause of *zakat* is an essential attribute of good *zakat* administrators.

Given all this, it is hoped that pertinent information, such as comprehensive surveys on relevant issues, organized data filing, up-to-date audited financial statements, and assessment of the impact of *zakat* mobilization on community welfare, can be developed.

2. Serious efforts on the legal front have to be made by the federal and state governments to facilitate *zakat* administration. This should include the adoption of common *zakat* laws and regulations, increased jurisdictional scope for the *zakat* administrators, reordered priorities of *zakat* payment over income-tax obligations for the Muslim community, and more rigorous supervision over possibilities of violations of *zakat* laws by *zakat* payers and *amilin* and misuses of *zakat* funds.

3. A more cohesive and integrated form of co-ordination and co-operation, as highlighted in previous sections, is needed to bring about more systematic procedures in the states. Undue discrepancies in *zakat* administrative procedures should be avoided for the sake of facilitating planning at the federal level.

4. There is a need to review the interpretation of the *asnaf*, especially for *ar-riqab, al-gharimin, fisabilillah,* and *muallafutil-qulubuhum*. This is imperative if one is not to deny the rights of others over the *zakat* funds solely because of indifference and insensitivity over the possibility of widening the definitions of the eight *asnaf*. For example, for how long a period after conversion to Islam can a person be called a *muallaf*?

The above list of proposals covers only what the writer observes as the main issues. This list is not exhaustive.

## Conclusion

*Zakat* may have been institutionalized in Malaysia. However, this study reveals that where the concepts of *zakat* in particular and *Baitul-Mal* in general are concerned, areas of confusion and lack of understanding still remain. As stated earlier in this chapter, the colonial legacy is largely responsible for the present apathy reflected in the attitude and commitment of many Muslims towards the *zakat* obligation. The factors causing this apathy have already been discussed at length. The status of the legal base relevant to *zakat*, too, is hindered by facts such as the dichotomy which exists between so-called religious matters and administration of the other aspects of a Muslim's life.

Another matter of concern is over the almost dormant thinking in efforts towards extending a wider interpretation and appreciation of concepts in *zakat*. Most important among this is the interpretation of the *asnaf*. It is due to this that we find states such as Negeri Sembilan, Kelantan, and Johor not having expenditures for *ar-riqab* and *al-gharimin*; Melaka has no expenditure for *ar-riqab* while Perlis and Pulau Pinang have only token allocations for *ar-riqab* and *al-gharimin*. These states, however, are not the only ones guilty of this. However, this does reflect a need to extend the interpretation of the *asnaf*. It is difficult to accept the claim that some of the *asnaf* were only applicable in the early days of Islam and not for today and the future.

It is not wrong to say that the full potential of *zakat* in Malaysia has still not been reaped and mobilized. Any further indifference and insensitivity towards this matter is only to the detriment of the Muslim community, given the fact that poverty and income and wealth disparities leave much to be desired.

# APPENDIX

## Results of Survey Conducted in Eight States of West Malaysia on the Informal Channels of *Zakat* Payment Phenomenon

### A. Number of Respondents by State

| State | Number of Respondents |
|---|---|
| Kedah | 296 |
| Perak | 250 |
| Kelantan | 171 |
| Trengganu | 203 |
| Selangor | 100 |
| Negeri Sembilan | 151 |
| Melaka | 193 |
| Johor | 150 |
| Total | 1,514 |

### B. Occupational Structure of the Respondents
(In numbers)

| State | Occupation | | | |
|---|---|---|---|---|
| | Labourers | Farmers/Fishermen | Own Business | Civil Service |
| Kedah | 19 | 246 | 25 | 6 |
| Perak | 18 | 162 | 50 | 20 |
| Kelantan | 29 | 57 | 46 | 39 |
| Trengganu | 28 | 27 | 55 | 93 |
| Selangor | 22 | 50 | 18 | 10 |
| Negeri Sembilan | 32 | 17 | 45 | 57 |
| Melaka | 56 | 14 | 69 | 54 |
| Johor | 28 | 94 | 18 | 10 |
| Total | 232 | 667 | 326 | 289 |
| Percentage | 15 | 44 | 22 | 19 |

**C. Types of Zakat Paid**
(Number of respondents)

| State | Types of Zakat Paid | | | |
|---|---|---|---|---|
| | Fitr | Wealth | Commerce | Cereals |
| Kedah | 300 | — | 1 | 259 |
| Perak | 250 | — | 3 | 84 |
| Kelantan | 170 | 13 | 8 | 20 |
| Trengganu | 200 | 32 | 9 | 4 |
| Selangor | 100 | 2 | — | — |
| Negeri Sembilan | 150 | 11 | — | 3 |
| Melaka | 194 | 4 | — | 5 |
| Johor | 150 | — | — | — |
| Total | 1,514 | 62 | 21 | 375 |
| Percentage of respondents paying each type of zakat | 100 | 4 | 1.4 | 25 |

**D. Payment Channels Used**
(Number of respondents)

| State | Channels of Zakat Payment | | |
|---|---|---|---|
| | 100 Per Cent Formal Means | 100 Per Cent Informal Means | Combination of Both Formal and Informal Means |
| Kedah | 6 | 148 | 142 |
| Perak | 166 | 23 | 61 |
| Kelantan | 99 | 15 | 57 |
| Trengganu | 136 | 61 | 6 |
| Selangor | 99 | 0 | 1 |
| Negeri Sembilan | 143 | 2 | 6 |
| Melaka | 187 | 1 | 5 |
| Johor | 150 | 0 | 0 |
| Total | 986 | 250 | 278 |
| Percentage of respondents paying through each channel | 65 | 17 | 18 |

**E. *Zakat* Distribution through Informal Channels**
(Number of respondents)

| State | Needy Relatives | Needy Neighbours | Needy Friends | *Zakat* Recipients through Informal Channels | |
| --- | --- | --- | --- | --- | --- |
| | | | | Other People Known to be Needy | Those Recognized as Having Contributed to Society's Welfare |
| Kedah | 35 | 8 | 3 | 144 | 80 |
| Perak | 4 | 2 | 3 | 20 | 19 |
| Kelantan | – | – | – | 13 | 7 |
| Trengganu | 21 | 14 | 15 | 52 | 4 |
| Selangor | – | – | – | – | – |
| Negeri Sembilan | – | – | – | 3 | – |
| Melaka | – | – | – | – | – |
| Johor | – | – | – | 1 | – |
| Total | 60 | 24 | 21 | 233 | 110 |
| Percentage | 13.4 | 5.4 | 4.7 | 52.0 | 24.5 |

**F. Reasons for Informal *Zakat* Payments**
(Number of respondents)

| State | Lazy to Visit Council/Department | Lack of Confidence in Council's/Department's Administration of *Zakat* | Inefficiency of Council/Department in Collecting *Zakat* | Political Factor | More Confident with Own Efforts to Distribute *Zakat* |
|---|---|---|---|---|---|
| | | | Reasons for Paying *Zakat* through Informal Channels | | |
| Kedah | 3 | 9 | 2 | 23 | 124 |
| Perak | 1 | 11 | 7 | 8 | 12 |
| Kelantan | – | – | – | – | 14 |
| Trengganu | 2 | 31 | 17 | 11 | 35 |
| Selangor | – | – | – | – | – |
| Negeri Sembilan | – | 2 | – | – | 2 |
| Melaka | – | – | – | – | – |
| Johor | – | – | – | – | 1 |
| Total | 6 | 53 | 26 | 42 | 188 |
| Percentage | 2 | 17 | 8 | 13 | 60 |

NOTE: The reasons reflect multiple responses per individual.

**G. Sources of Information on *Zakat* to be Paid for
Those Paying *Zakat* through Informal Means**
(Number of respondents)

| State | Mosque | Council of Religion or Religious Department | Individual Assessment | Self Enquiry from Religious Teachers |
|---|---|---|---|---|
| Kedah | 6 | 8 | 9 | 29 |
| Perak | 16 | 20 | 68 | – |
| Kelantan | 19 | 43 | 22 | – |
| Trengganu | 16 | 13 | 28 | 10 |
| Selangor | – | – | – | – |
| Negeri Sembilan | 1 | – | 2 | – |
| Melaka | 4 | – | 2 | – |
| Johor | – | 1 | 1 | – |
| Total | 62 | 85 | 132 | 39 |
| Percentage | 19 | 27 | 42 | 12 |

# 6 *WAQF* MANAGEMENT IN MALAYSIA

*Syed Othman Alhabshi*

## Introduction

Wealth is one of the things which man covets. It can either lead him astray (away from God) or bring him closer to God. Islam has repeatedly exhorted its adherents to spend out of what they love for the sake of God.[1] Allah has promised in the Qur'an a multitude of rewards for those who generously spend in His way (Al Baqarah [2]: 245). Since the earliest period of Islam, the Muslims have given out of their wealth for the benefit of others.

Voluntary charities can take different forms, one of which is *waqf*. A tradition[2] of the Prophet (peace be upon him) described *waqf* as a benevolent act of setting aside part of one's wealth, mainly in the form of fixed assets, whose income is continuously used for charitable deeds. As such, most of the *waqf* properties have been in the form of land (estates or orchards), residential and commercial buildings, schools, mosques, and books of knowledge, which could generate income or confer benefits on society. These properties, which could not be inherited, sold or given away, tended to accumulate over time and formed the main source of income for various charitable and educational institutions. One such institution which to this day is well-endowed with *waqf* properties is the institution of Al-Azhar in Cairo, which provides free education from the primary to the university level. Al-Azhar is also known for its financial contribution towards the development of Islamic education and missionary activities throughout the world.

*Waqf* is by no means an insignificant institution in Islam. Its potential can be discerned by the very insistence on the non-transferability of the ownership rights of the property. Once a piece of property is given for a charitable purpose, the owner ceases to have any claims over it, because the property is said to belong to no one but Allah. A trustee in the form of a single person or group of persons will have to be constituted to manage the property for the generation of income which is distributed as specified by the donor. This concept is of great importance for the development of the poorer sections of society if such *waqf* properties would be managed to generate income for distribution or even for further accumulation of assets. Thus, *waqf* itself can be regarded as an important economic institution for the purpose of generating economic activity whilst at the same time ensuring that the benefits will accrue to some specific sections of society.

Since the advent of Islam in Malaysia, the practice of *waqf* among Muslims has been quite widespread. It is on record that most of the mosques and other places of worship for Muslims in this country are gazetted under *waqf*. There are also a considerable number of assets, particularly in the form of land, which have been donated by individuals as *waqf* lands. Such *waqf* properties are found in every state, particularly in Peninsular Malaysia. Although most of the *waqf* properties have been donated before the turn of this century and their administration has been mostly left to the trustees, efforts towards the centralization of *waqf* property administration have been made in the middle of this century. The present status of *waqf* administration in the country has an important bearing on the extent to which the *waqf* institution contributes towards the development of the Muslims, particularly the specific beneficiaries.

This chapter intends to delve in considerable depth into the management of *waqf* properties in Malaysia. Its significance in the development of the Muslims will be of great interest, judging from the amount of properties gazetted under *waqf* and its long history of practice in the country. The chapter is divided into eight sections. The second section, following the introduction, provides the religious and historical factors motivating Muslims in Malaysia to give away properties for *waqf* purposes. The types of *waqf* properties arising from such motivations are also discussed in the same section. The third section deals with the administrative set-up of *waqf* properties, both pre- and post-1950. It is in this section that an attempt is made to underscore the significance of *waqf* in the development of Muslims in Malaysia. Section 4 provides estimates of *waqf* properties which are currently available. The estimates would not only reflect the quantum but also their estimated value and potential capital for generating the economic activity. Section 5 provides estimates of the revenues and expenses of *waqf* properties. An effort is made in this section to gauge how effective *waqf* management currently is. Section 6 discusses property developments on *waqf* lands. Section 7 is devoted to a discussion of the problems pertaining to *waqf* management. The final section will provide some insights and suggestions for improvement.

## Religious and Historical Perspectives

The coming of Islam to the Malay Archipelago had brought about dramatic changes in the lives of the people, particularly those in Peninsular Malaysia, where all the so-called Malays were Muslims. Islam as a comprehensive way of life was not confined to the rituals of worship but was manifested in the application of Islamic injunctions in every facet of life. Islam, therefore, influenced their customs, traditions, language, literature, eating habits, and even the law of the land. For example, Muslims found guilty of fornication or adultery were condemned to death. Typically, the Malays were keen to eulogize their predecessors and counterparts in the other parts of the then Islamic Empire.

Like other people in the past, the Malays too settled themselves in centres of activities or towns. These towns were normally located at the confluence of rivers for easy communication into the hinterland, or by the river mouths which were conducive for international trade. The historical city of Melaka was a typical example. Since Melaka was the centre of international trade between South Asia (and later Western Europe) and the Far East, it was only natural that Islam came to the peninsula through Melaka as well. This was due to the fact that traders, particularly from India, were also devout Muslims. History has it that Islam spread through Melaka around the eleventh or twelfth century and through the east coast state of Trengganu at around the same time.

Islam managed to set foot very firmly since then, for not less than two to three centuries before the arrival of Christian colonialists. The Malay States were gradually colonized after the arrival of the Portuguese in 1511 until independence in 1957. Although they could not colonize the Malays in their faith, they subsequently secularized them in almost every respect. The very nature of Islam as a comprehensive way of life was reduced to mere religion as a belief. The mundane matters of material life were not supposed to be influenced by the Islamic injunctions. This drastic change was clearly visible when the British confined the authorities of the sultans to matters of religion and culture whilst they took charge of the rest. These included the administration, security, maintenance of law and order, finance, and education.

Vehement resistance against these changes occurred, though sporadically, from time to time. It was not resistance to change but rather against the kinds of changes which were taking place. The gradual and systematic secularization of the lives of the Malays resulted in almost everything being dichotomized into secular and religious dimensions.

The scenario briefly described in the preceding paragraphs had great influence on the practice of *waqf* among the Muslims in the peninsula. Firstly, it was the firm and honest desire to eulogize the benevolent acts of others.

The concept of *waqf* itself was well understood, at least in terms of the flow of income to be generated from time to time. It was also an act of worship which was certainly considered to be most rewarding, particularly in the hereafter. There was obviously no hesitation among the well-endowed to sever any claim on their wealth as long as it could benefit the Muslim society. This commitment is most apparent in the quantum of assets which were on *waqf* prior to the twentieth century.

The second significant factor was the fear of the secularization process which was taking place so steadily. The main fear was that the process may encroach into the freedom of worship itself. In order to ensure that the freedom of worship was always maintained, it was generally felt necessary to have proper places of worship with a constant stream of income for their upkeep. The best guarantee available was to provide lands for mosques and *surau*. This practice was apparently so common that a very high proportion of *waqf* lands to this day are meant for the construction of houses of worship. In fact, it is generally true that the plots of land on which mosques or *surau* have been constructed are *waqf* lands.

A *waqf* property for such a specific purpose is called specific *waqf*, whilst those for general benefits of the Muslim society are called general *waqf* or *waqf khairiah*. In most cases, *waqf* properties in Malaysia are tied to some specific purposes.

The belief was, and indeed still is, very strong that any benevolent act associated with the worship of Allah would be considered most desirable. This is another plausible reason why most mosques have been constructed on *waqf* lands. It is also believed that *waqf* properties which are not properly utilized by the beneficiaries may incur the wrath of Allah. In order to avoid this wrath, the donors preferred to make their *waqf* properties specifically for the construction of mosques.

In cases where enough plots of land have been earmarked for mosques and *surau*, the *waqf* endowments were aimed at generating income to meet the expenses on maintenance of the mosques. This was true particularly with *waqf* properties in the form of land or buildings from which rent could be regularly collected.

*Waqf* lands are also commonly used for cemeteries. These lands are either alienated by the government for cemeteries or actually donated by individuals for that purpose. In any case, most of those individually donated lands for cemeteries were meant for the families of the donors.

The third use of *waqf* properties is for the construction of schools, particularly religious schools. However, the amount of *waqf* land for schools is quite limited and is mostly available in areas where *pondok* type of education is common. *Waqf* properties have also been made specifically for orphanages. The latter category is by far quite limited.

It is clear then that most of the *waqf* properties belonged to the specific *waqf* and very few were meant for general purposes. Most of these properties were specifically donated to be used as houses of worship, schools, and orphanages.

## Administration of *Waqf* Properties

Despite the fact that rich Muslims had given away part of their property for *waqf* since the advent of Islam in this country, the administration of such properties had been left to the trustees without any legal safeguard or organized administrative machinery. Selangor was the first state to enact, in 1952, the Laws on the Administration of Islamic Shariah which contains, *inter alia*, the relevant clauses on *waqf*. It is, therefore, very pertinent to compare the pre-1950 administration of *waqf* properties in Malaysia with that of post-1950.

### Pre-1950 Administration of Waqf Properties

As described in Section 2 above, most of the *waqf* properties were specific for mosques, *surau*, religious schools, and cemeteries. Very few of them were meant for orphanages or other purposes. As such, most of the trustees were the relevant committees of the mosques, *surau*, religious schools, orphanages, and so forth. Apart from the committees, the *penghulu* or village headmen were also entrusted to manage *waqf* properties.

In most cases, the ownership grants of *waqf* properties were handed to the relevant trustees without any documentation to support that such properties were intended for the specific purpose. Verbal instructions given by the donors and accepted by the trustees were considered sufficient for the purpose. The ownership grants were then expected to be changed to the relevant trustees by the trustees themselves, since the donors believed they had no more claims on such properties.

When the *waqf* land was given for the construction of mosques, *surau*, religious schools, and so forth, the construction of such buildings was sufficient evidence for the donor that his donation was properly utilized. No queries would ever be made against the trustee. Similarly, when the *waqf* land was meant for a cemetery, there were no qualms about its use.

*Waqf* properties in the form of land or residential and commercial buildings which generate income for mosques, *surau*, religious schools, and so forth, were similarly administered by the relevant authorities in the form of committees. The donors did not put any claim on them and the income generated through rentals would usually go to meet the recurrent and development expenditures.

This kind of loose practice resulted in the loss of some of the *waqf* properties for several reasons. First, the ownership grants were not changed from the original owners to the relevant authorities. After the death of a donor and the trustee (usually the *penghulu*), the descendants of the deceased donor would claim the property as the rightful inheritors. The absence of any documentation to substantiate that the *waqf* was made earlier clearly favoured the claimants. Secondly, the trustees conveniently transferred the ownership grants to themselves. Although they might not have intended to lay any claim on the property, their children might do so after the trustees expired, but such cases of misappropriation were not rampant.

### Post-1950 Waqf *Administration*

The problems pertaining to the management of *waqf* properties which were held in trust by the trustees, particularly individuals, made it imperative for the State Religious Councils to enact the relevant laws. The first state which enacted the laws on *waqf* properties, as contained in the Laws on the Administration of Islamic Shariah, was Selangor in 1952. Almost all other states followed suit subsequently. For example, Trengganu enacted the same laws in 1955, Melaka in 1959, Perak in 1965, and Johor in 1978. Among the pertinent clauses were the following:

1. The Council of Islamic Religion is the sole trustee of all *waqf* properties;
2. All documents pertaining to *waqf* properties must be kept by the council;
3. The council must take the necessary steps to transfer the ownership of all *waqf* properties to itself;
4. All monies received from specific *waqf* properties must be used according to the purpose for which such properties were intended;
5. All monies received from general *waqf* properties must be kept in the general fund of the *majlis* or the *Baitul-Mal*.

The general situation of *waqf* properties in every state today has improved subsequently. Steps have been taken to ensure that the ownership of all *waqf* properties is transferred to the State Religious Councils. However, owing to various problems, particularly the difficulty in tracing the *waqf* lands in each state and the lack of competent personnel and administrative facilities, there are some *waqf* properties still being held in trust by the original trustees.

### Administrative Set-up

Since the sultan of each state is the head of religion and culture, the state Islamic Religious Councils of the former Federated and Unfederated Malay States are directly under their respective sultans. The states without sultans, namely Melaka, Pulau Pinang, Sabah, and Sarawak, and the Federal Territory are all under the charge of the Yang Di Pertuan Agong, the King. The council, not being an integral part of the government machinery, has its own authority and powers. The Islamic Religious Department, however, is an integral part of the government administration. With the exception of Sabah and Sarawak, the chairmen of the councils are either the sultans or their representatives. In most states, however, the State Executive Councillor for Religious Affairs represents the sultan or the Yang Di Pertuan Agong as the chairman of the council. In Sabah and Sarawak, the council is presided by the head of the Religious Department, who is a civil servant.

Since the council is the sole trustee of all *waqf* properties, its management is delegated either to a committee or an officer appointed by the council. In most states *waqf*, *zakat*, and *Baitul-Mal* are managed by the same committee or officer. It is only in some states, like Melaka, that each of the three divisions (*waqf*, *zakat*, and *Baitul-Mal*) is managed by a separate committee.

The number of administrative staff undertaking the management of *waqf* properties ranges from one to seven, depending on the property size. In most states, the officer-in-charge is also the Secretary of the Council. He is, therefore, not a full-time officer managing the *waqf* properties. He is normally assisted by a clerk and a typist only.

Almost none of the officers managing the *waqf* properties have any training or competency in investment analysis, project management, property evaluation, or any such experience relevant for the job. They are usually pure administrators who are assisted by clerks, typists, and at most an accounts officer. The Pulau Pinang and Melaka Religious Councils seem to have more competent staff than in other states. Figure 1 shows the organizational chart of Waqf, Zakat, and Baitul-Mal (LUKMAL) Council of Melaka State. The committees of the two mosques (Kampong Hulu and Kampong Kling mosques) have been included in the organizational chart because most of the *waqf* properties in Melaka are meant for these two mosques.

The administrative set-up in other states is somewhat similar, with the Secretary of the Council being the officer-in-charge, assisted by a few clerks and typists. It is only in Pulau Pinang where an investment committee has been set up comprising officials from within and outside the council who could contribute towards the profitable investment of *waqf* properties. In Melaka, the Waqf Committee or Council makes investment policies and is responsible for the overall management of *waqf* properties.

The administrative set-up of the *waqf* section of the State Islamic Religious Councils seems to require some drastic review in terms of size, structure, and personnel. This is apparently necessary if *waqf*, as an Islamic institution for development, were to make a significant contribution to the welfare of the *ummah*.

FIGURE 1

**Organizational Chart: Waqf, Zakat, and Baitul-Mal Council (LUKMAL)**

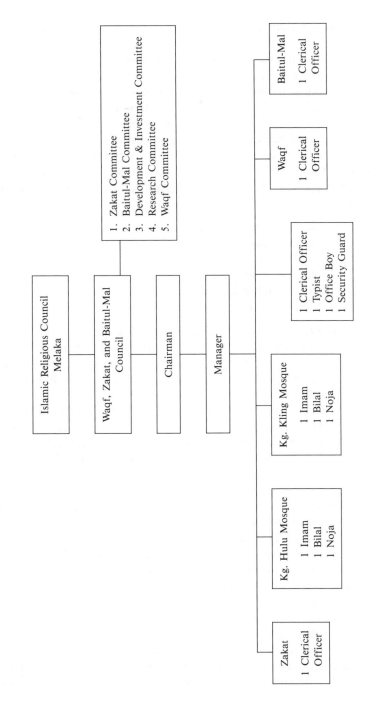

## Estimates of *Waqf* Properties

At the outset, it must be pointed out that there is virtually no complete listing of all *waqf* properties in any state as yet. Any attempt at estimating, or worst still evaluating, the *waqf* properties would, at best, amount to no more than a very rough guesstimate. This section can only provide a rough idea of the amount of *waqf* properties available in various states where data are available.

Sources of data are from the *waqf* section of the Islamic Religious Council for each state. Interviews were conducted with the officials in charge in each state and attempts were made to collect the various pertinent information, wherever possible. The types of *waqf* properties commonly available are as follows:

1.  land for commercial or agricultural purposes;
2.  land for mosques, *surau*, religious schools, cemeteries, and orphanages;
3.  funds for the maintenance and upkeep of mosques, *surau*, religious schools, orphanages, etc.;
4.  commercial and residential buildings;
5.  mosques, *surau*, religious schools, etc.

Since the object of this chapter is to look into the potential of *waqf* as an Islamic development institution, it is important to estimate the amount of assets which could contribute towards the generation of income for the benefit of the target groups. Those assets which are not investible should be excluded from this estimate.

A very peculiar fact about *waqf* land is that all lands used as cemeteries for Muslims are considered *waqf* lands. This is so, irrespective of whether the lands have been donated by members of the public or alienated by the government. The main reason for this peculiarity is that all *waqf* lands for cemeteries are exempted from quit rent. Assets used for other purposes will be subject to quit rent and/or assessment.

The second important fact is that most of the *waqf* lands used for the construction of mosques, *surau*, and religious schools are usually the *waqf* of the specific type. This implies that they cannot be used for any other purposes except for what they have been intended. Their use cannot be changed at all except under extremely special conditions, in accordance with Islamic Shariah, especially that of the Shafie school of thought which is dominant in Malaysia.

Thirdly, *waqf* lands for such specific purposes, especially for cemeteries, form a sizeable proportion of the total land under *waqf*. For example, in Perak, out of a total of 1,161 hectares of *waqf* land, 911 hectares or 78 per cent are reserved for cemeteries. In Johor, out of 529 hectares of *waqf* land, about 375 hectares or 71 per cent are reserved for cemeteries, about 100 hectares or 19 per cent for mosques, 36 hectares or 6.9 per cent for *surau*, and about 0.4 hectare for other purposes.

Taking the above facts into consideration, we may conclude that at most only about 10 per cent of the *waqf* lands have income-generating potentials. Table 1 gives the estimates of *waqf* properties which have the potential for generating income. They comprise residential, agricultural, and commercial plots of land and residential and commercial buildings. In most cases, these properties are rented out at usually below the market rates.

TABLE 1
*Waqf* **Properties by Type and State**

| State | Investible Land (Hectares) | Residential/Commercial Buildings |
|---|---|---|
| Johor | 70.8 | 5 |
| Melaka | 56.3 | 20 |
| Negeri Sembilan | n.a. | n.a. |
| Selangor | 14.2 | n.a. |
| Perak | 129.1 | 23 |
| Pahang | n.a. | n.a. |
| Trengganu | 104.4 | n.a. |
| Kelantan | 97.1 | n.a. |
| Pulau Pinang | n.a. | n.a. |
| Kedah | n.a. | n.a. |
| Perlis | n.a. | n.a. |
| Sabah | n.a. | n.a. |
| Sarawak | n.a. | n.a. |
| Federal Territory | n.a. | n.a. |

n.a. — not available.

Despite the huge amount of *waqf* properties available, around 90 per cent of the fixed land assets are *waqf* for specific purposes which seem to be confined to the rituals of worship or death. Only around 10 per cent of such assets are under the general-purpose *waqf* with potentials for development. It is, therefore, very misleading indeed to look only at the total area of *waqf* lands.

Another problem of concern is that not all *waqf* properties have been transferred to the State Islamic Religious Councils. This is because of various problems pertaining to tracing the *waqf* properties which are still under the original trusteeship. The above data, therefore, suffer from gross underestimation.

## Revenues and Expenses of *Waqf* Properties

Most of the *waqf* properties which could generate income are in the form of residential buildings, agricultural land, and land lots for commercial or residential buildings.

The buildings under *waqf* are those which were donated by individuals or built in recent decades on *waqf* land. The plots of land for construction of residential or commercial houses have not been developed. One striking feature of these properties is that they are mostly located in the towns. The fact that most of these properties were donated by rich Muslims more than a century ago, suggests that the towns were then dominated by the Muslims. The commercial value of these properties has increased many fold, thanks to their prime location.

However, these properties have been generally rented out as they were. Plots of land in the towns have been given out on 99- or 66-year leases at very cheap prices. For example, most of the centrally located plots of land in Kuala Kangsar and Taiping have been on 99-year leases at M$1.00 per month. Only the more recent leases were made at the rate of M$10.00 a month. It is on these plots of land, which are strategically located, that the tenants have constructed two or three storeys of shoplots to carry out their business. About 98 per cent of the tenants are non-Muslims.

The rentals on residential buildings are often lower than the market rate. One reason for this low rate is that they have been rented out before the turn of the century. The Rent Control Act seems to protect these tenants from being charged higher rents. In fact, some of the principal tenants sublet the buildings to other sub-tenants at rates higher than what they have to pay to the *waqf* authorities. These incidents seem to happen rampantly in Melaka, Pulau Pinang, and Perak where a sizeable proportion of *waqf* properties are in the form of buildings or plots of land.

The expenses of *waqf* properties usually comprise payments of salaries to the mosque officials, electricity and water rates, quit rents, assessments, and maintenance and upkeep of mosques/*surau*. In most states, the total income is just sufficient to cover the expenses. In some cases, however, particularly in Perak, the expenses exceed income owing to the low rates of rentals and high rates of quit rent and assessments. Table 2 gives the annual revenues and expenses of *waqf* properties in Melaka from 1970 to 1978.

Both the revenues and expenses of *waqf* properties in Melaka have generally been growing annually. This is so because the surplus of revenue over expenses had been used to construct a number of residential buildings, particularly low-cost houses or flats, to be rented out. Secondly, the rent deals concluded in recent years have tended to yield more reasonable rents. Table 3 gives the monthly rental rates of *waqf* properties in Melaka. It will be noticed

TABLE 2
**Revenue and Expenses of *Waqf* Properties in Melaka, 1970–78**

| Year | Revenue | Expenses |
|------|---------|----------|
| 1970 | 38,454.50 | 29,748.47 |
| 1971 | 37,850.60 | 33,531.90 |
| 1972 | 38,012.10 | 36,323.27 |
| 1973 | 39,678.02 | 29,761.19 |
| 1974 | 42,354.35 | 49,693.57 |
| 1975 | 44,236.52 | 33,762.50 |
| 1976 | 53,705.50 | 35,060.35 |
| 1977 | 50,419.60 | 37,434.43 |
| 1978 | 54,181.80 | 36,463.44 |
| Total | 398,892.99 | 321,779.12 |

TABLE 3
**Monthly Rentals of *Waqf* Properties under Islamic Religious Council, Melaka**

| No. | Address | Type | Monthly Rental M$ |
|-----|---------|------|-------------------|
| 1. | Kampung Ketek, Melaka | Land | 1.00 |
| 2. | 91, Jalan Hang Kasturi, Melaka | Shophouse and Land | 94.00 |
| 3. | 52, Kampung Pantai, Melaka | Shophouse and Land | 100.00 |
| 4. | 50, Kampung Pantai, Melaka | Shophouse and Land | 170.00 |
| 5. | 9, Temenggong, Melaka | Shophouse and Land | 430.00 |
| 6. | 45, Bunga Raya, Melaka | Shophouse and Land | 75.00 |
| 7. | 30, Jalan Laksemana | Shophouse and Land | 220.00 |
| 8. | 32, Jalan Laksemana | Shophouse and Land | 260.00 |
| 9. | Jalan Tok Kong, Melaka | Land | 14.00 |
| 10. | Jalan Tebgkera | Land | 4.00 |
| 11. | Jalan Bali Panjang | Land | 4.00 |
| 12. | Jalan Bukit Cina Pengkalan Rama | Land | 1.00 |
| 13. | Kampung Ketek | Land | 1.00 |
| 14. | Kampung Kuli | Land | 150.00 |
| 15. | Jalan Tengku | Land | 3.00 |
| 16. | 82, Hang Kasturi | Shophouse and Land | 17.75 |
| 17. | 84, Hang Kasturi | Shophouse and Land | n.a. |
| 18. | 86, Hang Kasturi | Shophouse and Land | n.a. |
| 19. | 88, Hang Kasturi | Shophouse and Land | n.a. |
| 20. | 90, Hang Kasturi | Shophouse and Land | n.a. |

n.a. − not available.

that the rentals shown in Table 3 are much higher than those in Kuala Kangsar and Taiping, as depicted in Table 4.

It is to be noted that the revenues and expenditures of *waqf* accounts for each state were not easily available for the following two reasons. Firstly, not all *waqf* properties have been transferred to the State Islamic Religious Councils, the legal trustees of all *waqf* properties in the country. Some are still in the custody of the original trustees, mainly the mosque committees. As such, the accounts have been kept by the original trustees and the State Islamic Religious Councils have not taken the necessary steps to supervise or oversee the accounts.

Secondly, most of the *waqf* properties have not been generating the expected income. As such, the accounts have not been updated or kept in proper order.

The surplus over the years does increase, but only marginally. Accumulation of surplus for capital formation is not very significant. It is important to collect the more recent data to see the actual situation, because it is during the last few years that efforts to develop the *waqf* properties for the purpose of generating income have been stepped up. It is, therefore, relevant to discuss the programmes undertaken for developing the *waqf* properties, to which we now turn.

## Development on *Waqf* Lands

Despite the fact that most of the individuals who donated their properties, particularly land, merely specified that any income derived from them should be used for the mosque in the neighbourhood, more often than not such assets were simply rented out. Most of these *waqf* lands are located in towns and their use are categorized for buildings. Only some of these lands are located in the rural areas under the agricultural category. Some of these lands have not been well taken care of. Squatters have occupied some of them.

Most *waqf* lands in Perak have been rented out on 99- or 66-year leases at incredibly cheap rates. Taking advantage of such long and cheap leases, the tenants had erected permanent structures/buildings, either for residential or business (retail shops) purposes or both. However, there are some plots of land which are left vacant or settled by illegal squatters. In Melaka and Pulau Pinang, the lands in the towns have also been rented out at cheap rates. The buildings, too, have been rented out at rates which are normally lower than the market rates.

Indeed, these lands which are strategically located in town centres could have been developed and then rented out to generate higher revenues. Surpris-

TABLE 4
**Rented *Waqf* Properties in Taiping and Kuala Kangsar**

| No. | Lot *Waqf* | Monthly Rental M$ | Lease Period | W.E.F. |
|-----|-----------|-------------------|--------------|--------|
| 1. | 1 | 1.00 | 99 years | 6.6.1896 |
| 2. | 2 | 1.00 | 99 years | 6.6.1896 |
| 3. | 3 | 1.00 | 99 years | 6.6.1896 |
| 4. | 4 | 1.00 | 99 years | 6.6.1896 |
| 5. | 5 | 1.00 | 99 years | 6.6.1896 |
| 6. | 6 | 1.00 | 99 years | 6.6.1896 |
| 7. | 7 | 1.00 | 99 years | 6.6.1896 |
| 8. | 8 | 1.00 | 99 years | 6.6.1896 |
| 9. | 9 | 1.00 | 99 years | 6.6.1896 |
| 10. | 10A | 1.00 | Temporary Rental | 1.6.1864 |
| 11. | 10B | 1.00 | Temporary Rental | 1.6.1864 |
| 12. | 10C | 3.00 | Temporary Rental | 1.6.1864 |
| 13. | 10D | 3.00 | Temporary Rental | 1.6.1864 |
| 14. | 10E | 3.00 | Temporary Rental | 1.6.1864 |
| 15. | 10F | 3.00 | Temporary Rental | 1.6.1864 |
| 16. | 11 | 1.00 | 99 years | 6.6.1896 |
| 17. | 12 | 1.00 | 99 years | 6.6.1896 |
| 18. | 13 | 1.00 | 99 years | 6.6.1896 |
| 19. | 14 | 1.00 | 99 years | 6.6.1896 |
| 20. | 15 | 1.00 | 99 years | 6.6.1896 |
| 21. | 16 | 1.00 | 99 years | 6.6.1896 |
| 22. | 17 | 1.00 | 99 years | 6.6.1896 |
| 23. | 19 | 1.00 | 99 years | 6.6.1896 |
| 24. | 20 | 1.00 | 99 years | 6.6.1896 |
| 25. | 21 | 1.00 | 99 years | 6.6.1896 |
| 26. | 22 | 1.00 | 99 years | 6.6.1896 |
| 27. | 23 | 1.00 | 99 years | 6.6.1896 |
| 28. | 24 | 1.00 | 99 years | 6.6.1896 |
| 29. | 25 | 1.00 | 99 years | 6.6.1896 |
| 30. | 26 | 1.00 | 99 years | 6.6.1896 |
| 31. | 27 | 1.00 | 99 years | 6.6.1896 |
| 32. | 28 | 1.00 | 99 years | 6.6.1896 |
| 33. | 29 | 1.00 | 99 years | 6.6.1896 |
| 34. | 30 | 1.00 | 99 years | 6.6.1896 |
| 35. | 31 | 1.00 | 99 years | 6.6.1896 |
| 36. | 32 | 1.00 | 99 years | 6.6.1896 |
| 37. | 33 | 1.00 | 99 years | 6.6.1896 |
| 38. | 34 | 1.00 | 99 years | 6.6.1896 |
| 39. | 35 | 1.00 | 99 years | 6.6.1896 |
| 40. | 36 | 1.00 | 99 years | 6.6.1896 |
| 41. | 37 | 1.00 | 99 years | 13.1.1897 |
| 42. | 38 | 20.00 | Temporary Rental | 1.3.1952 |
| 43. | 39 | 20.00 | Temporary Rental | 1.3.1952 |

TABLE 4 (*continued*)
**Rented *Waqf* Properties in Taiping and Kuala Kangsar**

| No. | Lot *Waqf* | Monthly Rental M\$ | Lease Period | W.E.F. |
|-----|------------|--------------------|--------------|--------|
| 44. | 40 | 20.00 | Temporary Rental | 1.3.1952 |
| 45. | 41 | 20.00 | Temporary Rental | 1.3.1952 |
| 46. | 42 | 20.00 | Temporary Rental | 1.3.1952 |
| 47. | 43 | – | Vacant land not rented yet | – |
| 48. | 44 | – | Vacant land not rented yet | – |
| 49. | 45 | – | Vacant land not rented yet | – |
| 50. | 46 | 1.00 | 99 years | 1.1.1901 |
| 51. | 47 | 1.00 | * 99 years | 1.1.1901 |
| 52. | 48 | 1.00 | 99 years | 1.1.1901 |
| 53. | 49 | 1.00 | 99 years | 1.1.1901 |
| 54. | 50 | 1.00 | 99 years | 1.1.1901 |
| 55. | 51 | 1.00 | 99 years | 1.1.1901 |
| 56. | 52 | 1.00 | 99 years | 1.1.1901 |
| 57. | 53 | 1.00 | 99 years | 1.1.1901 |
| 58. | 54 | 1.00 | 99 years | 1.1.1901 |
| 59. | 55 | 53.50 | – | Sept. 1945 |
| 60. | 56 | 53.50 | – | Sept. 1945 |
| 61. | 57 | 20.00 | Temporary Rental | 1.5.1953 |
| 62. | 58 | 1.00 | 99 years | 28.1.1897 |
| 63. | 59 | 1.00 | 99 years | 28.1.1897 |
| 64. | 60 | 1.50 | 99 years | 25.5.1912 |
| 65. | 61 | – | *Waqf* house for *Imam* | – |
| 66. | 62 | – | *Waqf* house for *Imam* | – |
| 67. | 63 | – | *Waqf* house for *Imam* | – |
| 68. | 64 | 2.50 | 99 years | 1.12.1909 |
| 69. | 65 | 2.50 | 99 years | 1.12.1909 |
| 70. | 66 | 2.50 | 99 years | 1.12.1909 |
| 71. | 68 | 1.00 | 99 years | 1.12.1909 |
| 72. | 69 | 1.00 | 99 years | 1.12.1909 |
| 73. | 70 | 1.00 | 99 years | 1.12.1909 |
| 74. | 72A | 3.00 | Sewa Sementara | 1.12.1909 |
| 75. | 111 | – | Vacant land not rented yet | – |
| 76. | 112 | – | Vacant land not rented yet | – |
| 77. | 113 | – | Vacant land not rented yet | – |
| 78. | 114 | – | Vacant land not rented yet | – |
| 79. | 115 | – | Vacant land not rented yet | – |
| 80. | 116 | – | Vacant land not rented yet | – |
| 81. | 119 | – | Vacant land not rented yet | – |
| 82. | 120 | – | Vacant land not rented yet | – |
| 83. | 121 | – | Vacant land not rented yet | – |
| 84. | 122 | – | Vacant land not rented yet | – |
| 85. | 123 | – | Vacant land not rented yet | – |
| 86. | 124 | – | Vacant land not rented yet | – |

TABLE 4 (*continued*)
**Rented *Waqf* Properties in Taiping and Kuala Kangsar**

| No. | Lot *Waqf* | Monthly Rental M$ | Lease Period | W.E.F. |
|---|---|---|---|---|
| 87. | 2438 | 10.00 | 66 years | 1.9.1965 |
| 88. | 2439 | 10.00 | 66 years | 1.9.1965 |
| 89. | 2440 | 10.00 | 66 years | 1.9.1965 |
| 90. | 2441 | 10.00 | 66 years | 1.9.1965 |
| 91. | 2442 | 10.00 | 66 years | 1.9.1965 |
| 92. | 2443 | 10.00 | 66 years | 1.9.1965 |
| 93. | 2444 | 10.00 | 66 years | 1.9.1965 |
| 94. | 2445 | 10.00 | 66 years | 1.9.1965 |
| 95. | 2446 | 10.00 | 66 years | 1.9.1965 |
| 96. | 2447 | 10.00 | 66 years | 1.9.1965 |
| 97. | 2448 | 10.00 | 66 years | 1.9.1965 |
| 98. | 2449 | 10.00 | 66 years | 1.9.1965 |
| 99. | 2450 | 1.50 | 99 years | 23.6.1919 |
| 100. | 2451 | 10.00 | 66 years | 1.3.1966 |
| 101. | 2452 | 10.00 | 66 years | 1.3.1966 |
| 102. | 2453 | – | Vacant land not rented yet | – |
| 103. | Lot 50 Mukim Pupai | | | |

W.E.F. – With Effect From.

ingly, it was not until the 1970s did the trustees of these lands realize the need to develop them by constructing buildings for rent. A number of the State Islamic Religious Councils (Pulau Pinang, Melaka, and Trengganu) undertook development projects in the midst of the construction industry's boom period (1980–84). Such councils are assisted by panels of advisors on investment, comprising officials from various state departments and other professionals. They include, among others, project managers of the State Economic Development Corporation, architects and engineers from the Public Works Department, other professionals, and politicians. These panels are to provide expert advice on investments, construction, and the financing of the projects. The Urban Development Authority (UDA) and Majlis Amanah Rakyat (MARA)[3] have been actively involved in providing the finance for the construction of buildings.

The Melaka State Islamic Religious Council had formed a special committee on *waqf* for the purpose of overseeing the overall management of all *waqf* properties under its jurisdiction as well as to explore and undertake development of *waqf* lands. The members of the committee are drawn from professionals serving government departments or statutory bodies, religious scholars, and so forth. One of the projects which has been successfully completed is a four-storey complex of shoplots and office space which was constructed on 1,951 square metres of *waqf* land in Melaka Town in 1979. It was a joint-venture between the council and the Urban Development Authority. The committee has also indicated its desire to identify other plots of land which are suitable for development. Apart from this significant development, the various trustees of *waqf* lands had erected low-cost residential houses for rent. Most of the finance comes from the mosque committees, the *de facto* trustees of the *waqf* lands.

In Pulau Pinang, a panel of advisors has been constituted to advise the council on the feasibility, financing, and management of development projects on *waqf* lands in the state. Unlike in Melaka where the special committee on *waqf* is completely responsible for the *waqf* properties, the Pulau Pinang State Islamic Religious Council has appointed an investment committee. The function of this committee, which includes businessmen and professionals, is to provide regular advice on investments.

In 1979, the council extended an existing block of 22 flats and 13 shoplots by constructing 6 additional units of flats. Another project of constructing a four-storey complex of shoplots and office space on a 5,593-square-metre plot of land in the city centre was also completed in 1985. This project, which cost around M$2 million financed by MARA, is now generating a rental revenue of around M$13,200 a month. Apparently, the council is receiving M$2,000 a year for thirty years as rental on the land. At the end of the period, the building will be given to the council. The projected revenue when the council takes over the building in thirty years' time is expected to be about half a million ringgits a year. Reference must also be made to another construction project — four-storey, low-cost flats, shoplots, and office space on a 1,579-square-metre plot of land located in the town centre. The total cost is estimated at M$700,000. The council hopes to undertake the project, which is to be financed by a loan from the federal government. The project has already been approved by the Georgetown City Council. The expected revenue is about M$85,000 a year.

The council has also invested *waqf* assets of M$1,065,500 in fixed deposits. Now that the Islamic Bank has been in operation, the money has been transferred into the Investment Account of the Islamic Bank.

In Perak, the council has been looking into the development of a four-storey shopping complex, a four-storey hostel complex, and a mosque on a 6.1-hectare piece of land in Taiping. The project is still underway. Although there are many plots of *waqf* land available in the state, they are uneconomical in size and shape and are sporadically distributed.

In other states, very little has been done to develop the *waqf* properties. Efforts towards this end are apparent relatively more markedly in Trengganu and Johor.

## Problems of Management

Most of the *waqf* properties in Malaysia have been donated prior to the turn of this century. The trustees had been the village headmen, other respectable individuals, or mosque committees. It was the realization that *waqf* properties had not been properly managed or executed according to the donors' intentions which led the State Islamic Religious Councils to enact the law that the council become the sole trustee of all *waqf* properties. This move took place not earlier than the middle of this century.

The major problem of *waqf* property management is the transfer of ownership titles of *waqf* properties to the council as the sole trustee of all *waqf* properties in a given state. This seems to be the major obstacle, particularly with regard to *waqf* properties for general purposes. *Waqf* properties for specific purposes are very clear and easily traceable since they are meant for cemeteries, mosques, *surau*, religious schools, and so forth. When a piece of property has been donated for a general purpose, the original trustee may not have transferred the ownership title to the proper trustee. In such cases, the property was claimed by the descendants of the donor after the donor's death. Conversely, a trustee could transfer the ownership title to himself and his heirs would conveniently claim ownership of such property in due course. All such properties have been completely untraceable.

The second major problem is the shortage of qualified and competent personnel in the *waqf* section of almost every state council. The mood seems to be that the amount of revenue derived from *waqf* properties is so small to even cover the expenses of managing them. As such, it smacks of the chicken and egg problem. The small number of staff curtails their ability to even compile the full list of *waqf* properties in the state.

In the absence of a proper record of *waqf* properties, it is conveniently assumed that the available list of *waqf* properties is a comprehensive one. The list is collected simply by requesting all mosque, *surau*, or religious school committees to submit the necessary information. Very little follow-up work is done to ensure the accuracy of the information.

The third problem involves the process of transferring the ownership titles. The process, which has to go through the Land Offices, is a very slow and tedious one. This becomes a problem particularly because of the incompetence and understaffing of the *waqf* units.

Fourthly, the state council has to incur costs in terms of quit rent and sometimes assessment on the property whose title is under the name of the council. The only property which is exempted from quit rent is a *waqf* for cemetery. The council would not, therefore, be in favour of transferring the ownership title to itself when the property is not income-generating or when the cost exceeds the revenue. The way to solve the problem is to register the title under the President of the State Religious Department, thereby making it a piece of government property and hence exempted from quit rent or assessment. But this method would make the list of *waqf* properties even shorter.

Lastly, there seems to be very little understanding of the potential of *waqf* as an Islamic development institution within the circle of those involved in managing the *waqf* properties. There is, however, a glimpse of hope stemming from the efforts of a few states like Pulau Pinang, Melaka, Perak, and Trengganu, which are relatively more active in undertaking income-generating projects on *waqf* lands.

## Some Insight and Suggestions

*Waqf* not only plays a religious role but also represents an economic institution designed for the benefit of the Muslims. The institution of *waqf* has played a key role in the accumulation and development of assets for the common good of the Muslims. Although the earlier generation of Muslims the world over had attached a great deal of importance to the institution of *waqf*, the present generation of Muslims has not been able to exploit the potentials of such *waqf* properties to the fullest, let alone increase them through their own wealth.

One of the main obstacles is the inability to comprehend and appreciate such benevolent acts. It is perhaps not incorrect to say that the limited amount of property given out as *waqf* these days is partly due to the weak economic position of the Muslims. However, it would be difficult to accept an explanation in terms of shortage of personnel, funds, and expertise for managing *waqf* properties these days. It is an economic waste to allow *waqf* properties unattended. And, it is un-Islamic to do so.

A rethinking on this matter has to be done immediately. There is a need to overcome the problems of Land Control Act, the long and tedious process of transferring titles of ownership, the shortage of competent staff, the limited financial resources, and so forth. Several seminars on *waqf* have been held in Malaysia. One of these, held in Ipoh in November 1986, has called for the setting up of a Special Steering Committee or a Task Force to look into these problems. It is heartening to report that such a Task Force has been constituted lately.

## NOTES

1    "By no means shall ye attain righteousness unless ye give [freely] of that which ye love" (Al Imran [3]: 92).

2    Umar was reported to have inquired of the Prophet (peace be upon him) how he could be closer to God through his wealth, an amount of which he never obtained before. The Holy Prophet replied, "Stop the capital and give the fruits", after which Umar prevented his property from being inherited, sold, or given away. This tradition as reported by Ash Shafie and Al Hanbali has been considered as the very basis of *waqf*. Indeed the multitude of rewards from Allah is obviously commensurate with the charity which would be extended continuously out of the generated income.

3    A statutory body instituted by the government to undertake developments for the benefit of the Bumiputra (indigenous people).

# 7 THE MALAYSIAN PILGRIMS MANAGEMENT AND FUND BOARD AND RESOURCE MOBILIZATION

*Radiah Abdul Kader*

## Introduction

Pilgrimage (*hajj*) is the threshold of a Muslim's spiritual experience. As it is the supreme expression of the belief in Allah, it is, therefore, an obligation on all Muslims to perform the *hajj* at least once in their lifetime if their circumstances permit. It requires tremendous preparation on the part of the believers, both spiritually and materially, so that the *hajj* can be performed in its complete form. Financially, in the Malaysian case, the journey to Mecca in the 1950s had cost most pilgrims their lifetime savings, a lot of sacrifices, and hardship. Their economic plight after the *hajj* was even more distressing. Having sold everything to perform the *hajj*, some returned to nothing. To meet the needs of the pilgrims before, during, and after the *hajj*, the Pilgrims Management and Fund Board (hereinafter referred to as the board or PMFB) was set up in 1969.

The board was established to serve two functions — as a financial institution and as a pilgrims' management body. After being in operation for two decades, the board seems to have reorientated its activities more along commercial lines. Nonetheless, its original goal of enabling its members to perform the *hajj* and safeguarding their welfare during the pilgrimage continues to be served. It has been mentioned that "the functions of the Board as a savings institution is secondary to its main function as a pilgrims' management institution".[1]

This chapter attempts to examine the role of PMFB as a mobilizer of voluntary savings among Malaysian Muslims and also to evaluate its contributions to the welfare of the Muslim community.

## A Review of PMFB

### Historical Evolution

Looking at its current role as a monopoly in pilgrims' welfare management, perhaps very few knew that the board originally started purely as a savings fund for prospective pilgrims. The historical evolution of PMFB can thus be divided into two stages. The first stage was the setting up of the Malayan Muslims Pilgrims Savings Corporation in 1962. The original idea behind the creation of this corporation was initiated by Royal Professor Ungku Abdul Aziz of the University of Malaya who, after an extensive study of the rural economy in the 1950s, presented a memorandum to the government suggesting the need for a corporation which will assist Muslims to perform the *hajj* without impoverishing them or imposing financial hardships after the pilgrimage. In the memorandum he mentioned that

> the biggest single motive for savings that is evident in any part of Malaya where there are Malays is that of saving for pilgrimage. This plan will create a new institution that will not only help them to achieve their desire in a more efficient way but it will enable them to do it in less time and with less loss to themselves and to the national economy particularly the rural economy.[2]

It was often assumed in those days that there was hardly any savings to be mobilized in the rural sector. Ungku Aziz, however, estimated that about M$3 million was spent each year by pilgrims, a steady source of savings which the government could not afford to neglect. But the ways by which this huge sum was saved were unsuitable for a monetized economy and harmful to national progress. Savings for the purpose of pilgrimage were typically hoarded in pillowcases and under the mattresses and floorboards or invested in land or livestock which would be later sold to meet the expenses for the *hajj*. Hoarded cash not only decreased in value over time but was vulnerable to theft and fire, while land as a form of saving was affected by subdivision, fragmentation, neglect, and so forth.

Such a saving behaviour among Muslims was not without justification. The main reason for resorting to saving outside the financial framework was to ensure that the money to be spent on the *hajj* was completely free from *riba* (interest). The savings facilities in any bank or financial institution at that time were unacceptable to these Muslims because of the presence of interest. "The solution", as perceived by Ungku Aziz, "was an institution to mobilise savings, not to involve interest, but to involve profits".

The plan was lauded, but could not be implemented then as the government was unable to resolve the question of *riba*. Nevertheless, it was finally carried out in 1962, following the recommendation of Sheikh Mahmoud Al-Shaltout who, on his visit to Malaysia, studied the plan and found it absolutely *riba*-free and technically sound. The Pilgrims Savings Corporation was incorporated in August 1962 and launched on 30 September 1963. From the *Shariah* (Islamic law) point of view, this constituted a major effort to rescue the Malaysian Muslim community from interest and hoarding, both of which are forbidden in Islam.

The second stage in the development of PMFB was marked by the merger between the Pilgrims Savings Corporation and the Pilgrims Affairs Office which had been in operation since 1951. Even though the former was largely a financial institution, from time to time it had to cater for the welfare of prospective pilgrims who were members of the corporation. Thus to avoid duplication and overlapping of functions between the two bodies, the government found it worthwhile to form a new body which would incorporate the functions of both. This led to the establishment of PMFB by statute in August 1969.

## Corporate Organization

*Aims and objectives.* Under its Act of Incorporation, the administration of PMFB would encompass three broad areas of operation, namely: (1) savings mobilization and maintenance, (2) savings utilization (investments), and (3) pilgrimage welfare management.

Each of these areas aims to accomplish the following goals correspondingly:

1.    to enable Muslims to save gradually so as to provide for their expenses in performing the pilgrimage or for other expenses that are beneficial to them;
2.    to enable Muslims, through their savings, to participate in investments in industry, commerce, plantations, and real estates, as approved by *Shariah*; and
3.    to provide for the protection, control, and welfare of Muslims while on pilgrimage through the various facilities and services of PMFB.

The clarity of the above goals enabled the formulation of the following objectives:

1    to render the best and most satisfactory services to Malaysian pilgrims on matters pertaining to the performance of the *hajj*; and
2.    to give maximum investment returns to depositors on their savings.

In short, the objectives of PMFB pertaining to public service and profits are quite specific and clear-cut, which give the organization a very good foundation for performance.

*Organizational structure.* The organizational structure of PMFB is shown in Appendix A. PMFB is a semi-government body under the Prime Minister's Department. Its organizational structure reflects a fully autonomous body which is able to exercise its statutory powers and executive policies for the benefit of its depositors. Its highest authority, the board of directors, is empowered under the Act to formulate policies and implement programmes in the interest of the organization and its depositors. Additional power is also given to administer the funds and all other matters pertaining to the welfare of the pilgrims. Members of the board comprise a chairman, a deputy chairman, a representative of the Prime Minister's Department, a representative of the Treasury, a director-general, not more than five other members appointed by the Prime Minister, and a representative from the Ministry of Health (by invitation).

Despite its vast powers, the board of directors would only act upon the advice of two advisory councils, namely the Financial Advisory Council on matters regarding finance and investments, and the Hajj Operations Advisory Council on matters pertaining to the welfare of the pilgrims. Decisions made are then delegated to the management for implementation and are supervised by two statutory committees, namely the Finance Committee and the Welfare Committee. Thus, elements of check and balance are inherent in almost all processes and procedures to ensure efficiency and trustworthiness.

At the headquarters level, the management is divided into four departments, each specializing in specific activities:

1.  The Department of Finance and Investment — responsible for all financial transactions in accordance with provisions stipulated in the Act of Incorporation.
2.  The Department of Hajj — responsible for discharging all services pertaining to *hajj* affairs whether in Malaysia or Saudi Arabia.
3.  The Department of Administration and Information — responsible for matters pertaining to personnel recruitment, training and career development, and dissemination of information regarding PMFB activities.
4.  The Department of Corporate Affairs and Research — dealing with all corporate matters, such as promotion of corporate image and evaluation of corporate strategies, so as to ensure that PMFB activities fulfil the needs of its clientele groups.

Each of the above departments is divided into divisions which are further subdivided into branches, units, and sections to provide for better supervision and control.

*Financial structure.* The funds needed to cover operating expenses are available from two sources: in the form of grants from the federal government and funds from PMFB itself.

The federal government's contributions are allocated only to the Department of Hajj and the Department of Administration and Information, which receive 100 per cent and 50 per cent financial aid, respectively. Operating expenses incurred by the Department of Finance and Investment are wholly met from funds generated by PMFB, which consist mainly of profits and income from investments and fees for services rendered.

## Financial Activities of PMFB

*Mobilization of deposits.* PMFB currently provides only one form of saving facility, that is, deposit facility. It accepts deposits from members on the *Shariah* principle of *al-wadiah*, whereby depositors grant permission to PMFB to use their deposits for investment purposes. Profits from the investment are then distributed among depositors in the form of bonus after the payment of *zakat* and other allocations have been made.

Membership is limited to Malaysian Muslim individuals only (excluding religious organizations such as *Baitul-Mal* where *zakat* funds are kept). The minimum deposit required to open an account is M$2.00. No savings account book is issued on opening an account. Instead, each member is given an account number which is used when subsequent deposits are made. Statement of account is sent to depositors twice yearly, that is, as at 30 June and 31 December. Bonus is calculated at the end of the year and credited to the account of individual depositors after the net distributable profit for the year minus *zakat* has been determined.

Deposits can be made at the PMFB head office or branch offices, through the post office, or by monthly salary deductions. These methods of savings have been devised on the premise that they are fool-proof, convenient for all members, and can be easily administered with least possible expenditures.

To attract new depositors, various saving schemes for schools, government departments, and the private sector have been launched from time to time. These include:

1. Saving schemes for school-children by introducing coin-boxes which were sold at M$5 each.
2. Saving schemes for dependants where a depositor is encouraged to extend his monthly salary deduction to his dependants.
3. Monthly Bonus Payment Scheme for accounts exceeding M$10,000 for at least a year. Bonuses credited at the end of each year will be paid in equal monthly instalments the following year. This scheme is specially devised for depositors in the lower income group who receive compensation from the government for their land and property forgone for development purposes. Through this scheme, they are ensured a fixed monthly income.

*Withdrawal of deposits.* PMFB is one of the very few financial institutions that provide a direct link between saving and purpose. As such, under the Act, savings deposited with the board cannot be withdrawn for reasons other than to defray all or part of the depositor's pilgrimage expenses, except in the following cases: (1) the death of the depositor; (2) when age, health, and so forth, make it difficult to undertake pilgrimage; and (3) on production of satisfactory evidence of intending emigration from Malaysia.

On principle, withdrawals are allowed only once in six months, with a maximum withdrawal of up to 80 per cent of the individual's credit balance. However, 100 per cent withdrawals are allowed for the exceptional reasons stated above. In addition, a member who is registered for pilgrimage in a certain year cannot make withdrawals within six months before his departure but is permitted to withdraw his savings in Mecca or Medina. On his return to Malaysia, withdrawals can only be made two months after the *wukuf* date (the day of the *hajj*).

All withdrawals are processed at the PMFB head-office and it normally takes a week or ten days before payment can be made. It may be noted that the rules governing withdrawals of deposits accord a long-term character to the deposits. This is to ensure that the primary aim of enabling the members to save for the *hajj* is achieved. Moreover, funds of the board could be invested in long-term investments which usually take at least six months for profits to accrue.

*Utilization of funds.* Since the funds lodged with PMFB are being held for the *hajj*, the areas of investments have to be within the framework of the *Shariah*. This, therefore, rules out investment in government securities, other interest-bearing securities, or shares in companies producing goods which are forbidden in Islam. Nevertheless, the scope for investment is still broad. At present, there are four types of investments undertaken by PMFB, viz:

1.   investment in shares (equity participation);
2.   investment in subsidiary companies;
3.   investment in land and building; and
4.   short-term investment.

To ensure that investment operations are in compliance with the *Shariah* rules, PMFB was brought under the advice of the National Advisory Council, which was later replaced by the Religious Supervisory Council of Bank Islam Malaysia.

1.   Investment in shares
        Investment in shares is limited to selected Malaysian equities, as permitted by *Shariah*. These include shares of companies in major sectors

such as plantation agriculture, manufacturing, trade, transport, mining, and properties. The amount of equity participation depends on the amount being offered but generally the PMFB does not participate as a major shareholder. In cases where PMFB is a substantial shareholder (that is, holding more than 5 per cent equity of a company), PMFB officials are represented on the company's board of directors. Constant reviews are made by PMFB officials on the activities of the companies to ensure that they comply with the *Shariah* rules. If found otherwise, PMFB will sell off its shares in the company.

Methods of share acquisition are as follows:

(a)   Quoted shares are directly bought in the Kuala Lumpur Stock Exchange while unquoted shares are acquired when issued to the public.

(b)   Shares allocated for Malays are purchased through the Ministry of Trade and Industry.

(c)   Four commercial banks are elected as nominee companies to purchase shares for PMFB.

(d)   Equity shares are also acquired through partnership or joint-ventures with other companies.

2.   Investment in subsidiary companies

As a statutory body, PMFB is constrained both by its own Act and by government regulations in its direct involvement in commercial activities. However, the Act provides for the incorporation of companies under the Companies Act of 1965. Currently, five subsidiary companies have been incorporated and wholly owned by PMFB, two of which operate in the plantation industry while the rest are involved in transport and trading, construction and housing, and property management.

3.   Investment in land and building

Activities under this heading involve the construction of buildings for the use of PMFB offices as well as for rental purposes. Potential lots of land for future development are also bought to form a land bank. Investment on the basis of sale and lease-back method is also undertaken whereby PMFB buys a building and leases it back to its original owner for a specific period.

4.   Short-term investment

The establishment of the Islamic Bank in Malaysia provides PMFB with an avenue to invest its temporary short-term funds in accordance with the Islamic principles. Short-term funds meant for *hajj* expenses are invested in a special investment account with the Islamic Bank on a profit-sharing ratio of 75:25 in PMFB's favour. On the other hand, normal short-term surplus is maintained in the current account and invested by the bank, and profits are shared in the ratio of 70:30.

## PMFB as a Financial Institution — an Evaluation of Performance

### Branch Network and Employment Structure

An index of development for any institution may be the size of its branch network, its work force, and its structure. In the early years of its incorporation, PMFB started off with very few branch offices and a staff of hardly twenty. After two decades, its branch offices have increased to 65, with 15 divisions under 4 departments at the headquarters level. As at 31 December 1985, the total number of staff stood at 841 with a high proportion of semi-skilled workers, including clerks and technicians. The proportion of professional and semi-professional staff is still small, comprising less than 20 per cent of total employees (Appendix B).

### Profile of Deposits

*Growth of deposits and the number of depositors.* As at 31 December 1986, PMFB had accumulated M$1.7 million worth of deposits with the number of depositors almost reaching the target of one million.

Table 1 provides data relating to total deposits and depositors and their growth for the period 1969–86. Major trends in growth of deposits are described below. With the exception of 1975 and 1976, the growth of deposits during the past two decades shows an increasing trend. Savings were in the range of M$7–70 million a year during the 1970s, and M$100–250 million a year in the 1980s.

The most remarkable growth occurred between the third and fifth year of PMFB's existence with deposits growing at an average rate of 69 per cent. This may be attributed mainly to the success of publicity measures undertaken in the rural areas beginning in 1972. Grand-scale campaigns were launched in four major states where the majority of the rural Malay population concentrates. In 1974, small-scale campaigns were extended to mosques and schools and exhibitions were held in various government agencies. The success of the publicity drive was followed by the opening of new branch offices in twelve states.

The years 1975 and 1976, however, witnessed a sharp decline in the volume of deposits (falling at an average rate of 30 per cent per year). One major factor causing this situation was the radical change in the implementation of the Sheikh System in Mecca and Medina in 1975 when pilgrims were not allowed to choose a particular sheikh as their guide. This new ruling

TABLE 1
**PMFB — Growth of Deposits and the Number of Depositors, 1969–86**

| Year | Deposits Received | | No. of Depositors | |
|------|------------------|---------------------|--------|-------------------|
| | M$ million | Percentage Change | ('000) | Percentage Change |
| 1969 | 7.0 | | 7.1 | |
| 1970 | 9.4 | 34.3 | 12.4 | 74.6 |
| 1971 | 10.7 | 13.8 | 12.9 | 4.0 |
| 1972 | 18.4 | 72.0 | 23.9 | 85.3 |
| 1973 | 29.4 | 59.8 | 42.0 | 75.7 |
| 1974 | 51.7 | 75.9 | 82.6 | 96.7 |
| 1975 | 42.7 | − 17.4 | 35.8 | − 56.7 |
| 1976 | 22.8 | − 46.6 | 15.5 | − 56.7 |
| 1977 | 26.9 | 18.0 | 27.1 | 74.8 |
| 1978 | 47.8 | 77.7 | 30.6 | 12.9 |
| 1979 | 68.8 | 43.9 | 34.7 | 13.4 |
| 1980 | 108.4 | 57.6 | 51.6 | 48.7 |
| 1981 | 150.3 | 38.7 | 58.4 | 13.2 |
| 1982 | 182.7 | 21.6 | 66.4 | 13.7 |
| 1983 | 195.9 | 7.2 | 75.1 | 13.1 |
| 1984 | 209.5 | 6.9 | 133.4 | 77.6 |
| 1985 | 226.7 | 8.2 | 123.8 | − 7.2 |
| 1986 | 275.0 | 21.5 | 126.4 | 2.1 |

SOURCE: Savings and Withdrawal Division, PMFB.

proved unpopular among pilgrims because it often meant separation from friends and relatives during the *hajj*. Another major factor was the worldwide inflationary situation which caused a rise in *hajj* expenses. Air fare in 1976 was relatively higher than in 1975. Coupled with the rise in the prices of daily essentials in Saudi Arabia, total *hajj* expenses escalated from M$1,500 to M$2,800 per person. This led to a decrease in the number of pilgrims, which in turn affected the volume of deposits.

Deposits started to rise again in 1977, following the annulment of the Sheikh System and has continued to increase ever since. However, the rate of increase has slowed down beginning 1981, which may be due to the economic recession.

Trends in the growth of depositors more or less follow the trend in deposits' growth, with peaks in 1972–74 and troughs in 1975–76. Growth between 1978 and 1983 was rather moderate, with average increases of 13 per cent per year (excluding 1980). The huge increase in the number of depositors in 1984 consisted mainly of school-children[3] and new deposits recruited through the salary deduction scheme.[4]

An examination of PMFB deposits can also be viewed from various categories of depositors, which can be classified mainly as:

1. intending pilgrims;
2. employees in the government and private sectors;
3. ordinary depositors; and
4. students/children.

Tables 2 and 3 show data on deposits accumulated by various methods of collection and the categories of depositors based on their methods of saving, respectively. It is evident that the salary deduction group represents the largest category, although it is smaller in terms of deposits collected. Employees in the government sector are the major depositors, while response from employees in the private sector has been quite poor. This may be attributed to the fact that almost 90 per cent of employees in the public sector are Muslims who could provide a steady flow of funds into PMFB each month. The poor response from employees in the private sector may be due to lack of co-operation by non-Muslim employers in making deductions for their Muslim workers.

TABLE 2
**PMFB — Deposit Accumulation, 1985–87**
(As a percentage of total deposits each year)

| Method of Saving | | 1985 | 1986 | 1987* |
|---|---|---|---|---|
| 1. | Non-Salary Deductions | | | |
| | Pilgrimage purpose | 35.0 | 32.9 | 40.2 |
| | Students | 0.2 | 0.2 | 0.2 |
| | Ordinary: | | | |
| |   Post office | 8.3 | 6.6 | 5.5 |
| |   Counter collection | 25.1 | 28.3 | 30.4 |
| 2. | Salary Deductions | | | |
| | Government | 21.3 | 22.0 | 15.8 |
| | Private | 2.3 | 2.7 | 3.7 |
| | Schools† | 7.8 | 7.3 | 4.2 |
| | Total | 100 | 100 | 100 |
| | Total Deposits (million) | M$226.7 | M$275.2 | M$96.3 |

* Until March 1987.
† Staff and teachers only.

Source: Savings and Withdrawal Division, PMFB.

TABLE 3
**PMFB — New Depositors, 1985–86**
(As a percentage of total new depositors each year)

| Method of Saving | 1985 | 1986 |
|---|---|---|
| Salary deduction | 31.2 | 31.0 |
| Students and children | 27.8 | 28.5 |
| Pilgrimage purpose | 5.6 | 5.2 |
| Ordinary* | 35.4 | 35.3 |
| Total | 100 | 100 |
| Total Number of Depositors | 123,997 | 127,660 |

* Comprises campaign, counter, and post office collections.

SOURCE: PMFB Annual Report, 1986.

Apparently, only 5 per cent of the depositors in a given year open accounts for the sole purpose of performing pilgrimage. Further examination shows that a common tendency among these intending pilgrims is to deposit a substantial lump sum (often to the tune of M$5,000) several months before making registrations for the *hajj*. This has several implications. This indicates that intending pilgrims have not used the savings facility of PMFB which is designed to mobilize savings on a gradual incremental basis. The lump sum deposited could come from conservative savings outside the financial framework or from the sale of assets. This shows that a preference for holding assets in liquid or semi-liquid form is still inherent. Thus, first of all, one may surmise that the saving habit of the Muslims has not changed much. Secondly, since PMFB does not allow withdrawals before the intended pilgrimage, some savers are quite reluctant to lock up a large sum of deposits with the board. It is preferable for them to save elsewhere and then transfer their funds into PMFB just before pilgrimage. Thirdly, for intending pilgrims who are pensioners, on attaining the age of fifty-five, the lump sum deposited in PMFB could come from compulsory savings withdrawn from the Employees Provident Fund.

Viewed from the investment angle, the short-term nature of these deposits implies that a substantial amount of investible funds cannot be channelled into relatively profitable long-term investments. In the absence of an Islamic money market, a substantial proportion of deposits (about 30 per cent) has been left idle, which benefits neither PMFB nor the depositors. However, with the establishment of the Islamic Bank in 1983, PMFB could undertake permissible short-term investments.

As regards savings among students and the young, the sum involved seems insignificant and its growth has been sluggish over the three-year period. However, the proportion of depositors from this group is quite significant, accounting for more than a quarter of the total depositors. Considering that this group consists of potential long-term savers, more should be done by PMFB to encourage Muslim children to save with the board. The value of such measures does not lie so much in the additional savings they will generate but rather in the development of the saving habit among the young.

The role of the post office as a collection agent has been declining, compared to its importance in the 1970s when the post office collected over 50 per cent of the deposits each year. One possible reason for this is the availability of more PMFB branches all over the country. Apart from the purpose of making deposits, depositors may find it more convenient to go to the PMFB branch offices where they can get answers to problems which cannot be solved by the postal clerks.

As noted earlier, PMFB came into existence to remedy the defects in the methods of saving among the Muslims in the rural areas. It would be interesting to examine how far this objective has been achieved. Table 4 shows the distribution of depositors in six representative states in Peninsular Malaysia which have high percentages of Muslim population and where the rural-urban areas can be clearly distinguished. It can be seen that depositors are more concentrated in the urban areas, to the extent of 60 to 80 per cent of depositors in each state. The proportion of rural depositors does not reflect the number of Muslims living in the rural areas. It is estimated that 67 per cent of the rural population of Peninsular Malaysia is made up of Malays and other indigenous groups. The low percentage of rural depositors is perhaps due to the generally low income levels of the rural population. Even though their propensity to save is not low, the opportunity to save is substantially restrained by the very limited resources that they hold. It is estimated that a substantial proportion of the rural Malay population (48 per cent) earns a monthly income of below M$500.[5]

The distribution of depositors by the size of their credit balance is shown in Table 5. The distribution is slightly skewed, with more than 80 per cent of depositors having accumulated balances of less than M$500. This shows that a large proportion of PMFB members are small savers. About 5.7 per cent of the depositors have balances between M$1,000–M$1,500, and only 2 per cent have balances of more than M$5,000. In a majority of cases, those accounts with small balances of less than M$100 belong to depositors who have not made any contribution for more than a year. These dormant account holders are mostly ex-pilgrims who have discontinued making savings after performing the *hajj*. Whatever increases in their balances consist of bonuses credited to their accounts.

TABLE 4

**PMFB — Distribution of Depositors by Area of Residence (Rural/Urban) in Selected States as at 31 December 1986**

(As a percentage of total depositors in each state)

| State | Urban Areas* | Rural Areas | Total Depositors |
|---|---|---|---|
| Kedah | 83.6 | 16.4 | 104,367 |
| Kelantan | 60.4 | 39.6 | 100,569 |
| Trengganu | 69.7 | 30.3 | 63,004 |
| Pahang | 65.6 | 34.4 | 76,184 |
| Negeri Sembilan | 67.8 | 32.2 | 52,757 |
| Perak | 59.0 | 41.0 | 117,980 |

\* Urban Area is defined as an area with more than 10,000 people.

SOURCE: Savings and Withdrawal Division, PMFB.

TABLE 5

**PMFB — Depositors by Size of Their Credit Balances as at 31 December 1986**

| Size of Credit Balance (M$) | Percentage of Total Depositors | No. of Depositors |
|---|---|---|
| Below 2 | 2.7 | 27,100 |
| 2–99 | 51.8 | 515,000 |
| 100–499 | 25.6 | 255,000 |
| 500–999 | 8.5 | 85,000 |
| 1,000–1,999 | 5.7 | 56,500 |
| 2,000–3,999 | 3.1 | 30,700 |
| 4,000–4,999 | 0.6 | 6,300 |
| 5,000–7,499 | 1.5 | 14,600 |
| 7,500–9,999 | 0.2 | 2,100 |
| 10,000 and above | 0.3 | 2,500 |
| Total | 100 | 994,800 |

SOURCE: Savings and Withdrawal Division, PMFB.

*Withdrawal of deposits.* Total withdrawals for 1986 are shown in Table 6. On the whole, withdrawal of deposits tends to be motivated primarily by the need to defray expenses for the pilgrimage. One can also conclude here that the rules governing withdrawals have to some extent helped PMFB achieve its objective of enabling Muslims to save for the *hajj*. PMFB should, however, improve the withdrawal procedures by shortening the period of processing each withdrawal form. With computerization, it should also be possible to make withdrawals at PMFB branch offices. It has also been suggested that PMFB could consider allowing withdrawals of up to M$200 on demand, especially in the rural areas.[6]

TABLE 6
PMFB — Total Withdrawals for 1986

| Type of Withdrawal | M$ (Million) | Percentage |
| --- | --- | --- |
| Pilgrimage purpose | 121.85 | 55.5 |
| Normal withdrawal | 85.35 | 38.9 |
| Death of depositor | 2.5 | 1.1 |
| Withdrawal at Holy Land | 9.84 | 4.5 |
| Total | 219.54 | 100 |

SOURCE: Savings and Withdrawal Division, PMFB.

*Investment Activities*

The investment activities of PMFB are currently carried out under the *Shariah* principles of *mudaraba* (profit sharing), *musharaka* (equity participation), and *ijara* (leasing). As at 31 December 1985 PMFB had invested M$464.3 million, the bulk of which (about 49 per cent) was in the form of equity participation. About 36.2 per cent of the funds were invested in land and building mainly for leasing, 12.6 per cent went into subsidiary companies, and 2.2 per cent were channelled to the Islamic Bank under a *mudaraba* arrangement.

As at 31 December 1985 a substantial portion of PMFB investment in stocks and shares (about 60 per cent) went into the acquisition of shares in the manufacturing, processing, and trading industries, as against the 8 per cent and 6 per cent invested in the plantation and property sectors, respectively. This preference has been largely based on the future prospects of industrial development in the country, reinforced by the investment incentives given by the government. Falling prices of primary commodities, especially palm oil and tin, and the slack in the property market have also forced PMFB to adopt a more conservative business approach towards these two sectors.

As a semi-government body and a religious-welfare organization, PMFB has been accorded certain privileges in the field of investment. Until 1986,[7] dividends were granted tax exemption which meant that gross dividend was taken as income when it was paid out. Secondly, since almost all of its members are Malays or other *bumiputera*, PMFB is recognized as a source of Malay capital and has been offered special allocations for company shares under the New Economic Policy.[8] This has enabled PMFB to invest in established companies as well as buy shares from newly established companies at par value, which give a good profit if PMFB has to sell these shares in the market in future.

PMFB's total investment in land and building as at 31 December 1985 amounted to M$168 million, with forty buildings all over the country and a very sizeable land bank. It is the aim of PMFB to have its own building in every major town in Malaysia either for its own use or for rental purposes. PMFB's biggest investment in this field is the construction of its thirty-eight-storey headquarters building which was completed in 1985 at a total cost of M$109 million (including the cost of land). This building is expected to generate 8.5 to 10 per cent annual rate of return on capital from rentals, and the pay-back period of capital investment is estimated to be twelve years.

Investments in subsidiary companies are undertaken to enable PMFB to participate actively in economic activities. To date, PMFB has formed five subsidiary companies:

1.  The Plantation Corporation;
2.  Sabah Plantation Corporation;
3.  The Transport and Trading Corporation;
4.  The Property Management Company; and
5.  The Construction and Housing Company.

The Plantation Corporation was formed in 1982 with an authorized capital of M$10 million. Its paid-up capital as of May 1986 stood at M$45 million and would be increased to M$50 million for financing additional projects. The corporation is actively involved in agricultural activities covering oil-palm, cocoa, and rubber plantations. Its fixed assets as at 1985 totalled more than M$69 million.

The Transport and Trading Corporation was formed in 1972 for the purpose of arranging charter flights with the national airline carrier to transport pilgrims to Mecca. At present, PMFB charges M$2,400 for return air fare, compared to other airlines which charge only M$1,800. This higher fare has invited criticisms regarding PMFB services for the welfare of the pilgrims. However, PMFB has justified reasons for the higher air fare. While other airline fares cover routine commercial flights, PMFB's air fare covers special charter flights which return to Malaysia without any passengers. Thus each plane has to make four flights to and from Jeddah for each load of passengers. This accounts for the extra payment imposed on the pilgrims.

Other services provided by The Transport and Trading Corporation include supplies of essential items such as the *ihram* (the *hajj* attire), belts, containers for 'zamzam' water, and other sundry goods which are sold to the pilgrims at minimum prices.

The Construction and Housing Company was incorporated in 1983 with the main objective of building houses and commercial buildings for sale to PMFB members and the public. To date, the company has successfully developed two housing projects consisting of 1,000 units and 3,000 units of houses.

The Property Management Company supervises the management of buildings belonging to PMFB, including the construction of the PMFB headquarters building and the provision of security services to the building.

*Income from Investments*
Income received by PMFB is derived from its investments. There are four types of major income, namely:

1.   dividend from investment in shares;
2.   rent from buildings;
3.   profit from short-term investment in Bank Islam; and
4.   profit from the sale of shares.

As shown in Table 7, the income of PMFB has been stable over the three-year period (1984–86), around M$40 million. Dividends from investment in shares make the largest contribution to income. In 1985, more than three-fourths of PMFB income came from this source. Rental income constitutes the second major source and has been increasing steadily over the period. Profits from short-term investment in the Islamic Bank seem to be declining, which could be attributed to the problem of excess liquidity faced by the bank itself.

TABLE 7
**PMFB — Composition of Income from Investments, 1984–86**

|  | Percentage of Total Income | | |
| --- | --- | --- | --- |
| Type of Income | 1984 | 1985 | 1986 |
| Dividend from shares | 65.2 | 76.5 | 72.1 |
| Rental income | 12.3 | 15.3 | 25.5 |
| Profit on sale of shares | 17.3 | 4.5 | – |
| Profit from short-term investment | 5.3 | 3.7 | 2.4 |
| Total | 100 | 100 | 100 |
| Total Income (million) | M$42.9 | M$42 | M$45 |

SOURCE: Finance Division, PMFB.

## Appropriation of PMFB Profits

Table 8 shows that profits made in the first half of the 1980s have been stable, with a slight fall in 1985 owing to the economic recession.

TABLE 8
**Distribution of PMFB Profits, 1981–85**

| Year | Profits (before *Zakat*) (M$ Million) | *Zakat* (M$ Million) | Bonus (after *Zakat*) (M$ Million) | Rate (Per Cent) |
|---|---|---|---|---|
| 1981 | 32.4 | 1.57 | 10.3 | 9.0 |
| 1982 | 32.2 | 2.32 | 12.7 | 8.0 |
| 1983 | 29.4 | 2.77 | 15.2 | 8.5 |
| 1984 | 29.8 | 1.35 | 34.5 | 8.5 |
| 1985 | 25.9 | 1.17 | 27.1 | 9.0 |

SOURCE: PMFB Annual Reports, 1981–85.

Under its Act of Incorporation, PMFB is required to maintain statutory reserves amounting to not less than a certain percentage of its total eligible liabilities (total deposits plus bonus payable). Unlike the statutory reserves of commercial banks which are fixed by the Central Bank, the reserves in PMFB are determined by the board, subject to approval by the Ministry of Finance. As at 31 December 1984, PMFB statutory reserves stood at M$20 million (about 5.2 per cent of PMFB total liabilities). This ratio fell to 5.1 per cent as at 31 December 1985. In short, the statutory reserve ratio maintained by PMFB is almost similar to that of commercial banks (5 per cent and 4 per cent in 1984 and 1985, respectively).

For the purpose of prudent financial management policy, PMFB has also appropriated a portion of its profits as general reserves, depending on the amount of profits made annually. As at 31 December 1985, the amount was M$36.6 million. Adding its statutory reserves of M$22.5 million, the total reserves of PMFB as at 31 December 1985 amounted to M$59.1 million.

## Payment of Zakat

PMFB has been paying *zakat* (on wealth and commerce) since 1980. The rate of *zakat* is 2.5 per cent on the sum of profits earned and the amount of working capital at the end of the *zakat* financial year. The question of *zakat* was raised some years ago but a clear *fatwa* (decree) was issued to the management of PMFB only in 1979. *Zakat* payments are made to the Islamic Religious Department in each state which in turn redistributes the *zakat* fund among the various beneficiaries. The amount received by each state is based on the credit balance of the depositors in the respective states. *Zakat* payment by PMFB for 1985 amounted to M$1.17 million, as shown in Table 8.

*Payment of Bonus*

A large proportion of PMFB net profits are distributed to depositors in the form of bonuses. The annual rate of bonus varies, depending on profits made. However, at times when profits are very low, part of PMFB general reserves are used to pay a reasonably high bonus. This practice is evident in 1984 and 1985 when the bonus payments amounted to 115 and 104 per cent of the total profits, respectively (see Table 8). As a result, PMFB has been able to offer a competitive rate of return to depositors at 8 per cent, which is comparable to the return from other types of investments in the country. As a matter of fact, this rate is relatively higher than the 5 per cent rate of profit paid on savings account in the Islamic Bank as at December 1985.

Until 1984, the amount of bonus paid to individual accounts was based on the minimum balance credited within a period of six months. However, now that PMFB is able to invest in short-term investments at the Islamic Bank, the amount is currently calculated on the minimum balance credited each month. By this method, active accounts will receive relatively higher bonuses than before. This is an incentive for depositors to increase their rate of savings or at least make more regular savings with PMFB. Bonuses are not paid in cash but are credited to the depositors' accounts. In addition, bonuses on deposits exceeding M$10,000 are tax-exempted.

*Evaluation of Performance and Recommendations*

PMFB is a financial institution of a special kind. Although it mobilizes funds from savers and channels them to investors, it is not a financial intermediary. PMFB is essentially a service organization. It acts as a banker to its members and when they decide to perform the pilgrimage, PMFB caters for their needs before departure, such as handling visa requirements, arranging for transportation, and giving information and education on pilgrimage. Services at the Holy Land include the provision of accommodation, food, and medical and health care. The economic activities of PMFB emanate from its role as a banker to its members whereby it attempts to convert their deposits into profitable investments.

PMFB performance can be evaluated from two aspects, viz: (1) its success in achieving its aims and objectives and (2) its contribution to the development process.

Looking at the growth of the size of its deposits and the number of its depositors over the years, it is apparent that PMFB has been successful in achieving its aim of enabling Muslims to save for the purpose of performing the *hajj*. When it was first formed in 1963, the organization had only 1,281 members with a total savings of M$46,600. As at 31 December 1986, its members totalled 995,000 with total savings of M$470 million. The concept of pilgrim management through PMFB has also been well accepted, as shown by the fact that a very high percentage of Malaysian pilgrims were members of the board. For instance, in 1985, of the 24,415 pilgrims 24,299 or 99.52 per cent were PMFB members.

In terms of economic development, PMFB's major contribution "comes from the means and opportunity it provides for the gradual institutionalization of savings"[9] among Muslims. Prior to its establishment, savings by traditional methods were not made available for investments that could contribute to development. With its formation, Muslims were motivated to hold their savings in a form which is socially desirable. Funds started to flow from two sources: from a reduction of unproductive non-institutional forms of savings and from savers who were motivated purely on religious grounds, which was to save only in an institution which conformed to the *Shariah*. As a result, resources which could have been hoarded or held in the form of semi-liquid assets have now entered the financial network available for developmental purposes.

With respect to the number of depositors, of the approximately 7.5 million Malays in the country, only about 900,000 or 13 per cent are members of PMFB, as at the end of 1986. Even though 13 per cent is a large figure, in which PMFB can take pride, it is disappointing that it has not exceeded the one million mark yet, considering that the organization has been in operation for about two decades. This shows that there is still a bigger segment of the market to be tapped.

One of the major failures of PMFB, in terms of deposit mobilization, is in the recruitment of membership from the rural sector. Although the organization serves both the urban and the rural communities, greater significance should be attached to the latter for it was the economic plight of this sector which prompted the establishment of PMFB. One way to attract the potential rural savers is to devise appropriate savings programmes which would meet their needs and abilities to save.

It is well noted that a common saving behaviour among the rural people is the preference to keep funds in forms within their immediate control. It would be, therefore, more appropriate to introduce an arrangement similar to that of saving deposits of commercial banks, which would permit withdrawal on demand subject to certain conditions. No doubt, this could defeat the purpose of saving for the *hajj*, but as an inducement PMFB could design and provide a guide-line to depositors on the amount of monthly savings required, given the target timing of the proposed pilgrimage. Appendix C gives an example of such a guide-line. A regular review of the amount saved in relation to the target date may discourage frequent withdrawals and call for higher rates of depositing.

An appropriate instrument which would meet the ability of rural savers is the saving stamp[10] which, on reaching a certain amount, could be exchanged for an equivalent deposit with the board. It is an inexpensive method of mopping up small and irregular savings from the huge rural sector. Instead of building branches in the rural areas when it will not be able to compete with the government post office saving bank as well as the Islamic Bank which is now moving into these areas, PMFB could introduce the saving stamp scheme with the help of local post offices and mobile postal units. Thus, the additional cost arising out of the dispersed and inaccessible locational character of the rural-saving group can be minimized. Even among the urban Muslims, the performance of PMFB in terms of savings mobilization is not satisfactory. Although depositors are concentrated in the urban areas, they comprise less than half of the total number of depositors in each state. Response from employees in the government and private sectors for the salary deduction scheme is not very encouraging for only less than 10 per cent of total depositors come under this scheme.

Within the rural-urban category mentioned above, there are two groups of potential depositors which need to be motivated to become members of PMFB. These comprise (1) members of religious and political organizations whose aspirations are different from those of the government and (2) depositors in the existing interest-based banks. The latter are concentrated in towns and cities, while the former are predominant in the rural northeastern states of Peninsular Malaysia.

Apart from political differences, one factor which explains the reluctance of the former to save with PMFB is the establishment of savings funds of their own. For instance, the PAS opposition party, whose members are all Muslims, has established the Darul-Mal, a savings fund akin to PMFB. Its activities include the management of members' pilgrimage through the private sector, acquisition of properties for its members, and equity participation in rubber and oil-palm plantations. Thus, the need to save in another institution such as PMFB would seem redundant for this group. Nevertheless, there is still scope for PMFB to compete for this group of potential depositors. Emphasis on the relative merits of saving with PMFB could form the main strategy. The possible selling points include the government guarantee of liquidity to PMFB, the privilege of investing in established companies which give relatively higher returns, certainty of flights to Jeddah, protection against fraud by travel agencies, and the provision of free medical services by PMFB medical team during pilgrimage.

With respect to Muslim depositors in the existing interest-based banks, it appears that this group of potential depositors is purely motivated by economic rationality and is sensitive to the rates of return given by financial institutions. They are not likely to transfer their deposits until the rate of return of Islamic financial intermediaries like PMFB exceeds the market interest rate. This is another challenge to PMFB which it could overcome either by increasing its operational efficiency or by seeking more profitable investments which pay better returns, subject of course to *Shariah* rules. As mentioned by the Director-General of PMFB, "if one out of fifteen Muslims saves in PMFB by transferring his fixed deposits from the commercial banks, the one million depositors target will be accomplished before 1990".[11]

Another feature which tends to discourage potential depositors is the restriction placed on the withdrawal of deposits. The rigid conditions and the observance of a six-month time interval put the organization at a relatively disadvantageous position. With the Islamic Bank savings facility close by, PMFB is likely to lose in the competition for deposits. Depositors should be allowed special withdrawals of a specified percentage of deposits to meet unforeseen contingencies. Even though at present such withdrawals are allowed in practice at the discretion of the board of directors, a formal statement of the regulation could go a long way in attracting new depositors.

It is beyond the scope of this chapter to discuss PMFB's *hajj* management. Nevertheless, an important factor which contributes to the low percentage of depositors pertains to the way in which PMFB handles the pilgrimage of its members. At the end of almost every pilgrimage season, complaints were raised about the unsatisfactory PMFB services at the Holy Land. Among them were poor accommodation facilities, inconvenient transport services, late flights, and the indifferent attitudes of PMFB officers. Some of these complaints were considered trivial, while others were beyond the control of PMFB. Nonetheless, it is the responsibility of PMFB to ensure that the welfare of member-pilgrims is well catered for. In relation to this, the organization has often been accused of only being concerned with profit-making and neglecting the welfare of its members. Moreover, past observations also show that those pilgrims who went through private organizations were given better services and facilities at a lower price. The 'extras' provided by the private sector might induce future pilgrims not to use the services of PMFB, which would in turn reduce the number of its would-be depositors.

Preventing pilgrims from going by private agencies is not the answer to get more people to become members of PMFB.[12] Instead, problems faced by pilgrims should be noted and overcome in the subsequent seasons. Such evaluations are imperative to maintain PMFB's sense of direction so that a balance is struck between profit-motivated and service-oriented modes of operations. The present services and facilities still need to be upgraded to match, if not exceed, those provided by other organizations. For instance, during the present recession, the public would appreciate it more if PMFB uses its profits to provide better services at lower prices rather than invest in the construction of prestigious buildings.

The above are but only a few of the moves that could be undertaken by PMFB to mobilize more savings among the Muslim population in Malaysia. It should be stressed that, for the successful implementation of such measures, PMFB needs to adopt imaginative methods of disseminating information to the public. What is obvious now is that there is very little awareness among the general public of what is really going on at PMFB. The organization has not made full use of the mass media to promote its image. Thus far, there has been no advertisement on PMFB as compared to the National Unit Trust Scheme.[13]

PMFB's second main contribution to the development process lies in its role as the user of investible funds deposited with it. Its average annual inflow of M$40 million illustrates the significant role it plays, as an investment organization, in the economic development of the country. Thus far, PMFB has been successful in channelling its resources to specified areas and giving high returns to depositors on their savings.

Besides giving direct benefits to its depositors, PMFB has also brought various benefits to the Malaysian Muslims at large. Direct investments undertaken by its subsidiary companies in the agricultural and real estate sectors provide employment to more Muslims, in addition to increasing Muslim property ownership in the country. It is also apparent that PMFB's investments are currently geared towards achieving the restructuring objective of the New Economic Policy which specifically aims to foster Malay participation in business activities so that by 1990 the Malays and other indigenous people would manage and own at least 30 per cent of the total commercial and industrial activities in all categories and scales of operation.

In other words PMFB, like other trust agencies, acts as an instrument in hastening the process of reducing the Malay 'capital deficiency gap' in the above-mentioned sectors, while at the same time avoiding unequal distribution of ownership amongst the Muslims. For, the bulk of PMFB's investments take the form of share equities in companies engaged in manufacturing, the leading growth sector in the Malaysian economy. As the minimum amount of subscription to share issues is generally beyond the means of most Muslim savers at any one time, PMFB plays the supporting role of buying these shares on behalf of its many depositors. Thus, it is possible to spread ownership over a large number of individuals, lest it will be confined to a small group of rich Malay individuals with higher income and propensity to save.

If internal corporate control (defined as the legally enforceable power to select, change, or dictate the management of the company)[14] is justified solely by ownership, the figures on PMFB's share ownership in the respective listed manufacturing companies (see Appendix D) tend to suggest that it is not the policy of PMFB to assume control in any of the companies. Of the thirty-three manufacturing companies, PMFB holds less than 2 per cent equity in twenty-two of them. This further implies that its role is confined to that of an investor rather than a major shareholder. Holdings are geared towards spreading ownership over many companies rather than gathering control within a few. This is justifiable in view of PMFB's stated objective which is to give maximum investment returns to depositors on their savings. Obviously, risks would increase if PMFB equity were made in a few companies only. Thus, some appropriate spread is required to attain a balance in its investment portfolio. The risk of investment in a company can be neutralized by investments in other companies. However, this does not imply that PMFB should keep its equity investment in any company absolutely or relatively small.

If PMFB holds a bigger stake in some of the companies, it has the right to select and influence the management of the company. Some influence could be exerted in terms of providing employment to Muslims and, more importantly, in ensuring that the activities of the companies and their subsidiaries adhere to the *Shariah*.[15]

The distribution of PMFB share ownership is quite dispersed in the manufacturing sector, covering various types of industries such as petroleum, foodstuffs, textiles, and electrical and engineering works, while in the other sectors the distribution is rather narrow and limited. Investment in the agricultural sector is confined only to a few companies involved in the cultivation of primary export crops. This uneven distribution may be attributed to the fact that investments in agriculture involve higher economic risks and lower returns. Another possible reason could be that one of PMFB subsidiary companies (The Plantation Corporation) is already involved in the cultivation and processing of oil-palm (five plantations ranging from 900 to 4,000 hectares each and two palm oil mills), and in the management of agricultural joint venture plantation projects in various parts of the country.

PMFB could play a more effective role in financing economic development by extending its investments into other agricultural activities besides primary commodities. Small-scale and agro-based industries in the rural areas are in dire need of finance. PMFB could help cover this deficiency through project-financing using *Shariah*-based techniques of *mudaraba* and *musharaka* or by financing the purchase of inputs using the *murabaha* (mark-up) or *bai salam* (formal purchase) modes of finance. Several prerequisites will have to be fulfilled before PMFB could execute this role. It would require the establishment of subsidiary companies and the recruitment of staff with project appraisal skills.

In the short term, PMFB can still play an indirect role by investing in the Special Investment Account at the Islamic Bank. Since the conditions for investment in this account are negotiable, request can be made by PMFB that its investment is specifically channelled to finance entrepreneurs in the agricultural sector.

At the institutional level, close co-operation between PMFB and the Islamic Bank is also feasible. Since both organizations share a common value system, co-ordination of activities between them can enhance the welfare of the Muslim community in the country. The Islamic Bank could assist PMFB in the investment field by providing technical and professional assistance. Nevertheless, several constraints will have to be ironed out, given the different nature of both institutions — PMFB being a statutory body compared to the Islamic Bank which is commercial in nature.

One of the main problems faced by PMFB relates to the profitable disbursement of its surplus liquid funds. In the absence of an Islamic money-market, interest-free short-run financial instruments are not available. The only channel open to PMFB is to invest in the Islamic Bank but returns are relatively low as the bank itself is saddled with excess liquidity.

PMFB also needs to keep a close watch on the activities of companies in which it invests so as to avoid involvement in activities contrary to *Shariah.* Hesitation shown by PMFB in the past in withdrawing its investments from such companies has led some members to question the importance attached to profit-making as well as the effectiveness of the Religious Supervisory Council.

Last but not least, there is still much scope for PMFB to improve its services and facilities to its member pilgrims.

Despite its shortcomings, PMFB has proved its success and can take pride in the fact that it is the only one of its kind in the world.

**APPENDIX A**
**Pilgrims Management and Fund Board**

**Organizational Structure**

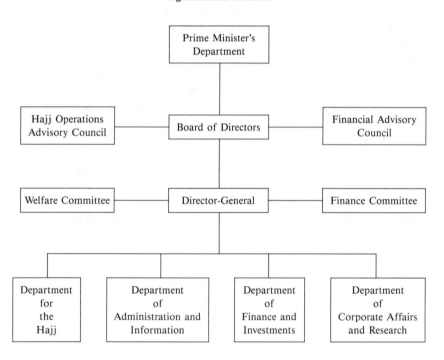

**APPENDIX B**
**PMFB Personnel by Category of Service, 1981–85**

| Category | 1981 | 1982 | 1983 | 1984 | 1985 |
|---|---|---|---|---|---|
| Managerial & Professional | 30 | 36 | 44 | 51 | 57 |
| Executive & Semi-Professional | 43 | 60 | 65 | 80 | 85 |
| Clerical/Technical | 166 | 227 | 270 | 334 | 394 |
| Industrial & Manual Group | 180 | 214 | 256 | 270 | 289 |
| Others (Temporary) | 10 | 15 | 12 | 13 | 16 |
| Total | 429 | 552 | 647 | 748 | 841 |

SOURCE: PMFB Annual Report, 1985.

### APPENDIX C
### Proposed Guide-line to Save for the *Hajj*

Assume that A starts saving in PMFB at the age of twenty-five with the intention of performing the *hajj* when he retires at fifty-five. He saves for thirty years.

Total *Hajj* Expenses (at current market price) = M$5,500
Current Rate of Annual Inflation: 10 per cent

On the assumption that the inflation rate remains constant throughout the period, the amount required (Pn) at the end of the thirtieth year to cover expected *hajj* expenses will be

$$Pn = Po [1 + i (n)],$$

where
$$Po = \text{amount of } hajj \text{ expenses required currently}$$
$$i = \text{rate of inflation}$$
$$n = \text{number of years}$$
$$= M\$5,500 [1 + 0.1 (30)]$$
$$= M\$22,000$$

The annual bonus is assumed to be constant at 8 per cent on the end of the year balance (see Table 8).

The following formula may be used to calculate the annual savings required to achieve a target annuity of M$22,000 at the end of the thirtieth year.

$$R = \frac{rA}{(1+r)^{n+1} - (1+r)}$$

where
$$R = \text{fixed annual payment}$$
$$A = \text{annuity} = M\$22,000$$
$$r = \text{bonus rate} = 0.08$$
$$n = \text{number of years} = 30$$
$$= M\$179.82$$

Monthly savings required $= \dfrac{179.82}{12}$
$$= M\$14.98$$

## APPENDIX D
### Percentage of Company Share Units Held by PMFB
### as at 31 December 1986 (Quoted Shares)

| Name of Company | Percentage of Units Held |
|---|---|
| *Manufacturing* | |
| 1.  Aluminium Co. of Malaysia | 8.85 |
| 2.  Bata Malaysia Berhad | 1.11 |
| 3.  Berjaya Kawat Bhd. | 1.68 |
| 4.  Chemical Co. of Malaysia Bhd. | 1.53 |
| 5.  Chocolate Products (M) Bhd. | 0.86 |
| 6.  Cycle & Carriage Bintang Bhd. | 1.43 |
| 7.  Dunlop Malaysian Industries Bhd. | 0.64 |
| 8.  Esso Malaysia Bhd. | 3.86 |
| 9.  Federal Flour Mills Bhd. | 0.58 |
| 10.  Hume Industries (M) Bhd. | 10.0 |
| 11.  Malaya Glass Factory Bhd. | 4.5 |
| 12.  Malayan Cement Bhd. | 1.19 |
| 13.  Malayawata Steel Bhd. | 1.17 |
| 14.  Malaysian Containers (1974) Bhd. | 0.70 |
| 15.  Malaysian Oxygen Bhd. | 1.43 |
| 16.  Malaysian Tobacco Co., Bhd. | 2.38 |
| 17.  Matsushita Electric Co., Bhd. | 1.41 |
| 18.  The N.S.T. Press (M) Bhd. | 5.49 |
| 19.  Oriental Holding Bhd. | 0.15 |
| 20.  Paramount Corporation Bhd. | 1.87 |
| 21.  Perlis Plantations Bhd. | 3.23 |
| 22.  Rothmans of Pall Mall Bhd. | 12.60 |
| 23.  Roxy Electric Industries (M) Bhd. | 8.76 |
| 24.  Shell Refining Co., Bhd. | 1.01 |
| 25.  Sime Darby Bhd. | 0.82 |
| 26.  South Pacific Textiles Ind. Bhd. | 6.33 |
| 27.  Sateras Resources (M) Bhd. | 0.97 |
| 28.  Tasek Cement Bhd. | 0.45 |
| 29.  Textile Corp. of Malaya Bhd. | 0.11 |
| 30.  Tractors Malaysia Holdings Bhd. | 0.53 |
| 31.  UAC Bhd. | 5.00 |
| 32.  United Motor Works (M) Bhd. | 0.72 |
| 33.  Wilkinson Process Rubber Co., Bhd. | 0.09 |
| *Real Estates* | |
| 34.  Bandar Raya Development Bhd. | 2.58 |
| 35.  Bolton Properties Bhd. | 6.93 |
| 36.  IGB Corporation Bhd. | 1.87 |
| *Oil-Palm* | |
| 37.  Batu Kawan Bhd. | 0.97 |
| 38.  Consolidated Plants Bhd. | 0.04 |
| 39.  United Plantations Bhd. | 2.77 |

**APPENDIX D** (*continued*)
**Percentage of Company Share Units Held by PMFB**
**as at 31 December 1986 (Quoted Shares)**

| Name of Company | Percentage of Units Held |
|---|---|
| *Rubber* | |
| 40.   Dunlop Estates Bhd. | 0.29 |
| 41.   Guthrie Ropel Bhd. | 2.84 |
| 42.   Highlands & Lowland Bhd. | 0.54 |
| 43.   Kuala Lumpur Malaysia Bhd. | 0.53 |
| 44.   Kulim Malaysia Bhd. | 0.12 |
| 45.   Malaysian Plantation Bhd. | 1.67 |
| *Tin* | |
| 46.   Berjuntai Tin Dredging Bhd. | 1.59 |

SOURCE: *Annual Company Handbook* Vol. 12, 1986.

## NOTES

1   Wan Mohd. Ismail Bin Wan Hussain, *Tabung Haji as an Islamic Savings Institution* (Kuala Lumpur: PMFB, 1986), p. 3.

2   Ungku Abdul Aziz, *Pilgrims Economy Improvement Plan* (Kuala Lumpur: 1959).

3   The Student Saving Scheme and The Children Coin-box Scheme were launched in 1984 to attract young depositors.

4   1984 was named 'The Salary Deduction Year'.

5   *Household Income Survey* 1984 (Kuala Lumpur: Economic Planning Unit).

6   *Berita Harian*, 8 April 1978.

7   As from 1987, dividends are liable to 40 per cent tax.

8   Under this policy, companies are required to restructure their equity to reflect local participation in equity ownership.

9   Lee Hock Lock, *Household Savings in West Malaysia and the Problem of Financing Economic Development* (Kuala Lumpur: University of Malaya, 1971), p. 197.

10   Ibid., p. 292.

11  *Berita Harian*, 9 May 1981.

12  Under the PMFB Act (Amended) 1973, Section 67A and B states that any party that wishes to perform the *hajj* through the private sector is required to get written approval from PMFB.

13  A scheme to enable Malay participation in the investment of company shares.

14  Sieh Lee M.L., "The Structure of Ownership and Control of Manufacturing Companies in Malaysia 1974–1975" (Ph.D. thesis, University of Sheffield, 1975), p. 13.

15  A survey of the *Annual Company Handbook* Vol. 12 (Kuala Lumpur Stock Exchange, 1986) reveals that the subsidiaries of two companies in which PMFB is a shareholder are engaging in credit and hire-purchase activities which involve interest.

# 8 ZAKAT AND SADAQQA PRACTICES AMONG THE MOROS OF THE PHILIPPINES

Carmen A. Abubakar*

## Introduction

This study on *zakat* and *sadaqqa* involves the Moros of southern Philippines who number approximately 5 million, in a total population of 56 million.

The Moros today are found predominantly in Regions IX and XII which comprise the following provinces: Lanao del Sur, Lanao del Norte, Maguindanao, Sultan Kudarat, North Cotabato, Tawi-Tawi, Basilan, Sulu, Zamboanga del Sur, and Zamboanga del Norte. Since 1979, these two regions have become autonomous regions, as a result of the Tripoli Agreement signed in 1976 between the Philippine government and the Moro National Liberation Front (MNLF).

There are thirteen Moro ethnolinguistic groups, the major ones of which are the Maranaos of Lake Lanao, the Maguindanaos of Cotabato, the Tausug of Sulu, and the Sama of Tawi-Tawi. The smaller groups are the Bajao of Sulu, Ilanun or Iranun of Maguindanao province, Jama Mapun of Cagayan de Sulu, Kalagan of Davao, Kolibugan of Zamboanga del Sur, Molbog of Balabac Island, Palawani of southern Palawan, Sangil of Sarangarin Island, and Yakan of Basilan Island.

*Zakat* and *sadaqqa* institutions are well-established in Moro communities owing to Islamization around the thirteenth century. However, there has been no study on these institutions except some mention of them in the local literature. *Zakat* and *sadaqqa* are, nevertheless, extensively discussed in Islamic texts. Among local literature, for example, Peter Gowing[1] observed that the Tausugs, Yakans, and Maranaos conscientiously pay *zakat* to the leaders of the mosque and recognize the merit of *sadaqqa*, especially during the Hari

Raya Puasa Festival (Feast of Edi'l Fitr). Thomas Kiefer,[2] on the other hand, noted that the Tausugs gave legal alms (*zakat*) as well as voluntary alms (*sadaqqa*) to the poor and to religious leaders. Kiefer further noted that although there was no formal organization in charge of enforcing the fee, the Tausugs endeavour to give *zakat* in the belief that failure to comply, especially in a good harvest, would mean bad luck in the next. Inger Wulff,[3] who studied the Yakans of Basilan Island, states that the Yakans considered *zakat* as *pitla*, a fee to be paid at the end of the month of fasting by every member of a Muslim household in the amount of 50 centavos paid to the *imam* for the use of the community. Andrew Sherfar[4] mentions the various rewards that Yakans believe are attached to the giving of *zakat* and *pitla*. For instance, Yakans are of the belief that non-compliance of *pitla* means that "all their good deeds are as nothing". As to the giving of *zakat* on one's wealth, harvests, or crops, the Yakans believe that "those who comply will enjoy long life on earth as well as material blessings, and in heaven will have special rewards". Mashur Bin-Ghalib Jundam's field report on the Yakans points out that only the financially able Yakans pay the yearly *zakat* and *pitla*.[5]

While these various bits of information establish the presence of *zakat* and *sadaqqa* institutions in Moro societies, there appears to be some confusion of terms. Many of the researchers have identified *zakat* and *pitla* as two distinct types of categories. The distinction, however, should be made clear. *Pitla* is *zakat al-fitr* (*fitrah*) which is given at the end of Ramadhan; while *zakat* on property or wealth is *zakat maal* and usually given after a harvest in farming communities.

Owing to the dearth of substantive materials on this subject, field-work was conducted in three areas, namely, Cotabato City, Marawi City, and Jolo. Cotabato City is found in Maguindanao, Marawi City is in Lanao del Sur, and Jolo is the main island of Sulu province. Since there is a growing Muslim community in Metro Manila, namely in Taguig, Quiapo, and San Andres, these were included in the study. However, only selected communities in these areas were studied.

The study represents largely a pioneer work and, therefore, tends to be highly descriptive and exploratory. It is limited to the practice of *zakat* and *sadaqqa* in Moro communities as part of the internal mobilization of resources but excludes external resources coming from the *zakat* and *sadaqqa* of foreign Muslim nationals.

## Islamization of Mindanao and Sulu

Since Islam is integral in contextualizing the principles of *zakat* and *sadaqqa* in Moro communities, a brief historical background on the Islamization of Mindanao and Sulu is in order.

Islam first came to Sulu in the early thirteenth century through the efforts of traders and *sufi* missionaries following the trade routes which passed through the Moluccas to China, India, and to the Middle East.

By the middle of the fifteenth century the Muslim community, initially established at Buansa, Sulu, had grown and flourished to such an extent that when a noted Arab scholar named Abu-Bakr arrived, he could introduce the sultanate as a new socio-political structure. This further consolidated and strengthened Islamic consciousness in the area.

Abu-Bakr, who became the first sultan of Sulu, laid the foundations for a cohesive Muslim community by building Islamic institutions which ordered the lives of the people. Thus, he introduced not just a political system but the entire legal, educational, and economic institutions that reinforced Islamic values and fortified the Muslim community in its subsequent struggle against colonialism and imperialism.

The spread of Islam to Maguindanao and Lanao is generally attributed to Sharif Kabungsuan, a prince from Menangkabaw who arrived at the Pulangi River in the sixteenth century. Through judicious use of alliances and marriages, as well as through active proselytization, Kabungsuan was able to Islamize the Maguindanaos in the seventeenth century and the Maranaos in the nineteenth century. Islam, therefore, became the common bond among these people and a force in their socio-political development.

After the establishment of Islam in the thirteenth century, the history of the Moros was one of unmitigated struggle for national survival in a world that was quickly being swallowed and overrun by western colonialists.

Spanish conquistadores found their way to the area now known as the Philippines by accident in 1521. Magellan's discovery fired Spanish imperial adventurism and subsequent expeditions were sent to consolidate Spanish gains. In 1565, Miguel Lopez de Legazpi was given royal orders to establish a colony and to Christianize the Indios.

Prior to the coming of the Spaniards, Islam had already been present in Sulu and Mindanao for three centuries and was moving to Luzon. Muslim states had been established and these had enjoyed sovereign state powers for more than a century. The coming of Legazpi, therefore, placed the Muslims and the Spaniards in a state of war that was to last for more than 300 years. In 1898 Spain, under the Treaty of Paris, ceded its Philippine territory to the United States.

Under American colonial rule Moro society began to change, as western institutions were imposed and allowed to undermine indigenous ones. With the introduction of secular public education, the Torrens system of land titling, a western legal structure, and new economic and political processes, the fabric of Moro society began to alter. The sultanate was abolished in 1915 and with its demise other Muslim institutions began to suffer and decline.

One institution, however, remained strong in the lives of the people. The Moros were Muslims and their faith had been their strength in the struggle against both Spain and America. The religious institutions, therefore, took the full brunt of preserving the Muslim community mainly through the institutions of the *masjid* and the *madrasah*. To support these institutions, the religious authorities relied on the help of the people largely through *sadaqqa* and *zakat*. Throughout Moro communities, the moral and religious suasion of *sadaqqa* and *zakat* continued to operate, and this kept religious activities relatively self-reliant. Thus, even in the smallest or isolated Moro community the *azan*, or call to prayer, as well as young voices reciting the Qur'an can be heard. The *masjid* might be no more than a crude structure of bamboo and nipa or of more permanent materials of wood and cement but one thing remains common and that is, these were built through the people's efforts.

### The *Masjid* and *Madrasah* Institutions

The focus of inquiry naturally is on the *masjid* (mosques) where *zakat* and *sadaqqa* are collected and utilized and the *madrasah* (Muslim religious schools) which derive most of their operational funds from the same source.

#### The Masjid

As a Muslim institution, the *masjid* is found wherever there are Muslim communities since it is the centre of community life, whether in the urban or rural setting.

In 1981 there was a total of 1,729 *masjid* in Mindanao and Sulu, distributed as follows:[6]

| | | |
|---|---|---|
| Region IX | — | 325 |
| Region X | — | 9 |
| Region XI | — | 276 |
| Region XII | — | 1,089 |

As revealed by these figures, Region XII has the most number of *masjid*. Of the provinces in this region, Lanao del Sur and Maguindanao, including Cotabato City, have the highest number at 396 and 364, respectively. These provinces are the homes of the Maranaos and the Maguindanaos, two of the biggest Muslim ethnic groups in terms of population.

In Region IX, Sulu has the highest number of *masjid* (154), followed by Zamboanga del Sur, including Zamboanga City (95). It is worthwhile to bear in mind that Islam first came to the Philippines through the Sulu archipelago. For this reason, the oldest *masjid* is located at Tubig Indangan, Simunul Island, now part of Tawi-Tawi province. The original *masjid* is attributed to

Makdum Karim (fourteenth century). This *masjid* has been reconstructed several times but some of the original hardwood pillars still exist.[7]

In Metro Manila, where Muslim communities have established themselves in modern times, seven *masjid* can be identified. One of the biggest and most beautiful is the Blue Mosque at Maharlika Village, located in Taguig. Another is the Golden Mosque at Quiapo. These two *masjid* were constructed through foreign donations, notably from Libya and Saudi Arabia. There are smaller *masjid*: one at Tandang Sora, known as the Salam Mosque; one at San Andres Bukid; and one at the Islamic Center, Quiapo, known as the Manila Grand Mosque. Two smaller *masjid* are also found near Maharlika Village: the Bandar Inged Mosque in the Maranao Village and the Sama Mosque. Most of these smaller *masjid* were constructed through community contributions, together with some help from foreign funds.

*Masjid* construction is usually a community affair through the initiative of an individual or a family who has the financial capability to undertake the project while the rest of the community contributes labour. The 'founder' then becomes the primary administrator of the *masjid*, supported by the religious functionaries, collectively known as the *pakil* among the Tausugs. The term *pakil* refers to the *imam*, *bilal*, *khatib*, and *ustaz* (functionaries). If a *masjid* is constructed mainly by community effort, the administrator is usually the *imam*.

At present, the list of administrators of *masjid* in Mindanao and Sulu shows a wide range of personalities, which include Hujaz, Ustaz, Barrio Captains, Sultans, Mayors, Commanders, elders, Hatib, Tuan, Councillors, Vice-Mayors, Panglima, Salip, Habib, Datu, and Sheik. The list demonstrates, to a great extent, the integrative character of the administrative structure of the *masjid*, which allows both the religious and political (and at times even military) authorities of the community to take active part in their management.

Since 1981, many Muslim communities have sprung up outside Mindanao and Sulu. There are Muslim communities now in the Bicol region, in Baguio City and Dagupan City, just as there are now Muslim communities in the Visayan provinces of Cebu and Iloilo. In each of these communities, the centre of communal activities is the local *masjid*, usually constructed by the people through their own efforts, with little or no external funding.

There are two types of religious buildings: the *langgal* and the *masjid*. The *langgal* can be equated to a hamlet chapel usually smaller than the *masjid* and constructed of semi-permanent materials. The *masjid* is built only with the permission of the sultan and sanctified by the sultan's performing *salat* (prayer) in the *masjid*. 'Membership' in a *masjid* is formalized with the payment of *zakat*, other monetary contributions, and assistance in the various activities of the *masjid*.[8]

## The Madrasah

Another institution that benefits from *zakat* and *sadaqqa* is the *madrasah.* As educational institutions, the early *madrasah* were established around 1450 by Shariff Abubakar, the first Sultan of Sulu. These schools were actually small *maktab*, or Qur'anic schools, where the reading, reciting, and memorizing of the Qur'an was taught. Writing was also part of the curriculum. These schools were found in all Muslim communities, and until the opening of the public schools during the American regime, they constituted the only form of education in these communities. Higher instructions beyond the reading and reciting of the Qur'an were also given in the *madrasah.* Before World War II, there were three small *madrasah* in Sulu. In the 1950s *madrasah* education, which offered formalized religious instructions, became more common in the Moro communities. It is believed that this development was inspired by Indonesian Muslim teachers and Egyptian teachers from the Al-Azhar University (Cairo).

*Madrasah* are owned by individuals, families, or Islamic associations. Financial support comes from many sources: tuition fees of students, voluntary contributions from the community, personal funds of the founder, and more recently grants from Islamic countries and Muslim associations abroad. As Cesar Majul has noted, the institution of *madrasah* could not survive without the support of the community.[9]

In 1981 the Office of Muslim Affairs (OMA) put the number of *madrasah* in the Philippines at 1,137. Most of these are, of course, found in Regions IX and XII. Table 1 shows the distribution of *madrasah* in the four regions of Mindanao and Sulu.

TABLE 1
**Number of *Madrasah*, Number of Students, and Number of Teachers as of 1981**

|  | Total No. *Madrasah* | Percentage | Total No. Students | Percentage | Total No. Teachers | Percentage |
|---|---|---|---|---|---|---|
| Region IX | 137 | (12) | 12,364 | (8) | 324 | (10) |
| Region X | 17 | (1.17) | 2,500 | (2) | 63 | (2) |
| Region XI | 130 | (11) | 10,321 | (7) | 284 | (8) |
| Region XII | 850 | (75) | 120,447 | (82.8) | 2,746 | (80) |
| Total | 1,134 | | 145,632 | | 3,417 | |

SOURCE: Office of Muslim Affairs (OMA).

In Region IX the biggest number of *madrasah* are in Basilan (37) and Sulu (37), while in Region XII the biggest number are found in Lanao del Sur (435) and Maguindanao (169). South Cotabato in Region XI also has a good number of *madrasah*, totalling 51. The average ratio of students per teacher is about 40 to 1, which compares favourably with the student-teacher ratio in the public schools.

A *madrasah* established in any particular community may be in the form of a Qur'anic school mainly to teach the reading of the Qur'an, or it can be organized at the elementary, high school, and even college levels, depending on the resources of the community. The establishment of a *madrasah* is often a community endeavour and for this reason much of its financial resources come from community contributions. *Madrasah*, as private educational institutions, do not receive funding from the government, although some of them do get donations from abroad.

A recent study[10] on the *madrasah* institution in the Philippines provides some insights with regard to financial resources and other relevant information. This study surveyed 647 *madrasah* in the Philippines in 1985. It reveals that only one of them operates at college level, while most of them are at the primary and elementary levels (see Table 2).

TABLE 2
**Distribution of *Madrasah* by Highest Curricula Offerings, 1985**

|  | Frequency | Percentage |
|---|---|---|
| College | 1 | 0.2 |
| Complete Secondary | 34 | 5.3 |
| Secondary, 1–2 years | 68 | 10.5 |
| Elementary | 222 | 34.3 |
| Primary | 310 | 47.9 |
| Kindergarten | 10 | 1.5 |
| Others | 2 | 0.3 |
| Total | 647 | 100.0 |

SOURCE: Moracio Baransing et al. (1987).

This study further reveals that *madrasah* are concentrated heavily in Region XII (502), particularly in Lanao del Sur, which has 281, and Maguindanao with 82. In Region IX (118), the biggest number are found in Zamboanga del Sur, with Basilan and Sulu following.

With regard to financial resources, 88 (22 per cent) *madrasah* in Region XII operated on a budget of 5,000–9,000 pesos a year, while 74 (18.6 per cent) operated on a slightly higher budget of 10,000–14,000 pesos. Six *madrasah*, however, had budgets of over 100,000 pesos, with two having a high of over 300,000 pesos. Of these two, one is found in Lanao del Norte, founded in

1974 by Ustadz Abdul Malik Banding. It has 647 students and 24 teachers. Of this budget, 280,000 pesos come from community contributions, while 100,000 pesos are a grant from Bahrain. This *madrasah*, called Maahad Kornatan al-Islamie (MAKIS) Inc., operates up to the high school level. Another, found in Lanao del Sur, is called Madrasa Diniah Pataingud Bayabao Masium al-Islamiah, which was founded in 1973 by Said Comayag. It has 175 students and 14 teachers. The funding comes from the community and donations from Saudi Arabia. Its education level is elementary.

Two *madrasah* in Maguindanao had budgets of 200,000 pesos each. The one in Buldon, called Maahad Buldon al-Islamie, was founded in 1962, and all of its funding comes from abroad. The other is in Dinaig, known as Maahad al Da'wat al-Islamie, which is financed by the local community.

In Region IX, the picture is slightly different. The biggest *madrasah* that has become operational is the Sheik Makdum Islamic University, located at Pitogo, about 9 kilometres from Zamboanga City. The building was constructed through a grant from Islamic Development Bank (IDB), amounting to US$1.6 million. The 6-hectare land was donated by Mayor Harun Kiram of Alicia, Zamboanga del Sur. The school has become operational since 1986, with an initial total enrolment of 700 students from grade one up to second year high school. The plan to open the collegiate level is still pending owing to financial constraints. According to the school director, Nahjin A. Isahac, the school has an operational budget of 1.5 million pesos which the school finds hard to raise. Another *madrasah* at Sta. Barbara, Zamboanga City, the Mahad al-Nahdat al-Islamie, which was founded in 1981 by a Muslim association, has a budget of 150,000 pesos. Funds for this school come from community contributions, together with donations from Kuwait (80,000 pesos) and Saudi Arabia (70,000 pesos). It has 900 high school students. Central Arabic and Islamic Institute located at Campo Muslims, Zamboanga, founded in 1974, also receives funding from the same sources. In Tawi-Tawi, the Maahad Tawi-Tawi al-Islamie, founded in 1980 by Ustadz Abdulfadil Tiam Ang, has a budget of 100,000 pesos which come entirely from community contributions. It has a total enrolment of 615 students and 22 teachers.

From this survey, it is evident that most *madrasah* with funding of 100,000 pesos and above usually get financial help from abroad. Of course, this survey did not include *madrasah* with integrated curriculum, which means that Arabic language and Islamic courses are offered together with public school subjects. These types of schools have fixed the students' fees and their teachers receive salaries commensurate with their teaching hours and comparable to rates given to teachers in the government system. In the *madrasah*, the students are often admitted free or pay very minimal fees, while the teachers receive donations instead of fixed salaries.

### Zakat and Sadaqqa among the Moros

This section attempts to describe the practices and various processes which have taken place in selected Moro communities with regard to *zakat* and *sadaqqa*. In many instances, parallel developments have occurred; in others, some advances have been made in organization and planning.

#### Practices

*Zakat.* Traditionally, during the period of the sultanate, the sultan of Sulu was responsible for the maintenance and construction of mosques throughout the Sulu archipelago. An institution such as the *Baitul-Mal*, or House of Treasury, existed for the collection of revenues and the disbursement of expenditures. The sultan appointed the various religious functionaries such as the *imam*, *khatib*, and *bilal*. The sultan also appointed a chief *santili* (from Malay *santiri* — collector) who headed the *Baitul-Mal* and who was a member of the sultan's council. The chief *santili* appointed representatives who went around the different communities to collect *sadaqqa* every month and to accept *zakat*, especially during the harvest times.

Once *zakat* was collected, the sultan would issue an order for its distribution. The recipients were the needy of the communities, usually categorized as *ilo-balo* or orphans and widows. The sultan, however, had the privilege of keeping some part of the *zakat* for the state and for himself.

*Zakat* is classified into two types: *zakat al fitr* and *zakat al mal*. *Zakat al fitr* (*pitla* or *fitrah* in local terms) is given during Ramadhan, usually during Eid celebration at the *masjid*. This is a tax on persons to be paid either in kind or in cash. If paid in kind, it is valued at one ganta of rice convertible to its cash equivalent. At current market price, this would amount to around 16 to 20 pesos, depending on the quality of the rice. Among the Tausugs, the *zakat al fitr* is known as *pitla*. The Maguindanaons calculate *pitla* at the same value of one ganta or 12 glasses (12.7 centimetres tall) of rice. The *pitla* is usually given for all those who are seven years old and above. The Tausugs, however, paid *pitla* for everyone, including infants.

*Zakat al mal* is tax on property. Since Moros live in agricultural areas, this is usually given after harvest. *Zakat al mal* is calculated by the Tausugs according to the total harvest: for every 20 sacks of rice, 2 sacks are given as *zakat*. The Maguindanaon *zakat* calculation also follows the same formula: for every 100 sacks of rice, 10 sacks are given as *zakat*. Other crops such as corn, millet, and sorghum are not given *zakat* since these are not considered primary crops and are planted as intercrops. *Zakat* on fruit harvest amounts to 2.5 per cent of the money earned from the harvest. Thus for every 100 pesos earned, 2.50 pesos are apportioned as *zakat*. For *zakat* on cash, the same ratio is applied. *Zakat* on cash is usually given on the month of Jul-Hijjah, the tenth month of the Muslim calendar.

*Sadaqqa.* Institutionalized *sadaqqa* in Moro society finds expression in many varied ways. The more systematic collection of *sadaqqa,* however, is through the *santili,* who visits every house on set days to offer *dua* or prayers. He is given *sadaqqa* either in kind or in cash, depending on the resources of the household. Another systematic *sadaqqa* collection is that done at the *masjid* during *jamaah* prayers (congregations).

There are, however, other forms of *sadaqqa* that are more spontaneous in terms of the manner and nature of its operation. This type relates to varying situations and the recipients may not always be the poor. This kind of *sadaqqa* can be tentatively categorized into the following groups:

1. *Sadaqqa* in terms of donation or contribution directed to community projects, e.g., the construction of *masjid* and *madrasah.*
2. *Sadaqqa* given to religious people performing religious functions, i.e., wedding ceremonies, thanksgiving *dua,* burial, etc., including singers during the *maulid* (the Prophet's birthday) celebrations, and teachers of *madrasah* or Qur'an schools.
3. *Sadaqqa* in the form of sharing bounty harvests in both farming and fishing communities.
4. *Sadaqqa* in terms of services rendered to families, individuals, or to the community during festivities or emergencies, e.g., contributions toward expenditures associated with weddings and other constructions, burial services.
5. *Sadaqqa* in the form of lending utensils, vehicles, equipment, and even jewelleries, native costumes, and other apparel during times of need.
6. *Sadaqqa* as gifts, especially from travellers returning from abroad or pilgrimage (*hajj*). The most common item given are *tasbih,* or prayer beads, and zamzam water from Mecca.
7. *Sadaqqa* through meeting the needs of orphans and widows, students, and refugees by taking them in as part of the family, and the needs of guests and travellers.

Generally, many of these deeds are kinship-oriented, since most Moro communities are clan-based, especially in rural areas. The recipients, therefore, are essentially kins and relatives. In urban areas, however, the principle of Islamic brotherhood takes over kinship orientation and *sadaqqa* is offered on brotherhood basis. But, in both rural and urban areas, *sadaqqa* has been a strong support mechanism in maintaining the social cohesiveness and integrity of the Moro communities. It is, therefore, not surprising that, in spite of economic difficulties, beggary or prostitution has not become a problem in the Moro communities.

With the abolition of the sultanate, the systematic collection of *zakat* and *sadaqqa* has been degenerating. These have been largely replaced by direct taxes, first levied by the American colonial government, then by the Philippine government after 1946.[11] In spite of this, however, the Moros have kept the *zakat* and *sadaqqa* institutions alive. Some changes have naturally occurred in these institutions on account of the wider socio-political changes that have taken place.

*Changes and Innovations*

As mentioned earlier, with the abolition of the sultanate and the diminution of the sultan's powers and subsequently his role in Moro society, important changes have taken place in the collection and distribution of *zakat* and *sadaqqa*. As the sultanate's collection of *zakat* and *sadaqqa* fell into decline, religious leaders like the *imam* became the prime movers in the *zakat* and *sadaqqa* collections and the *masjid* emerged as the central locus of collection.

This development is not altogether surprising, since the religious leaders were directly involved in the *zakat* and *sadaqqa* institutions even during the sultanate. As the *masjid* had always been the focal point of communal activities, it is only logical and natural that it has become the centre for the collection and distribution of *zakat* and *sadaqqa*.

As a result of all this, what was previously a collective and communal effort has become somewhat individualized. People go directly to the *imam*, other religious functionaries, or recipients whom they consider deserving of their *zakat*.

Among the Tausugs, for example, the practice is to give *zakat* to recognized religious functionaries, some of whom are not actually qualified to receive *zakat* because they are already financially well-off. But tradition has established this practice and has been justified by the exhortation of the religious leaders to give *zakat* to the *pakil*. In many cases, the latter keep the *zakat* for themselves under the justification that these *zakat* are gifts from the people given to them personally. This apparent misunderstanding, according to Sayedy,[12] arises from a mistranslation of the word *faqir*, which in Arabic means 'needy', to the Tausug *pakil*, which refers to the religious functionaries. Sayedy also states that religion has become a profession so much so that religious functionaries now view gifts as their just compensation. For this reason, the beneficial effects of *zakat* and *sadaqqa* on the communal level are not readily manifested. This is true not only in the Tausug but also in the Maguindanao and Maranao communities.

Other changes have also occurred. The *santili*, once an important part of the *zakat* and *sadaqqa* institutions, has lost ground. It is already extinct in

Lanao and slowly becoming obsolete in Maguindanao. In Sulu, the *santili* can still be found. However, instead of submitting the collection to the *masjid* or to the *imam*, as was the practice during the sultanate, the *santili* keeps it for his own use. Since he is usually an old man and his collection constitutes part of his livelihood, his legitimacy as the rightful recipient of *sadaqqa* is not questioned by the donor. Among the Maguindanaons, the *santili* has been completely supplanted by the *imam* in the collection of *sadaqqa* and *zakat*.

It is in the realm of *sadaqqa* that some innovations are taking place. All of the *masjid* investigated have begun institutionalizing the collection of *sadaqqa* during Friday *jamaah*. An appointed person passes a box amongst the people for their *sadaqqa*, whereas before, a box was simply left at the door of the *masjid* for this purpose. The money collected is utilized for the upkeep and maintenance of the *masjid* as well as for the support of the Qur'an schools administered by Islamic workers.

One innovative approach toward systematization of *zakat* and *sadaqqa* has been the creation of community- or *masjid*-based organizations. This development has reached a relative degree of success among the three Moro groups.

Among the Maguindanao of Masulot, an organization known as the Cotabato Islamic Foundation, Inc. (CIFI) has taken responsibility for the mobilization and administration of *zakat* and *sadaqqa* since 1982. The organization has systematized the collection and management of the Friday *sadaqqa* since and has kept records of its incomes and expenditures.

The CIFI has also allowed direct appeal by individuals in emergency situations to the *jamaah* during Friday congregations. These people, however, are first screened by the *imam* or by officers of the CIFI to establish the authenticity of the emergency before an appeal is made on their behalf.

So far, the CIFI has utilized its funds to install water connection for the *masjid* and for the acquisition of a new sound system and plastic mats for use in prayers. It has plans to establish a library within the *masjid* compound.

Additional data obtained from the largest *masjid* in Cotabato City, known as the 'Supermarket Mosque', show the presence of a centralized system where everything is in the hands of the founder, Haji Amil Salamat, who administers the *masjid* with the help of the *imam* and selected associates. This informal body constitutes what can loosely be described as 'the management'.

Collection of *sadaqqa* by the management entails two systems: (1) by asking people to drop their donations for the *masjid* and the *madrasah* in a drop box located at the entrance gate leading to the *masjid*; and (2) through a monthly collection scheme involving all residents in the area. This monthly collection goes for the payment of electricity and water bills, averaging about 600 pesos.

Among the Maranaos, specifically at the Jamia Mindanao al-Islamie, the administration of the *masjid* rests with the board of directors elected by the *jamaah* on a yearly basis. The board is supported by two working committees: (1) the Constituent Commitment Committee whose main function is to enlist people who pledge a monthly donation to the *masjid*; and (2) the Administration Committee which looks after the fund and its usage.

The Jamia Mindanao al-Islamie derives most of its funding from its members, who are mostly government employees. They also include businessmen and well-known rich families such as the Alontos and the Lucmans who have made generous contributions amounting to thousands of pesos. Although the members of the Constituent Commitment Committee, comprising professionals, have pledged to contribute an average of 500 pesos a month each, the bulk of the contributions actually come from those members who are financially well-off.

As part of its mobilizing efforts, the organization has set up a *Baitul-Mal* at the *masjid* to which people may hand in their *zakat* and *sadaqqa*. Sometimes, the organization distributes envelopes and actively solicits donations from community leaders and friends. The maximum average collection of the *Baitul-Mal* ranges from 1,000 pesos to 1,300 pesos per day. This fund is intended for the maintenance and the on-going construction of the *masjid*. For instance, the collection from 1 January 1984 to 20 February 1985, amounting to 529,842.13 pesos, was spent mainly on materials and labour cost.

A similar organizational set-up occurs in the other Maranao *masjid* investigated; however, in some cases, like the Mahad Marawi al-Islamie Mosque, the organization is loosely constructed in the same manner as that of the Supermarket Mosque in Cotabato City. The custodian (Sultan Dalomangcob Rashid Sampaco) is also the chairman of the board of directors. There is an assigned *amil* (treasurer) who is in charge of the *Baitul-Mal*. To mobilize funds for the *masjid* construction, the organization once introduced a 'Beauty Queen' contest in which the pretty daughters of the clan were the candidates. The winner was decided by the highest amount of money she was able to raise. This method of raising funds was condemned as unIslamic by an *alim* (jurist) and was never repeated. *Zakat* and *sadaqqa* are now left to the individuals. The organization also distributes envelopes to friends and supporters and regularly collects a monthly contribution of 30 pesos from every household in order to raise additional funds for the maintenance of the *masjid* and its *madrasah*. The *masjid* has a *tabang* (help) system for emergency cases, which is financed out of contingency funds, as a service to the community.

In Jolo, no formal organization had been established in the three mosques investigated. But at Masjid Tulay, a board of directors has been operating since the 1970s. After the burning of Jolo town in 1974, it was this group that was instrumental in rebuilding the *masjid*, which is now the biggest in Jolo. The board consists of nine members headed by a president. Currently it is Haji Aisad Sali, former Mayor and Governor of Sulu. Prior to 1974 Habib Amin-kadra Abubakar, the then Municipal Mayor of Jolo, was in charge of the management of Masjid Tulay. The *masjid* does not rely on external funding, except when it was being rebuilt after the fire, and funding is provided by the Office of Muslim Affairs. The *imam* co-ordinates the voluntary services of the Islamic workers who help maintain the *masjid* or conduct religious activities, including classes in the *madrasah*.

*Sadaqqa* is collected after Friday *jamaah* prayers and the collection is kept by the *imam* who dispenses it for the upkeep of the *masjid*. No records are kept. In each *masjid* there is also a group of ten members who have pledged to make regular contributions.

*Masjid*-based organizations have sprung up in Lambayung and Kasulutan which intend to provide benefits for their members. The Lambayung Jamiyat Al Abidin has been in existence since 1985 and already has eighty-five members. The organization provides burial assistance to members who pay a 5-peso membership fee and 5 pesos monthly dues. The organization has plans to provide scholarships for deserving students.

A similar organization at Kasulutan has also been established, known as the Kasulutan Muslimin Parhimpunan. The monthly due is 2.50 pesos and the annual fee is 10 pesos. Initially the organization had only seventeen members; today, there are 110 members, attesting to the success of the organization in giving aid to the indigents.

In the Moro communities in Metro Manila, specifically in the Islamic Center at Quiapo and at San Andres Bukid, a parallel development is taking place. At the Islamic Center, a community-based organization has been established known as the Philippine Islamic Cultural Foundation, Inc. (PICFI). The main task of this organization is to undertake community development projects. Another organization called JAMA, which consists of male members only, takes care of the religious activities and the maintenance of the religious institutions. There is also a women's organization called Jamiatun Nisah.

Each of these organizations has drop-boxes at the entrance of the *masjid* to receive *sadaqqa*. Contribution of *zakat* to these organizations has been encouraged by the *imam* and *ulama* as well as by leaders of the community through announcement in the *masjid* but the residents prefer to send their *zakat* to deserving relatives in the provinces or, as is common among other communities, they give it to whom they consider lawful recipients. The reasons behind the direct approach include the lack of trust in people handling the funds and the presence of too many organizations undertaking similar projects.

In order to systematize the collection and utilization of *zakat* in the community, informants suggested the following:

1.  There should be only one *amil* (trusted collector) in the community.

2.   All residents should give *sadaqqa* and *zakat* in the community in which they reside.
3.   Community leaders should co-operate with each other and look into ways and means of using *sadaqqa* and *zakat* in accordance with Islamic principles in relation to community development and poverty alleviation.
4.   Community leaders should see to it that their programmes cater to public rather than personal interest.
5.   Community members should be educated on the collection and utilization of *sadaqqa* and *zakat*.
6.   Community leaders should establish trust between themselves and community members.
7.   Organizations should present annual financial statements, either posted on the bulletin board in the *masjid* or *madrasah* or circulated to the households.

At San Andres Bukid, the residents have organized themselves into a civic association called the San Andres Bukid Manila Islamic Foundation, Inc. Through a general consensus rather than an election, a president and secretary were designated as officials of the organization. Through this organization, funds were solicited from Muslim countries like Saudi Arabia and Libya for financial assistance in the purchase of the land and the construction of the *masjid*. Recently, the organization appointed an *amil* to collect *zakat* and *sadaqqa* for the maintenance of the *masjid* and the *madrasah*. The *amil*'s office would be at the *masjid* and residents have agreed that all their *zakat* and *sadaqqa* would be handed to this person. Prior to this development, about one-half of the residents' *zakat* was sent to the provinces to their poor relatives. *Sadaqqa* is collected through a box passed around only during *jamaah* prayers, or given directly to the *imam*.

Many of these innovations now taking place in the different communities began after the return of local *ulama* who were educated in the Middle East in the late 1960s. But, in some cases, the establishment of an organization is in itself a recognition that such an association would be an efficient instrument in the mobilization of funds. Certainly, there is the awareness that foreign funding would be facilitated through an officially recognized organization registered at the Security and Exchange Commission.

The presence of professionals in these organizations cannot be discounted as a factor in their establishments. However, in some instances, the professional members run into disagreements with the traditional leaders with respect to the management or policies of the organization. This occurred at the Jamaie Dansalan Amanao Al Islamie and the Masjid Lumbac Lilod Madaya at Marawi City.

These *masjid*- or community-based organizations exhibit a common element in that the 'owners' of the *masjid* are also usually the presidents of the boards of directors. Such is the case in Masulot where the Abas family was responsible for the construction of the *masjid*, as well as at the Mahad Marawi al-Islamie in Marawi City, where Sulotan (sultan) Dalomangcob Rashid Sampaco is identified as the 'owner' or the 'manager'. In most cases, these persons also have a great deal to say about how funds are to be spent, or on the policies and plans of the organization. The practice of individuals building *masjid* for the use of the community is quite common in many Moro areas. It is considered a great blessing for the individual to do so.

This introduces another facet of the Moro society, that is, the participation of prominent personalities in religious affairs. In many instances, these personalities are also political leaders who hold important positions in government, stressing the tie between the temporal and the spiritual leadership that used to prevail during the sultanate and which is still demonstrated today in the *masjid* set-up. Thus, the Alontos and the Lucmans, who are political leaders in Lanao del Sur, are not only the supporters of the Mindanao al-Islamie but also the members of the *masjid* standing committees. The same is true with the *masjid* in Masulot where the 'owner' is also a Barangay captain. In Jolo the contribution of the mayor, Aminkadra Abubakar, is counted on to help defray expenses for the maintenance and upkeep of the *masjid*, as well as pay the *madrasah* teachers.

The obvious advantage of these various organizations has been not only in re-establishing a system but also in earning the credibility and respect of the *jamaah* by making records of collection and expenditures available to the people through financial statements on a regular basis. Where this process has been adopted, public confidence has been greatly restored with regard to the usage of funds given to the *masjid*. In the past, the use of *sadaqqa* funds had been kept a secret and people had no way of knowing where the money went.

Another positive factor is that these organizations have been able to mobilize the scarce resources of the community, whether human or material, for the purpose of undertaking communal activities. At the moment, these efforts are concentrated on the *masjid*, the *madrasah*, and religious activities. But, in time, other communal benefits can also be pursued.

Let us now look briefly at some of the *madrasah* institutions as direct beneficiaries of *sadaqqa* and *zakat*. In the case of the three *masjid* in Jolo, *sadaqqa* is used mostly for paying teachers' fees. The Bus-Bus *masjid* has a *madrasah* called the Bus-Bus Islamic Institute and Guidance which offers Grade O to Grade IV, with a total student population of 134.

The classes are held for two hours in the weekends (every Saturday and Sunday evening). There are five full-time teachers and they get 100 pesos a month for teaching a maximum of around sixteen hours. These teachers' fees can by no means be considered wages since they are mere pittance; but the teachers' efforts represent their own *sadaqqa* to the community. They have their own main occupations during the day which provide them financial support for their families. There are no student fees but financial support is given by a businessman, Haji Ukkuh Jupli. These resources, however, cannot provide for books for the students, and there is no library to speak of; only the teachers have copies of the text which they use as references. Neither can the resources provide for a schedule which would make the *madrasah* full-time classes instead of being held only during weekends.

This situation also prevails at the Lambayung Madrasa Islamiyah which has sixty-three students distributed in Grades 0 and I. There are two full-time teachers handling two-hour classes every Saturday and Sunday night. The teachers' fees come from the mayor's monthly donation of 300 pesos.

At the Kasulutan Madrasa al Islamiyah there are five grades, including an adult class. The total student population is 191, including 100 attending adult classes. The classes are held in the day-time on Saturdays and Sundays from 8.00 to 11.30 a.m., then from 1.30 to 5.00 p.m. There is a monthly fee of 3 pesos; but even this is voluntary for regular students except for the adults. The money goes to pay the salaries of three full-time teachers.

The *madrasah* at Masjid Tulay, known as the Masjid Tulay Central Islamic Institute, has seven grade levels with a total enrolment of 254 students and 15 teachers. It holds classes only in the evenings for one hour and twenty minutes per class. No fees are paid by the students except 20 pesos at the time of enrolment. Based on this, the *madrasah* had 5,080 pesos as its income for 1986, which clearly was not enough even for teachers' salaries. The teachers each receives a nominal salary of 100 pesos a month which comes from the student fees and from the private funds of the founder, Ajuji T. Isnain.

In Cotabato City, the Madrasatu Alih-Amir Al Islamie founded in 1979 by Haji Amil Salamat, the 'owner' and the administrator of the Supermarket Mosque, derives most of its funding from tuition fees. Each student pays 120 pesos per year regardless of grade levels. This fund is used for the salaries of eight *ustaz* who receive 300 pesos a month each teaching half days four times a week. On the basis of a total enrolment of 250 students in 1986, the *madrasah* was able to collect 30,000 pesos. Out of this, 28,000 pesos were disbursed for teachers' salaries. The rest of the money went to the upkeep of the *madrasah*. As can be expected, this inadequate funding allows for very little or no facilities to enhance the learning process. Nevertheless, the *madrasah* continues to be self-reliant although its continued survival appears to be dependent on the strength of the enrolment. In 1987, only 120 students enrolled; consequently income of the *madrasah* was drastically reduced, forcing the management to seek public donations or *sadaqqa* to make up the shortfall.

In Marawi City, two *masjid* investigated also have *madrasah* as part of the *masjid* complexes. While these are self-sustaining, they also encounter funding difficulties. However, Marawi City abounds with *madrasah* functioning independently. The OMA 1981 survey noted the presence of twenty-two *madrasah* in the city alone. The biggest is the Mahad Matampay located just outside the city.

In Metro Manila, the Grand Mosque Madrasa located at the Quiapo Islamic Center, which occupies the second floor of the *masjid*, offers a programme from kindergarten to Grade VI. It has classes only on Saturdays and Sundays. It has more than 100 students with 11 teachers, including the principal. The source of funding comes from community contributions and a yearly community contest where all the municipalities represented in the community vie for the first place in terms of resource mobilization. In 1986, the winner was the municipality of Ditsaan, Ramain, whose actual location in Lanao del Sur is 17 kilometres from Marawi City. The *madrasah* gives a salary ranging from 500 pesos for kindergarten to Grade VI teachers, to 2,000 pesos for Grade XII, which includes the principal. The *madrasah* appears to be financially solvent although its physical facilities need improvement and its library is practically non-existent. No fees are paid by the students.

The Madrasatul Hudah al-Islamia, which occupies the ground floor of the San Andres Mosque, began with twenty kindergarten students in 1980 and one teacher who received 100 pesos monthly as salary. The student population increased to 118 in 1987 and the programme now includes kindergarten to Grade IV with five teachers. Three of the teachers receive 300 pesos each, and the other two receive 500 pesos each. Classes are held only on Saturdays and Sundays. The community finances this *madrasah* through *sadaqqa*, but in times of shortfall, it receives aid from the San Andres Bukid Manila Islamic Foundation. Owing to increased student population, the *madrasah* is already crowded and there are plans for expansion. But funding will be a problem and mobilizing resources will be the job of the San Andres Foundation.

As can be seen from this sample, funds available to *madrasah* that are housed within the *masjid* are inadequate and are used to defray expenses such as teachers' salaries with little or no funds left for facilities like libraries and reproduction of learning materials.

*Problems of Mobilization*

As the data suggest, the resources of the *masjid* are too small to provide for good *madrasah*. In Jolo, the approximate weekly incomes of the *masjid* are as follows:

Bus-Bus *masjid*    —  70 pesos
Lambayung *masjid* —  50 pesos
Kasulutan *masjid*   —  20 pesos

At this rate, Bus-Bus *masjid* can expect a monthly collection of 280 pesos; Lambayung, 200 pesos; and Kasulutan, 80 pesos. Their monthly approximated expenditures amount to 160 pesos, 50 pesos, and 120 pesos, respectively, which are accounted for mainly by electricity and other amenities. The amount that goes to the *madrasah* in terms of teachers' fees is insignificant. For example, the Bus-Bus *madrasah*'s allotment for teachers' fees is only 100 pesos a month. Without support in the form of *sadaqqa* from individuals in or outside the community, these *madrasah* can hardly exist. That they do, albeit even on a very limited budget and despite poor facilities, speaks highly for the commitment of the people to give religious instructions to their children. As already mentioned, many of the teachers render service as their *sadaqqa* to the community.

In so far as the Masulot Masjid is concerned, the monthly collection amounts to around 700 pesos, with a regular expenditure of about 400 pesos. It has a monthly surplus of 250 pesos and a total yearly savings of 3,000 pesos. However, in terms of its plans to improve the *masjid* and to build a library, these funds will be grossly inadequate.

The Jamia Mindanao al-Islamie shows by far a strong financial profile. According to its financial statement, its total collection for three months of 1986 (September to November) was 14,911.99 pesos. However, its budget for the construction of the *masjid* is US$1 million, and at the present rate of collection it would take many years before the total amount can be raised. Although the *masjid* administrators have been soliciting funds since 1969, they are still far away from the target. The other two *masjid* in Marawi City face similar situations.

However, the possibilities for increasing the flow of funds are not entirely absent, even with the present poor economic status of the Moros. Based on an overall attendance that each *masjid* in Jolo could accommodate, the small collection seems to indicate the very poor financial capacities of the congregants. At the Bus-Bus *masjid*, where an average of 300 people attend the Friday prayers, the collection totals only 70 pesos. If everyone contributes just 1 peso each, the *masjid* could easily raise 300 pesos every week and 1,200 pesos every month. That this expected income is not realized can be attributed either to the depressed economic conditions of the people or the absence of management expertise in resource mobilization.

There are indications that it is the lack of management that is by far the most telling factor. Although the people attending these *masjid* are fishermen and vendors, and their economic base is really low, a contribution of one peso a week is not totally outside their income range. But, because *sadaqqa* has been advanced as not only voluntary but also as a privilege of the rich, there is no real effort on the part of the masses to make *sadaqqa* a part of their expected expenditure and to provide for it. One reason is that religious leaders have not encouraged the Moros to think of *sadaqqa* as a source not only of spiritual rewards but also of communal benefits. The idea that the person who gives *sadaqqa* might, in return, also improve his own material way of life as well as that of others, has not been emphasized. Another reason is that there have been too many failure stories involving *sadaqqa*, especially where collections were taken up for particular projects which never came off. Thus, there has been a growing resistance to giving more unless the people, especially the rich, see proof that their *sadaqqa* has been put to good use. Organizations which have shown accountability and earned credibility in handling the *sadaqqa* funds have had little problem in soliciting for funds even outside their communities.

Another area where management of resources can be made more effective is in the collection and distribution of *fitrah*, which is easier to monitor as it is given at the end of Ramadhan. Taking the case of Jolo as an example, and based on a calculation of a maximum rate of 20 pesos per person, Bus-Bus would yield 282,020 pesos from 14,101 people, while the entire municipality of Jolo would yield 1,048,580 pesos, given a population of 52,429 residents. The whole province of Sulu should yield 7,211,790 pesos, given a total Muslim population of 360,582. This far exceeds the 1.8 million pesos collected in Sulu in 1983.

Thus, the huge resource base remains practically untapped. There is abundant proof that the Moros are conscientious about fulfilling *zakat* as a religious obligation so the question of non-payment does not arise. The problem rather centres on the practices that have grown up in the Moro communities where *zakat* is given to individual religious leaders who receive these funds for their own use. Even where an organization like the CIFI exists, *zakat* is considered a special collection and is not accounted for in its financial statements. The collection is given to the 'owners' of the *masjid* and the *imam* who dispense *zakat* according to their discretions. The same is true in Marawi City and in Jolo. Other sources of *zakat* and *sadaqqa*, such as those given by foreign nationals and handed directly to the *imam* of the *masjid*, also remain unaccounted. It is not rare for the religious functionaries to receive significant amounts as *zakat* and *sadaqqa* which, if properly managed, can finance development programmes for the benefit of the Moro communities.

In fact, the use of *zakat* for the general welfare of the community is one aspect of *zakat* that has not been well understood. According to Ismail R. Al-Faruqi,[13] religious leaders have become accustomed to thinking of *zakat* mainly to be given to the eight specified categories in the Qur'an, namely, the poor and the destitute, the wayfarers, the bankrupt, the needy converts, the captives, the collector of *zakat*, and those in the path of God. Faruqi claims that this last category has been left ambiguous to allow for the funding of community projects. These development projects are urgent in many remote Moro areas. In fact, such needs can account for the success that the organizations in Lambayung and Kasulutan have gained, since they attempt to meet the needs of the community.

The idea that *zakat* should be used for community development is already gaining ground, especially among the young Moros. An exploratory seminar paper[14] presented by a student at the Institute of Islamic Studies (University of the Philippines) showed that the majority of the respondents (41 out of 70), generally below 25 years old, considered *zakat* as a socio-economic institution for the poor and the needy as well as for community development. In contrast, the researcher noted that older respondents considered *zakat* as a religious obligation and to them the act of giving fulfils this obligation. Their main concern is not so much with how these funds can be put to use for the benefit of the community but rather with their being able to discharge this duty as a Muslim.

Obviously, there is a need for a change of attitude, first among the religious leaders and second, among the masses, in terms of *zakat* mobilization and utilization. More systematic plans must be put forward. In this connection, several attempts have been made. In 1973, when the Muslim Personal Laws were being codified, a proposal was submitted whereby an office to collect *zakat* would be established within the structure of the Office of Muslim Affairs. The proposal was turned down since there were fears that such a financial house would be used by the Moros for something else. The government suspects that *zakat* funds might be diverted to the Muslim secessionist movement.

Another proposal which is being worked out is the creation of an Office of the Mufti under the administrative supervision of the Supreme Court. Although the main functions of the office would be to deal with the legal system, it is envisioned that it can organize a body to supervise religious and cultural affairs. Such a body would be mandated with the collection of *zakat* and its disbursement on a nation-wide basis.

Actually such an office is already provided for in Article 164 of the Code of Muslim Personal Laws of the Philippines which is to be called the Office of the Jurisconsult. This office would be under the administrative supervision of the Supreme Court of the Philippines. Its suggested permanent station would be in Zamboanga City. Among its functions are: (1) to render legal opinions relating to Islamic Law; and (2) to compile and publish legal opinions.

Legal opinions relating to the systematic collection and dispensation of *zakat* are expected to be within the purview of this office. There is already a petition[15] to the Office of the President to implement this provision through the appointment of a Jurisconsult and the organization of the office itself. Meanwhile, there are already Darul Ifta (organization for Islamic Legal Opinion) chapters operating in Mindanao and Sulu composed of *ulama* and *ustaz,* many of whom are graduates of Al-Azhar, Cairo, and the University of Medina, Saudi Arabia. In the scheme of things envisioned by the creation of the Office of the Jurisconsult, these local chapters can be absorbed. Since these people are well-respected in the Moro communities, they are in the best position to spearhead a movement to revolutionize the *zakat* and *sadaqqa* institutions.

Another possible move would be to allow the Moros with fixed incomes to declare *zakat* as contribution to charity so that it is deductible from income taxes. Such a step would free professionals and other fixed income earners from carrying the burden of double taxation. This, however, would require approval from Malacanang or Congressional legislation, including the creation of an agency which would receive *zakat* and issue official receipts acceptable to the Bureau of Inland Revenue (BIR). With the installation of the New Congress, which has seven Moro members, such a legislative bill might become law.

From this standpoint, it goes without saying that the biggest obstacle in the systematic collection and management of *zakat* is the absence of a state machinery that can undertake this programme, together with a comprehensive plan for the use of *zakat* funds. This is what has developed in many Muslim countries. But the Philippine government is not likely to allow a state-supported machinery for this purpose, as it will be in direct contradiction to the constitutional provision regarding the separation of church and state. The best course, therefore, would be to establish an independent foundation by the Moros for this specific purpose.

One solution would be the establishment of the Moro autonomous government which would be able to enact its own legislative instrument in support of a systematic *zakat* collection and the efficient management of the funds to be collected. For example, the Tripoli Agreement signed between the Philippine government and the MNLF in 1976 provides for this kind of arrangement, to wit:

> The authorities of the autonomy in the south of the Philippines shall have their own economic and financial system. The relationship between this system and central economic and financial system of the state shall be discussed later.

Unfortunately, the Tripoli Agreement was not fully implemented and the substance of the agreement remained only on paper.

## Conclusion

There is no doubt that the presence of *zakat* and *sadaqqa* institutions in the Moro communities had been instrumental in maintaining a high degree of self-reliance which the Moros have enjoyed since the sultanate period. Today, these institutions are active at the individual rather than communal level, in the sense that their benefits tend to accrue generally to individual recipients rather than to the community as a whole.

The move to systematize *zakat* and *sadaqqa* collections is a recognition of the need to increase the capacity of Moro communities to undertake communal projects and to address pressing problems in the economic sector, especially the problem of poverty. At present, so much attention is devoted to the question of survival that the Moros are unable to use their native talents for the development of their art and culture.

The future prospects for systematizing *zakat* and *sadaqqa* collections, in spite of the present problems, appear positive as evidenced by the various moves both at the individual and group levels. At the moment, a nation-wide system may not be applicable, but the current developments at the *masjid* level are regarded as the necessary prerequisites that would make a wider system possible in the future.

The prospects would be even brighter if the negotiations for autonomy are again resumed and a final agreement is signed. As of this writing, Executive Order No. 220, creating the Cordillera Administrative Region (CAR), has been signed by President Corazon C. Aquino (16 July 1987), leaving Congress to enact the enabling laws to complete the process of empowering the autonomous government of the Cordillera. In due course, the same development may occur for the Moro Autonomous Region in the south.

In the meantime, greater awareness about *zakat* and *sadaqqa* and their role in the development of Moro society is called for.

## NOTES

\*    The author wishes to acknowledge gratefully the valuable assistance provided by Ms Shu-Jen Gonora, Mr Mustapha Kabalu, Mr Calimba Maulawi, Mr Isduri Adjili, Ms Raisalam Magondacan, and Mrs Maria Cabacungan in conducting this study.

1    Peter Gowing, *Muslim Filipinos: Heritage and Horizon* (Quezon City: New Day Publishing, 1969).

2    Thomas Kiefer, *The Tausug: Violence and Law in a Philippine Moslem Society* (New York: Holt, Rinehart and Winston, Inc., 1972), p. 42.

3    Inger Wulff, "Features of Yakan Culture", in *The Muslim Filipinos: History, Society and Contemporary Problems*, edited by Peter Gowing (Manila: Solidaridad Publishing House, 1974).

4    Andrew Sherfar, *The Yakans of Basilan Island: Another Unknown and Exotic Tribe of the Philippines* (Cebu City: Fotomatic (Phils.) Inc., 1976).

5    Mashur Bin-Ghalib Jundam, *Yakan, Asian Center Ethnic Research Field Report* Series II, no. 1 (Quezon City: Asian Center, U.P. Press, 1983).

6    Ministry of Muslim Affairs, List of Masajid and Madaris, 1981.

7    Cesar Adib Majul, *Muslims in the Philippines* (Quezon City: Asian Center, U.P. Press, 1973).

8    Kiefer, op. cit.

9    Cesar Adib Majul, *The Education of the Muslims in the Philippines: History, Present Situation*, 1976.

10   Moracio Baransing et al., *The Madrasa Institutions in the Philippines, Historical and Cultural Perspectives*, 1987.

11   The collection of taxes had been the cause of many Moro uprisings and rebellions against the Americans. The Moros vehemently resisted paying such taxes because these signified a state of subjugation. For more of these struggles against American colonial rule, see Samuel Tan, *The Filipino Muslim Armed Struggle 1900–1972* (Manila: Filipinas Foundation, 1977).

12   Prof. Abdulrafih H. Sayedy is a faculty member of the Institute of Islamic Studies (IIS) and an authority on Islamic Law and Jurisprudence.

13   Ismail R. Al-Faruqi and Loes Lamya al Faruqi, *The Cultural Atlas of Islam* (New York: Macmillan Publishing Co., 1986), p. 147.

14   Sapia B. Datukali, "The Concept of Zakah Among Muslim Maranao at Maharlika Village" (Seminar paper for I.S. 271, Institute of Islamic Studies, 1983).

15   The petition was spearheaded by the Maharlika Village Islamic Forum, Inc., Maharlika Village, Taguig, Metro Manila.

# 9  THE MANAGEMENT OF MUSLIM FUNDS
IN SINGAPORE

*Amina Tyabji**

## Introduction

Of the countries with Muslim minorities in Southeast Asia, Singapore is relatively more affluent. Singapore Muslims may be dichotomized into two groups: Malay Muslims, which comprise 90 per cent of the total, and the others, primarily of Indian and Middle Eastern origins. Malays as a group are more homogeneous than the others. This historical dichotomy and diversity are stamped on the origins and evolution especially of the early Islamic institutions in this country.

Since 1968, the Majlis Ugama Islam Singapura (MUIS), a statutory body, has occupied a central role in the administration of Muslim affairs. A distinct bureaucratization process has pervaded Muslim institutions. This is reflected in the mobilization and utilization of funds as well as in a number of other areas.

This chapter is concerned with the role of the voluntary sector in contributing to the welfare of Muslims in Singapore. It is divided into eight sections. Since both the early and post-1968 development and management of Muslim institutions are rooted in demography, a socio-economic profile of Muslims is presented first. Given the increasingly important role of MUIS, this institution and the legislation guiding its activities are examined next. This is followed by a discussion of *zakat* (wealth tax) and *fitrah* (poll tax), *waqf* (endowment), education, and welfare activities and new initiatives. The final section contains some concluding remarks.

**Socio-economic Profile of Singapore Muslims**

The foundation of modern Singapore is dated to 1819 when Sir Stamford Raffles entered into a treaty with the Sultan of Johore and the Temenggong of Singapore. Very quickly the island became a thriving commercial settlement attracting migrants not only from the neighbouring Indonesian archipelago but also from China, India, and even Arabia. Amongst these migrants were many Muslims. The ethnic diversity of Singapore's population, then and now, is reflected in its Muslim population which, while sharing a common religion, is separated by differences in language, culture, and customs.

The early nineteenth century Muslims were divided into two groups. The first group, referred to as the Malayo-Muslims, comprised migrants from the region, while the second consisted of two quite distinct groups, the Indian Muslims and the Arabs (primarily from the Hadramaut). One characteristic of the Malayo-Muslims was that they were, from the start, demographically more settled, exhibiting relatively more balanced sex ratios since their migration was characterized by family migration rather than adult, male migration typical of all other migrants to Singapore, including the Indian Muslims and Arabs. Marriages between the first and second groups propagated other Muslim communities — Malay-Arab and Jawi Peranakan (the children of Indian Muslim and Malay marriages). Despite the assimilation implied by these unions (how extensive these were is not easily determined), the early nineteenth century Muslims, because of their diverse ethnic origins, lived as separate Muslim communities, preserving their cultural identity, rather than as a homogeneous group. This is borne out, as will be discussed below, in the establishment of the early mosques and associations, many of which were based on ethnicity.

It is not possible to even offer a guesstimate as to how many Muslims there were in Singapore in the nineteenth century. There are no precise numbers even for the twentieth century. Even though population censuses have been conducted since 1901, a question on religion was asked only during the census in 1980. Tabulated in Table 1 are crude estimates based on the following assumptions: (1) 99 per cent of the Malays[1] are Muslims, and (2) Malays comprise 90 per cent of the total Muslim population.

Evidently, Muslims have formed a significant and sizeable minority in Singapore. Unlike the Muslim minorities in the Philippines and Thailand, Singapore Muslims are ethnically more heterogeneous. Since published information on religion is available only in the 1980 census, the following analysis of the socio-economic characteristics of Muslims is based on this census.

Table 2 shows not only the relative importance of Islam as a religion in Singapore but also the ethnicity of the Singapore Muslims among others. The data reveal that (except for the Malays who are overwhelmingly Muslims)

TABLE 1
**Estimated Number of Muslims in Singapore, 1901–80**

| Census Year | Number | Percentage of Total Population |
|---|---|---|
| 1901 | 39,580 | 17.4 |
| 1911 | 45,978 | 15.2 |
| 1921 | 58,951 | 14.1 |
| 1931 | 71,515 | 12.8 |
| 1947 | 125,183 | 13.3 |
| 1957 | 216,764 | 15.0 |
| 1970 | 342,516 | 16.5 |
| 1980* | 386,659 | 16.0 |

* This figure differs from that reported in the 1980 census which includes only population aged 10 and over.

SOURCES: Various censuses.

TABLE 2
**Singapore: Persons Aged 10 Years and Over by Religion and Ethnic Group, 1980**

| | Total | Chinese | Malays[1] | Indians[2] | Others[3] |
|---|---|---|---|---|---|
| **Religion** | | | Number | | |
| Total | 1,981,962 | 1,517,661 | 294,120 | 127,781 | 42,398 |
| Christianity | 203,517 | 161,068 | 805 | 15,879 | 25,765 |
| Buddhism | 529,140 | 520,174 | 317 | 1,268 | 7,381 |
| Taoism | 580,535 | 580,334 | 55 | 86 | 60 |
| Islam | 323,866 | 1,122 | 292,174 | 27,823 | 2,747 |
| Hinduism | 72,400 | 65 | 60 | 72,179 | 96 |
| Other Religions | 11,069 | 1,374 | 30 | 8,976 | 689 |
| No Religion | 261,433 | 253,524 | 679 | 1,570 | 5,660 |
| | | | Percentage | | |
| Total | 100.0 | 100.0 | 100.0 | 100.0 | 100.0 |
| Christianity | 10.3 | 10.6 | 0.3 | 12.4 | 60.8 |
| Buddhism | 26.7 | 34.3 | 0.1 | 1.0 | 17.4 |
| Taoism | 29.3 | 38.2 | — | 0.1 | 0.1 |
| Islam | 16.3 | 0.1 | 99.4 | 21.8 | 6.5 |
| Hinduism | 3.6 | — | — | 56.5 | 0.2 |
| Other Religions | 0.6 | 0.1 | — | 7.0 | 1.6 |
| No Religion | 13.2 | 16.7 | 0.2 | 1.2 | 13.4 |

[1] All persons of Malay and Indonesian origin.
[2] All persons of Indian, Pakistani, Bangladeshi, and Sri Lankan origin.
[3] Includes Eurasians, Europeans, Arabs, and others.

SOURCE: *Census of Population Singapore 1980*, Release No. 9, Religion and Fertility (Singapore: Department of Statistics, 1981).

religion is not wholly ethnic centred, and that no one religion is professed by the majority of the population. Cognizant of the potential socio-political conflict of a small Malay Muslim minority in the midst of a Chinese majority (over three-fourths of the population), the Singapore government, since independence, has attempted to integrate the Muslim population in the context of national development. Given the nature of Singapore's economy and polity (small, highly urbanized, and administratively highly centralized) such policies in the main have been successful.

An analysis of the socio-economic characteristics of the Muslim population aged 10 and over in 1980 should aid our understanding of some of the new initiatives undertaken by Muslims in the 1980s. Table 3 (a) compares the age distribution of the Muslim population with the total population. Generally

TABLE 3
**Singapore: Demographic Characteristics, 1980**

(a) By Age Group and Sex (in percentage)

|  | Total | Males | Females |
|---|---|---|---|
| Muslims | 100.0 | 52.9 | 47.1 |
| Total Population | 100.0 | 50.6 | 49.4 |

|  | Age Group | | | | | | |
|---|---|---|---|---|---|---|---|
|  | 10–19 | 20–29 | 30–39 | 40–49 | 50–59 | 60–69 | 70+ |
| Muslims | 31.5 | 28.2 | 14.2 | 11.3 | 9.0 | 4.2 | 1.7 |
| Total Population | 26.3 | 27.5 | 17.3 | 12.0 | 8.3 | 5.5 | 3.1 |

(b) Residential Status (in percentage)

|  | Singapore | | Non-Residents |
|---|---|---|---|
|  | Citizens | Residents |  |
| Muslims | 85.4 | 7.9 | 6.7 |
| Total Population | 90.2 | 4.0 | 5.7 |

SOURCE: Computed from *Census of Population Singapore 1980*, Release No. 9, Religion and Fertility (Singapore: Department of Statistics, 1981).

the Muslim population is younger than the rest due largely to differential fertility, especially of the Malays. This in turn has certain implications for education, particularly in view of the past backlog, as will be discussed later.

Educational characteristics are depicted in Table 4. Educational attainment of Muslims is significantly below that of the rest of the population as evidenced by the low share of those with tertiary qualifications and those attending tertiary institutions. This in turn affects the economic status of Muslims, as corroborated by the data of Table 5.

TABLE 4

**Singapore: Educational Characteristics, 1980**

(a) By Literacy[1] (in percentage)

|  | Literacy |
|---|---|
| Muslims | 86.7 |
| Total Population | 84.0 |

[1] Defined as the ability to read with understanding a newspaper in any of the four official languages or any other language.

(b) By Highest Qualification (in percentage)

|  | Full-Time Students | Primary and Below | Secondary and Upper Secondary | Tertiary |
|---|---|---|---|---|
| Muslims | 18.1 | 70.0 | 11.5 | 0.4 |
| Total Population | 17.3 | 65.1 | 15.3 | 2.3 |

(c) By Educational Level Attending (in percentage)

|  | Primary | Secondary | Upper Secondary | Tertiary |
|---|---|---|---|---|
| Muslims | 47.2 | 48.7 | 3.7 | 0.3 |
| Total Population | 39.4 | 50.0 | 8.6 | 2.0 |

SOURCE: Same as Table 3.

While the activity status of the Muslims in 1980 was no different from the rest of the population, their occupational and industry status exhibited considerable difference (Table 5 [b]). More than half of the Muslim working population fell into the production and related category, the so-called blue-collar jobs, compared to 40 per cent for the rest. This share is partly attributable to the rapid increase in the female (Malay) labour force participation rate[2] accompanying rapid industrialization[3] in Singapore. The large influx of Malay women in the labour force is indicative both of their changing role in the economy and modernization within the community. Due to their lower educational attainment, the Muslim share of 'professional and technical' and 'administrative and managerial' categories is well below that of the total population.

Separate data on income by race and religion have not been published. However, occupational status, educational attainment, and type of house are proxies for income. Based on these[4] it would seem that the economic status of the Muslims is relatively low in Singapore. There are, of course, differences within the group (intra-group income inequality) but the degree of this cannot be ascertained specifically in the absence of data. What is common knowledge is that amongst the Muslims, the Arabs and Indians are more affluent than the Malays.

## AMLA and MUIS

The Administration of Muslim Law Act (AMLA) of 1966 marks the latest stage in the evolution of legislation pertaining to the conduct of Muslim affairs in Singapore. More comprehensive and detailed than the earlier legislation it repealed, the act has ten parts[5] dealing with religious and legal affairs. It is not necessary for us to examine this act in its totality; only the sections relevant to this chapter will be noted. These are the creation of MUIS and the relevant sections of Part IV, which deals with financial aspects.

The act created MUIS as a statutory body with wide-ranging powers: to issue of *fatwa* (decree), to appoint religious officials, to oversee *waqf* and religious education, and to collect and disburse *zakat* and *fitrah*. Its creation represents the first facet of the process of bureaucratization of Islam in the country. Concommitantly with it, leadership in Muslim affairs passed from individuals of different ethnic Muslim communities to a body corporate representing larger collective interests.

MUIS's creation as a statutory body is not without significance. Parastatal organizations have been assigned pivotal roles in Singapore's social and economic development since it attained self-government in 1959. They are seen to provide a vital link between the community and government, partly to foster a sense of community and cohesion and partly as an instrument of control.

## TABLE 5
### Singapore: Economic Characteristics, 1980

(a) By Activity Status (in percentage)

|  | Economically Active | Working | Unemployed | Economically Inactive |
|---|---|---|---|---|
| Muslims | 57.1 | 96.5 | 3.5 | 42.9 |
| Total Population | 56.2 | 96.4 | 3.6 | 43.8 |

(b) By Occupation (in percentage)

|  | Professional and Technical | Administrative and Managerial | Clerical | Sales | Services | Agriculture and Fishing | Production and Related | Not Classifiable |
|---|---|---|---|---|---|---|---|---|
| Muslims | 4.6 | 1.0 | 14.3 | 6.6 | 16.7 | 2.5 | 51.8 | 2.5 |
| Total Population | 8.9 | 5.0 | 15.7 | 12.4 | 10.4 | 1.8 | 40.2 | 5.7 |

**TABLE 5** (*continued*)

**Singapore: Economic Characteristics, 1980**

(c) By Industry (in percentage)

| | Agriculture and Fishing | Quarrying | Manufacturing | Utilities | Construction | Trade | Transport and Communications | Financial and Business Services | Other Services | Not Classifiable |
|---|---|---|---|---|---|---|---|---|---|---|
| Muslims | 0.3 | 0.3 | 35.7 | 0.6 | 7.6 | 13.4 | 12.0 | 7.3 | 21.9 | 0.04 |
| Total Population | 1.3 | 0.09 | 30.5 | 0.7 | 6.6 | 21.6 | 11.2 | 7.4 | 20.6 | 0.03 |

(d) By Type of House (in percentage)

| | Public Flats | | | Private Housing | | | | |
|---|---|---|---|---|---|---|---|---|
| | 1- and 2-Room | 3-Room | Others | Bungalows, Semi-detached and Terrace Houses | Flats | Shop Houses | Attap/Zinc Roofed Houses | Others[1] |
| Muslims | 21.7 | 34.8 | 12.9 | 3.1 | 1.0 | 1.4 | 19.3 | 5.8 |
| Total Population | 16.8 | 34.6 | 16.6 | 9.7 | 3.1 | 4.3 | 13.4 | 1.6 |

[1] Includes labour lines or quarters, non-residential buildings used as living quarters, such as a room in a factory, warehouse, workshop, office or school garage, out-houses, and sheds at construction sites.

SOURCE: Same as Table 3.

MUIS's role in the polity and society of Singapore was clearly enunciated in a ministerial speech:

> ... it is vital for the *majlis* and the Muslim community to maintain good rapport with each other for only in this way can the *majlis* know the views and problems and convey them accurately and adequately to the government. Conversely, it enables the *majlis* to explain relevant government policy decisions to Muslims and to assist them wherever possible.[6]

Part IV of AMLA, as noted, deals with financial aspects. For our purposes it is sufficient to take note of the following sections:

1. Section 57 — creation of a General Endowment Fund (*Baitul-Mal*).
2. Section 58 — *waqf* or *nazar* — the act empowers MUIS to appoint and remove *mutawallis* (supervisors).
3. Section 59 — all property subject to *waqf* or *nazar* "shall if situate in Singapore vest in the Majlis, without any conveyance, assignment or transfer whatever ...".
4. Sections 64 and 65 — together with an annual report, the Majlis shall publish a balance sheet and income and expenditure account to be audited and certified as correct by the Auditor-General.
5. Section 66 — each year the Majlis shall publish in the *Gazette* a list of all properties, investments, and assets vested in the Majlis subject to any trust, *waqf*, or *nazar*.
6. Section 70 — collection of *zakat* and *fitrah*.

Section 70 of the act centralized statutory collections (*zakat* and *fitrah*) and their disbursement, and made them subject to audit. Accountability, useful in itself, has a special place in Singapore's political philosophy with a strong revulsion for corrupt practices. Since all *waqf/nazar* are to be vested in MUIS, whether actually managed by it or not, control and accountability are again given special focus.

Having identified the relevant financial provisions, we shall turn to the collection and disbursement of funds, both statutory and voluntary, beginning with *zakat* and *fitrah*.

### *Zakat* and *Fitrah*

Centralized collection of *zakat* and *fitrah* was introduced by MUIS in 1968. Before its inception, *fitrah* was collected by JAMIYAH[7] (All-Malaya Muslim Missionary Society, founded in 1932), presumably on a voluntary basis. It is not known how much was collected. While *fitrah* payments are now statutory, *zakat* has not been made mandatory for two reasons: first, it is claimed that it would constitute double taxation on Muslims who are liable for income tax, and second, the absence of some competent authority to rule on default and to settle disputes.[8] A more cogent reason is an administrative one: no assessment is required for *fitrah*, but the same cannot be said for *zakat*, the payment of which demands adequate record keeping. It is interesting to note that the MUIS Fatwa Committee has recently ruled that *zakat* must be paid on contributions to Singapore's compulsory savings scheme (Central Provident Fund). Implementation as yet remains unclear. It may be noted also that *zakat* is not mandatory in many other countries in Southeast Asia.

Even though voluntary, *zakat* payments to MUIS have shown a rapidly increasing trend, with an annual average growth rate of 58.8 per cent for 1974–85 (Table 6). However, since a sizeable portion of *zakat* may be distributed to the needy directly, the data understate actual *zakat* disbursement. Collections can be expected to increase in the future with a growing number of contributors, owing to *zakat* awareness and rising incomes.

TABLE 6
*Zakat* and *Fitrah* Collections by MUIS, 1968–85[1]

| Year | Fitrah | Zakat |
|------|--------|-------|
| | S$ | S$ |
| 1968 | 393,415 | |
| 1969 | 356,158 | |
| 1970 | 347,687 | |
| 1971 | 339,408 | |
| 1972 | 354,221 | |
| 1973 | 655,212 | |
| 1974 | 779,719 | 2,052 |
| 1975 | 757,596 | 4,303 |
| 1976 | 626,718 | 15,292 |
| 1977 | 639,792 | 18,992 |
| 1978 | 717,581 | 32,592 |
| 1979 | 740,231 | 41,582 |
| 1980 | 844,308 | 44,288 |
| 1981 | 970,847 | 62,358 |
| 1982 | 947,258 | 107,457 |
| 1983 | 928,947 | 156,480 |
| 1984 | 934,949 | 257,146 |
| 1985 | 940,412 | 331,455 |
| Annual Average Rate of Growth (in percentage) | | |
| 1968–85 | 5.3 | — |
| 1974–85 | 1.7 | 58.8 |

[1] Collections correspond to Muslim year.

SOURCE: MUIS, *Annual Report* (Various years).

*Fitrah* collections, on the other hand, show a more modest rate of growth (1.7 per cent per annum during 1974–85), although they have increased almost two and a half times in absolute terms since 1968. This is to be expected given the basis of collection, the basis being the price of grains. The collections more than doubled between 1972 and 1974, when the price of rice increased sharply from S$1.20 to S$2.20 per kilogram. In the near future, only marginal growth can be expected since the Muslim population is unlikely to expand rapidly and rice prices are expected to be fairly stable.

Table 7 sets out the disbursements of the above obligatory charities during the period for which data are available. There is no consistent trend for any one item. However, a ranking of the different expenditure categories reveals that 'Riqab' (those freed from ignorance) has each year fallen between first and third. In fact in seven out of thirteen years it ranked first. In five out of thirteen years, 'Fakir and Miskin' (the destitute) ranked first. 'Muallaf' (new converts) ranked second or third in eight years. Even so, there is no easy way to predict what the future distribution and ranking of these various recipients will be, particularly since distribution is discretionary.

As detailed in Table 8, the bulk of MUIS's funds are derived from *zakat* and *fitrah* collections. Substantial sums are, however, saved each year, although between 1982 and 1985 savings fell significantly from 44 per cent in 1981 to an average of 24 per cent for 1982–85. When queried on these funds in 1978, the Minister in charge of Muslim affairs informed Parliament[9] that MUIS plans to use them for two major projects, that is, a multipurpose religious centre and the construction of mosques. The former is nearing completion and the latter is discussed in the next section.

Besides the *zakat* and *fitrah* fund, other funds, including *waqf* funds, are maintained by MUIS for specific purposes. These are discussed below.

## Waqf

The role of *waqf*, long established as an instrument of community welfare and development, is almost as old as Islam. It is a means of providing permanent support for welfare activities. Three types of *waqf* are normally distinguished: (1) *waqf zurri* (private endowment for family), (2) *waqf khairi* (established for the public interest), and (3) *waqf mustarak* (quasi public, established for the benefit of specific individuals and the community).

Private endowments are of not much relevance to this chapter. Such endowments undoubtedly exist, but no attempt has been made to ferret them out. Of greater interest are the second and third types of *waqf*. These have in Singapore, as elsewhere, led to the establishment of mosques, burial

TABLE 7

MUIS Expenditure from 'Fitrah Account', 1973–85[1]

(In percentage)

| | 1973 | 1974 | 1975 | 1976 | 1977 | 1978 | 1979 | 1980 | 1981 | 1982 | 1983 | 1984 | 1985 |
|---|---|---|---|---|---|---|---|---|---|---|---|---|---|
| Amil (Administration of Fitrah) | 18.8 (3) | 18.2 (2) | 15.8 | 14.0 | 14.6 | 15.3 | 15.7 (3) | 15.9 | 15.0 | 10.9 | 12.1 | 11.5 | 11.2 |
| Fakir and Miskin | 27.5 (1) | 32.4 (1) | 24.0 (2) | 19.7 (2) | 21.8 (2) | 18.9 (3) | 14.6 | 15.2 | 18.5 (3) | 20.7 (2) | 31.4 (1) | 31.8 (1) | 30.4 (1) |
| Muallaf | 15.3 | 13.5 | 9.9 | 16.2 | 16.7 (3) | 22.2 (2) | 21.4 (2) | 18.5 (3) | 19.9 (2) | 15.2 | 18.7 (3) | 21.6 (2) | 18.4 (3) |
| Fisabilillah | 7.9 | 12.4 | 26.5 (1) | 18.3 (3) | 15.6 | 13.8 | 15.4 | 20.6 (2) | 13.4 | 11.3 | 11.0 | 11.0 | 12.9 |
| Riqab | 22.8 (2) | 16.2 (3) | 18.6 (3) | 22.8 (1) | 28.0 (1) | 27.2 (1) | 30.5 (1) | 29.2 (1) | 31.9 (1) | 21.8 (1) | 23.9 (2) | 21.3 (3) | 22.4 (2) |
| Ibnissabil | 0.1 | 5.8 | 1.0 | 3.6 | 1.4 | 1.3 | 1.2 | – | – | 0.09 | 0.04 | 0.2 | 0.8 |
| Gharimin | 7.5 | 1.5 | 4.2 | 5.3 | 1.8 | 1.2 | 1.2 | 0.6 | 1.4 | 20.0[2] (3) | 2.9 | 2.6 | 3.9 |

[1] The time period corresponds to Muslim year.

[2] This share is unusually high due to the large amount allocated for the settlement of debts.

Figures in parentheses show ranks for the three most important items.

SOURCE: Computed from MUIS, *Annual Report* (Various years).

TABLE 8
**MUIS: Sources and Uses of Funds, 1973–85[1]**
(In S$ thousand)

| | Sources | | | Uses | |
|---|---|---|---|---|---|
| | Total | Fitrah and Zakat | Others | Zakat and Fitrah Account | Excess of Income over Expenditure[2] |
| 1973 | 388.7 | 354.2 (91.1) | 34.5 | 235.6 | 153.1 (39.4) |
| 1974 | 699.1 | 655.2 (93.7) | 43.9 | 395.8 | 303.3 (43.4) |
| 1975 | 857.8 | 757.6 (88.3) | 100.2 | 558.0 | 299.8 (34.9) |
| 1976 | 750.5 | 651.2 (86.8) | 99.3 | 488.9 | 261.6 (34.9) |
| 1977 | 749.0 | 658.8 (88.0) | 90.2 | 409.6 | 339.4 (45.3) |
| 1978 | 843.9 | 750.2 (88.9) | 93.7 | 428.9 | 415.0 (49.2) |
| 1979 | 858.4 | 781.8 (91.1) | 76.6 | 430.1 | 428.3 (49.9) |
| 1980 | 1,030.0 | 888.6 (86.3) | 141.4 | 492.7 | 537.3 (52.2) |
| 1981 | 1,385.3 | 1,033.2 (74.6) | 352.1 | 776.4 | 608.9 (44.0) |
| 1982 | 1,323.8 | 1,054.7 (79.7) | 269.1 | 1,020.5 | 303.3 (22.9) |
| 1983 | 1,197.3 | 1,085.4 (90.7) | 111.9 | 905.1 | 292.2 (24.4) |
| 1984 | 1,261.8 | 1,192.1 (94.5) | 69.7 | 933.7 | 328.1 (26.0) |
| 1985 | 1,324.2 | 1,271.9 (96.0) | 52.3 | 1,034.0 | 290.2 (21.9) |

[1] Corresponding to Muslim year.
[2] Transferred to the Baitul-Mal and Accumulated Funds.
Figures in parentheses are percentages.

SOURCE: Compiled from MUIS *Annual Report* (Various years).

grounds, *madrasah* (religious schools), orphanages, and other welfare services. Unfortunately an accurate picture of the present situation regarding such *waqf* properties is not easy to obtain. Documentation is difficult to come by, and at times it is completely lacking. Often references to these endowments surface only in the event of a dispute. Even then the case material concentrates quite naturally on disputed aspects rather than on other substantive aspects which could be of interest to us. Often, what has been at issue is the meaning of charity.[10]

The paucity of information is not due to any lack of legislation, since power to make provision for the administration of Muslim endowments dates to 1905 with the passage of the Mohamedan and Hindu Endowments Ordinance. Endowment in the act was defined to include land or money given for the support of places of worship, shrines, schools, and other pious, charitable, or beneficial purposes. The basic form of this ordinance remained unchanged even though it was superseded by the Muslim and Hindu Endowments Ordinance of 1948. Under AMLA, as noted, power to administer *waqf* properties passed over to MUIS. While the MUIS annual reports publish a list of all mosque properties vested in MUIS pursuant to Section 74 (1) of AMLA as well as a list of all properties held by it, these lists by no means exhaust all *waqf* in Singapore. Attempts to trace others which may fall under the ambit of the Trustees and Charities Acts have proved unsuccessful as there is no central register for all, least of all Muslim, trusts and charities. Part of the problem may be due to the fact that some or many *waqf* are not registered at all or may be registered under some other legislation.

As far as this writer is aware, the only comprehensive and pioneering discussion on Muslim endowments was that by Ahmad Ibrahim[11] in 1965. In this account, the history of *waqf* for which information could be obtained is briefly recounted. Most of the *waqf* pertain to mosques which are by their very nature examples *par excellence* of this institution. The mosques described in the Ahmad Ibrahim study may be termed the first-generation mosques to distinguish them from the newer, post-1975 mosques which, as discussed below, are in many respects different. In the context of *waqf*, the first-generation mosques were endowed by individuals and whose sphere of influence was a relatively small Muslim community. The second-generation mosques are built on land purchased from the state. The construction of such mosques has emanated from a parastatal body, MUIS, and as detailed below funded in a unique manner. To put it differently, the first-generation mosques are a product of *laissez-faire*, whereas the second-generation mosques are the result of intervention which permeates to the management of these mosques.

From the Ahmad Ibrahim account of *waqf*, the following points emerge:

1.  Many of the endowments, and therefore the mosques, date to the nineteenth century.
2.  The majority of the mosques were, and still are, administered by trustees under trusts created by wills or deeds.[12]
3.  Several of the mosques and *waqf* included burial grounds all of which have been closed and even exhumed (since they were located in the city).

4.  Several of the *waqf* property leases have now lapsed (they were on ninety-nine-year leases).
5.  Almost all of the *waqf* presently managed by MUIS were endowed by Indian Muslims. Most of these were taken over by the Muslim and Hindu Endowments Board due to mismanagement.
6.  The Muslimin Trust Fund Association (MTFA), registered as a company in 1904, manages a number of mosques, many of which are Arab[13] endowments. The MTFA also runs two orphanages, the Madrasah Alsagoff (and at one time also the Alsagoff dispensary), and takes care of the burial of poor Muslims. The SMA Alsagoff Wakaf Fund and MTFA owe their foundation to a wealthy Arab trader, SMA Alsagoff, also the benefactor of the Madrasah Alsagoff. The SMA Alsagoff Wakaf Fund is reported to yield an annual income of S$120,000. Of this 21 per cent is allocated to MTFA, 8 per cent for the Madrasah, and 3 per cent for the maintenance of the Hajjah Fatimah Mosque.[14]
7.  The All-Malaya Muslim Missionary Society (JAMIYAH) manages several mosques, in addition to its other activities.

The only *waqf* for which relatively systematic information is available are those managed by MUIS. MUIS inherited ten such endowments from the Muslim and Hindu Endowments Board. Two have since been dissolved: Wakaf Khadijah in 1976 as "it was no longer possible to beneficially carry out its provisions";[15] and Wakaf Tantwalla, whose terms and objects were unclear, was wound up in 1977 and the balance was distributed in accordance with Section 62 (2) of AMLA.[16] Table 9 describes the nature of these *waqf*. As can be observed from this table, for the most part they comprise shops and dwelling houses frequently adjoining mosques. Table 10 details the sources and uses of the funds of these *waqf*. Excluding compensation for land acquired by the government from one *waqf*, the bulk of their income in 1985 was derived from 'interest from banks' (6.0 per cent). In the absence of an Islamic financial institution, fixed deposits are perhaps a convenient channel for the use of funds. Rent generated another 19.0 per cent. The low share of rent (gross) is attributable to the rent control to which the bulk of the properties were subjected. Redevelopment which is being planned[17] could augment this source of income.

Aside from the lapse of *waqf* properties due to the expiry of their leases, several others, including mosques, have been adversely affected by the compulsory acquisition of land by the government for urban renewal and development. Singapore Muslims have viewed with concern the demolition of their mosques as land upon which they stand is regarded as inalienable. Twenty-five mosques have been demolished since 1968, whereas between 1975 and 1986, eight new mosques have been built.[18]

Compared to other religious edifices, mosques are apparently less adversely affected by urban renewal. The MUIS 1973 *Annual Report* noted that:

In fact mosques are least affected as during the past 10 years only 11 mosques had to make way for public development schemes, while 172 temples were affected.[19]

Other mosques have been spared by the government bulldozer upon being declared national monuments; five fall into this category.[20] Others affected by urban renewal are allocated alternative sites. The first mosque to be built in Singapore, Masjid Omar Kampong Melaka, is to be retained even though not designated a national monument. The situation is, therefore, fairly varied.

We turn now to the second-generation mosques whose building and management are reflective of the institutionalized approach in fund mobilization. The unique feature of this second generation of mosques is the method of funding their construction cost. Other special features include their size, location, and role as mini-Islamic community centres.

In September 1975, MUIS inaugurated the Mosque Building Fund (MBF) into which Muslim employees, employers, and self-employed contribute voluntarily each month a specified minimum sum. When the scheme started, the minimum contribution was S$1.00; this has since doubled. MUIS utilizes the machinery of Singapore's compulsory saving scheme, the Central Provident Fund (CPF) for this purpose. This is not costless since it pays the CPF S$12,000 per month for the service.[21] Even so, this centralized collection not only ensures a regular flow of funds and facilitates planning, it also reduces transaction costs, since it is no longer necessary to solicit donations periodically. There is thus participation by Muslims en masse in the building of new mosques. It is a method reflective of Singapore's development philosophy — that of self-help, especially with respect to financing. For a country with a Muslim minority, Singapore is probably the only country in the world which has successfully systematized collections for the construction of mosques.

From its inception in 1975 till end-1985, MBF collections totalled S$26 million.[22] Ten mosques have been built; five more would be completed by the end of the 1980s. With the completion of the second phase of mosque building at the end of the 1980s, would the MBF scheme be disbanded? This seems unlikely, according to MUIS, which hopes to use the money for mosque maintenance and refurnishing.

At present the MBF can only be used for the purchase of land and construction of new mosques. Aside from the grants to *amil* (collectors) provided by MUIS, the operational costs of the new mosques are financed from public donations. Data available only for 1981 indicate that these are not insubstantial (see Table 11 [a]). The second-generation mosques are built on land leased from the government. Unlike the first-generation mosques, they do not have

## TABLE 9
### Properties Held by Majlis Ugama Islam Singapura as at 31 December 1985

| Situation of Property | Lot and Town Sub-Division or Mukim | Description | Cost of Land S$ | Cost of Building S$ |
|---|---|---|---|---|
| **A. *Waqf*/Endowments** | | | | |
| | **1. Coronation Road Mosque Endowment** | | | |
| (a) Land at Coronation Road (Jalan Haji Alias) | Lots 83, 84, and 85, Mukim IV | Al-Huda Mosque (34 Jalan Haji Alias) and vacant land | – | – |
| | **2. Alkaff Mosque Endowment** | | | |
| (a) Pheng Geck Avenue | Lot 4-37 Sub-division 2307, Mukim XXIV | Vacant land let to MTFA for building of an orphanage | 1 | – |
| (b) Pheng Geck Avenue | Lot 4-37 Sub-division 2308, Mukim XXIV | Vacant land | | |
| (c) 120, 120A, 122, 122A Upper Serangoon Road, and vacant land at Pheng Geck Avenue | Lot 869 pt (41.27) and Sub-division 488-1, Mukim XXIV | Shops, dwelling houses, Alkaff Mosque and vacant land (vacant land let to MTFA for building of an orphanage) | – | 1 |
| | **3. Arab Street Educational Trust Fund** | | | |
| (a) 63, 63A and 63B Temple Street | Lot 349-2 TS VI | Shops and dwelling houses | – | 1,255 |
| | **4. Gaffoor Endowment** | | | |
| (a) 21/39 (odd numbers) Dunlop Street 43/55 (odd numbers) Dunlop Street | Lot 85 pt TS XVI | Shops and dwelling houses Shops and dwelling houses | 1 | 1 |
| (b) 14 Mayo Street 36 Mayo Street | Lot 76 pt TS XVI | Dwelling house Dwelling house | | |
| (d) 25 Mayo Street | | Vacant land | | |
| (e) 41 Dunlop Street | Lot 85 pt TS XVI | Abdul Gaffoor Mosque and out-houses | | |

TABLE 9 (*continued*)

**Properties Held by Majlis Ugama Islam Singapura**
**as at 31 December 1985**

| Situation of Property | Lot and Town Sub-Division or Mukim | Description | Cost of Land S$ | Cost of Building S$ |
|---|---|---|---|---|
| 5. | Habib Noh Endowment | | | |
| (a) Land at Palmer Road | Lot 748 TS XXIII | Habib Noh Tomb and staircases, Haji Mohd Salleh Mosque, old cemetery (closed), and vacant land | 1 | — |
| 6. | Jamae Mosque Endowment | | | |
| (a) 196 Telok Ayer Street | Lot 233-2, TS III | Dwelling houses or quarters adjoining mosque | 1 | — |
| (b) 190/190A Telok Ayer Street | Lot 233-2 TS III | Dwelling house | | |
| (c) 192 Telok Ayer Street | Lot 233-2 TS III | Masjid Al-Abrar (Kuchupally Mosque) | 1 | |
| (d) 140 Telok Ayer Street | Lot 244-1, 244-2 TS III | Durgha Shrine | | — |
| (e) 117, 117A and 117B Telok Ayer Street 119, 119A and 119B Telok Ayer Street 121, 121A and 121B Telok Ayer Street | Lots 40-1, 40-2, and 40-3 TS II | Shops and dwelling houses | — | 1 |
| (f) 24 and 24A Pagoda Street 26 and 26A Pagoda Street 28 and 28A Pagoda Street 30 and 30A Pagoda Street | Lot 260 TS VI | Shops and dwelling houses | — | 1 |
| (g) 214 and 216 South Bridge Road | Lot 260 TS VI | Shops and dwelling houses | | |
| (h) 218 South Bridge Road | Lot 260 TS VI | Jamae Mosque | | 1 |
| (i) 226/232 (even numbers) South Bridge Road | Lot 260 TS VI | Shops and dwelling houses | — | |

TABLE 9 (continued)

**Properties Held by Majlis Ugama Islam Singapura
as at 31 December 1985**

| Situation of Property | Lot and Town Sub-Division or Mukim | Description | Cost of Land S$ | Cost of Building S$ |
|---|---|---|---|---|
| | 7. Kassim Mosque Endowment | | | |
| (a) Vacant land | Lots 343/27, 343/67, 343/64, 343/34, Mukim XXVI | Shops and dwelling houses | 1 | — |
| (b) 432/448 (even numbers) Changi Road | Lots 1375 (Lots 343/27 and 343/67) | Kassim Mosque | | |
| (c) 450 Changi Road | Lot 343-67 pt, Mukim XXVI | | | |
| (d) Land at Siglap Road | Lots 3-1, 3-2, 3-6, 3-7, Mukim XXVII | Burial ground (Kubur Kassim) (closed) | | |
| | **B. Baitul-Mal (General Endowment)** | | | |
| (a) 10 Gentle Road (Kg Pasiran) | Lot 89-1 and Lot 90 Town Sub-division XXVIII | Abdul Hamid Mosque and vacant land | 1 | — |
| (b) 24 Pheng Geck Avenue | Lot 514/125, Mukim XXIV | Land and semi-detached bungalow house | 1 | — |
| (c) Land at Toa Payoh | Lot 5340 (Resurvey), Mukim XVII | Site for Singapore Islamic Centre | 332,121 | — |
| (d) Land at Tiong Bahru | Lot 364, Mukim I | Additional land for Jamiyah Rabitah Mosque | 187,744 | — |
| | **C. Mosques Built under the MBF Scheme** | | | |
| (a) Muhajirin Mosque (Toa Payoh) Braddell Road | Lot 4180, Mukim XVII | Land and building for mosque | 86,879 | 832,819 |
| (b) Mujahidin Mosque (Queenstown) 590 Stirling Road | Lot 1510, Mukim III | Land and building for mosque | 129,158 | 898,534 |

TABLE 9 (continued)
## Properties Held by Majlis Ugama Islam Singapura
### as at 31 December 1985

| Situation of Property | Lot and Town Sub-Division or Mukim | Description | Cost of Land S$ | Cost of Building S$ |
|---|---|---|---|---|
| (c) Assyakirin Mosque (Jurong) Yung An Road | Lot 1082, Mukim VI (after resurvey) | Land and building for mosque | 127,931 | 1,143,020 |
| (d) An-Nur Mosque (Woodlands) Admiralty Road | Lot 1072, Mukim XIII (after resurvey) | Land and building for mosque | 146,959 | 1,862,219 |
| (e) Al-Ansar Mosque (Chai Chee/ Bedok New Town) | Lot 2393, Mukim XXVIII (after resurvey) | Land and building for mosque | 140,577 | 1,501,401 |
| (f) Al-Muttaqin (Ang Mo Kio) Avenue 6 | Lot 7975, Mukim XVIII (after resurvey) | Land and building for mosque | 169,987 | 1,839,470 |
| (g) En-Naeem Mosque (Tampines/ Hougang Avenue 3) | Lot 3788, Mukim XXII (after resurvey) | Land and building for mosque | 337,256 | 2,601,296 |
| (h) Proposed Darul Aman Mosque (Changi Road/Jalan Eunos) | Lot 1864 pt, Mukim XXIII | Land for construction of mosque | 380,805 | * |
| | | | 2,039,426 | 10,680,019 |

* Cost of construction has not been finalized yet.

Of the eight mosques mentioned above, the state lease for land occupied by Mujahidin Mosque, Assyakirin Mosque, An-Nur Mosque, Al-Ansar Mosque, and Al-Muttaqin Mosque only had been obtained.

SOURCE: MUIS, *Annual Report 1985.*

TABLE 10
Majlis Ugama Islam Singapura
*Waqf* Funds
Statement of Financial Position as at 31 December 1985

| | Al-Huda | Alkaff | Angulia | Arab Street Educational Trust | Gaffoor | Habib Noh | Jamae | Kassim | Total |
|---|---|---|---|---|---|---|---|---|---|
| | S$ | S$ | S$ | S$ | S$ | S$ | S$ | S$ | S$ |
| Balance at 1 January | 1,004 | 21,963 | 1,430 | 112,511 | 915,642 | 688,192 | 238,031 | 1,442 | 1,980,215 |
| Add: | | | | | | | | | |
| Rent | 240 | 2,004 | 1,208 | 3,135 | 6,316 | — | 24,941 | 9,614 | 47,458 |
| Chest Collection | — | — | — | — | 4,033 | 9,724 | 929 | — | 14,686 |
| Interest from Banks | 35 | 1,367 | 8,389 | 8,015 | 72,995 | 52,470 | 17,450 | 45 | 160,766 |
| General Donations | — | — | — | — | 3,183 | 7,306 | 1,250 | 2,615 | 14,354 |
| Grant from *Baitul-Mal* | — | — | — | — | — | — | — | 14,000 | 14,000 |
| Compensation for Land Acquired by Government | — | — | 616,511 | — | — | — | — | — | 616,511 |
| | 1,279 | 25,334 | 627,538 | 123,661 | 1,002,169 | 757,692 | 282,601 | 27,716 | 2,847,990 |
| Less: | | | | | | | | | |
| Expenditure on Manpower | — | — | 7,760 | — | 10,480 | 4,338 | 19,254 | 13,864 | 55,696 |
| Public Utilities | — | — | 6,150 | — | 6,638 | 860 | 9,287 | 6,776 | 29,711 |
| Property Tax | — | 427 | 179 | 252 | 897 | — | 5,744 | 374 | 7,873 |
| Audit Fee | 74 | 186 | 374 | 300 | 376 | 4,780 | 3,208 | 563 | 9,861 |
| Commission on Rent | 12 | 100 | 60 | 153 | 419 | — | 1,035 | 487 | 2,266 |
| Distribution of Rice | — | — | — | — | — | — | — | — | |
| Depreciation | — | — | — | — | — | 14,666 | — | — | 14,666 |
| Allowance to Descendants | — | — | — | 419 | — | — | — | — | 419 |
| Educational Grants | — | — | — | — | — | 2,800 | — | — | 2,800 |
| Valuation and Legal Fees | — | — | 10,165 | 1,500 | — | — | — | — | 11,665 |
| Maintenance and Renovation | 360 | — | 15,856 | — | — | — | 116 | 505 | 16,837 |
| Insurance Premium | 31 | 43 | — | 10 | 165 | 31 | 358 | 73 | 711 |
| Miscellaneous | — | — | — | — | 78 | 69 | — | — | 147 |
| | 477 | 756 | 40,544 | 2,634 | 19,053 | 27,544 | 39,002 | 22,642 | 152,652 |

TABLE 10 *(continued)*
**Majlis Ugama Islam Singapura**
*Waqf* **Funds**
**Statement of Financial Position as at 31 December 1985**

| | Al-Huda | Alkaff | Angulia | Arab Street Educational Trust | Gaffoor | Habib Noh | Jamae | Kassim | Total |
|---|---|---|---|---|---|---|---|---|---|
| | S$ | S$ | S$ | S$ | S$ | S$ | S$ | S$ | S$ |
| Balance at 31 December | 802 | 24,578 | 586,994 | 121,027 | 983,116 | 730,148 | 243,599 | 5,074 | 2,695,338 |
| Represented by: | | | | | | | | | |
| FIXED ASSETS | | | | | | | | | |
| Land and Buildings | 1 | 2 | — | 1,255 | 2 | 1 | 5 | 1 | 1,267 |
| CURRENT ASSETS | | | | | | | | | |
| Sundry Debtors, Deposits, and Prepayments | 161 | 43 | 7,446 | 91 | 6,350 | 31 | 6,938 | 2,743 | 23,803 |
| Fixed Deposits | — | 14,000 | 559,000 | 115,450 | 970,000 | 707,000 | 228,000 | — | 2,593,450 |
| Cash and Bank Balances | 764 | 11,570 | 21,208 | 5,385 | 8,038 | 30,559 | 14,098 | 3,863 | 95,485 |
| | 926 | 25,615 | 587,654 | 122,181 | 984,390 | 737,591 | 249,041 | 6,607 | 2,714,005 |
| CURRENT LIABILITIES | | | | | | | | | |
| Rent and Other Deposits | — | 157 | — | 575 | 591 | — | 500 | 350 | 2,173 |
| Sundry Creditors and Accruals | 124 | 880 | 660 | 579 | 683 | 7,443 | 4,942 | 1,183 | 16,494 |
| | 802 | 24,578 | 586,994 | 121,027 | 983,116 | 730,148 | 243,599 | 5,074 | 2,695,338 |

SOURCE: MUIS, *Annual Report 1985*.

TABLE 11
**Sources and Uses of Funds of Six New-Generation
Mosques in 1981**

(a) Average Monthly Donations Received (outside the MBF)

| Donation Sources | Combined Average S$ |
|---|---|
| Friday prayers | 2,980 |
| House-to-house | 1,070 |
| Public lectures | 660 |
| Religious events | 960 |
| Educational classes | 3,450 |
| Other donations and revenue | 5,270 |
| Total | 14,390 |

(b) Average Monthly Donations Received and
Average Monthly Operational Expenditure

| Donations Received | Expenditure* | Nett |
|---|---|---|
| S$14,390 | S$8,140 | + S$6,250 |

* With the exception of nominal subsidies received from the Muslim Religious Council (MUIS) to supplement the allowance of *imam* and religious teachers, the expenditures of the mosques are fully borne by the mosques. The finances required for meeting the operational expenditures are raised through donations and other fund-raising activities organized by the mosques themselves.

SOURCE: Mansor Haji Sukaimi, *Dynamic Functions of Mosques — The Singapore Experience* (Singapore: MUIS, 1982), pp. 12–13.

*waqf* properties set aside for their maintenance. Public donations are thus crucial for them. It is interesting to note that the new-generation mosques for which data are available appear self-sufficient in so far as their current expenditure requirements are concerned (see Table 11 [b]). Again, the philosophy of self-reliance speaks well for the mosque management committees and the generosity of the *ummah*.

In addition to the MBF, MUIS maintains several other 'Miscellaneous Funds' monies, some of which are used for mosque reconstruction and maintenance (see Table 12). This strategy augurs well for the mosque population in Singapore, many of which are now quite old.

TABLE 12
**Summary of MUIS Fund Balances, 1980–85**
(S$ million)

| | Baitul-Mal | Mosques and MENDAKI Fund | *Waqf* Funds | Mosque Reconstruction Fund [2] | Miscellaneous Funds [1] | |
| --- | --- | --- | --- | --- | --- | --- |
| | | | | | Satellite Town Mosque Maintenance Fund [3] | Other Mosque Maintenance Fund [4] |
| 1985 | 10.8 | 25.8 | 2.7 | 1.2 | 2.2 | 1.2 |
| 1984 | 9.5 | 22.5 | 2.0 | 1.1 | 1.5 | 0.9 |
| 1983 | 8.4 | 18.5 | 1.8 | 2.5 | n.a. | 0.9 |
| 1982 | 4.6 | 14.9 | 0.8 | 2.7 | n.a. | n.a. |
| 1981 | 4.0 | 11.2 | n.a. | 2.3 | n.a. | n.a. |
| 1980 | 1.6 | 8.5 | 0.6 | 0.6 | n.a. | n.a. |

[1] This comprises 18 separate funds, 13 of which are trust funds for purposes designated by the original benefactors. (For details see MUIS, *Annual Report 1985*, pp. 36–37.) The remainder are for mosque maintenance and missionary and welfare activities.

[2] Fund set up to finance renovation and reconstruction of mosques.

[3] This fund is to be used for the maintenance of satellite town (new) mosques.

[4] This fund represents compensation monies received for mosques compulsorily acquired by the government. The fund is used to finance repairs, renovations, additions, and alterations of mosques.

n.a. — not available.

SOURCE: MUIS, *Annual Report* (Various years).

The second-generation mosques were earlier referred to as Islamic community centres. One study describes these mosques as being dynamic[23] as they serve as focal points not only for worship, but also for education and other activities. Their regular activities and patronage are listed in Tables 13 and 14, respectively. Perhaps the range of activities provided is partly an attempt to reconstitute the fabric of community and religious life left behind due to resettlement.

TABLE 13
**Regular Activities of Second-Generation Mosques in Singapore**

| Educational | Religious | Family and Welfare |
| --- | --- | --- |
| Kindergartens | Daily prayers | Marriage counselling courses |
| Religious classes for children and adults | Friday prayers | Provision of free meals for the breaking of fast during Ramadhan |
| Courses on the management of the *jenazah* | Tarawih and the Eid-ul-Fitri/the Eid-ul-Adha congregational prayers | Meetings/dialogue sessions organized by local Muslim organizations |
| Courses for pilgrims | Aqiqah/Korban | |
| Religious forums | Religious lectures by local and foreign speakers | Visits by foreign and local Muslim delegations |
| Debates | *Fitrah* collections | Fund-raising activities |
| | Awal Muharam | Exhibitions on drug abuse |
| | Maulidin Nabi | *Akad Nikah* (Solemnization of Marriages) |
| | Israk Mikraj | |
| | Berzanji Competition | |
| | Qur'an Reading Competition | |
| | Thanksgiving Service | |

SOURCE: *New Generation of Mosques and Their Activities* (Singapore: MUIS, 1986), p. 10.

Table 14 indicates that mosque activities are widely patronized. This may be attributed to mosque locations which capture large population catchments. Based on *fitrah* collections for 1981, the estimated Muslim population around the six new mosques ranges between 8,000 and 35,000. This compares

TABLE 14
**Extent of Participation by Selected Mosque Activities, 1981**
(Combined averages for all six mosques)

| Activities | Number of Times Held in 1981 | Number of Participants Per Session |
|---|---|---|
| 1. Kindergartens | 230 | 75 |
| 2. Religious classes (children) | 170 | 970 |
| 3. Religious classes (adults) | 290 | 1,780 |
| 4. Courses for *hajj* pilgrims | 20 | 190 |
| 5. Circumcision | 2 | 45 |
| 6. Aqiqah Korban | 1 | 60 |
| 7. Religious events (e.g. Awal Muharam, Maulid, Israk Mikraj) | 4 | 1,300 |
| 8. Religious lectures | 10 | 1,230 |

SOURCE: Mansor Haji Sukaimi, *Dynamic Functions of Mosques — The Singapore Experience* (Singapore: MUIS, 1982), p. 10.

favourably with a range of between 1,000 and 6,000 for the older mosques.[24] The larger population bases generate various economies of scale and are reflected in both the variety of programmes offered and the high participation rates. Additional benefits include the large corps of volunteers who help run the activities and the substantial public donations.

While the spatial distribution (or perhaps redistribution) of population in Singapore around the public housing estates has led to ethnic integration, many traditional voluntary organizations (including Muslim) have lost their roots. In their place have emerged at the national level, community centres. At a subnational level, it seems as if the new mosques have assumed the form of community centres in another respect, that is, religious.

Like the community centres and residents' committees which are sponsored and controlled by the government, mosque activities are co-ordinated by MUIS through a facilitation committee named LARAS. This too differentiates them from the first-generation mosques which functioned largely as individual, local entities. Such co-ordination is viewed as being "consistent with the concept of the mosques being institutions that actively promote the collectivity of the 'Ummah'".[25]

But therein may lie a dilemma. As Muslims, especially the Malays, identify more with mosque activities, this affects their integration with the rest of Singapore society.

## Education

More than any other religion, Islam emphasizes the importance of learning and the acquisition of knowledge. It is, therefore, not surprising that Islamic education has always been a central concern of Muslims in Singapore from the time of their earliest settlement. This is manifest in a number of forms: at a formal, institutionalized level, there are full-time and part-time *madrasah*; informal (although institutionalized) support for education, religious and secular, is provided through bursary and scholarship schemes and most recently MENDAKI (Council for the Education of Muslim Children); and not the least through missionary activities which may be regarded as a recommended charity. Until fairly recently, traditional voluntary organizations were largely responsible for Islamic education. This *laissez-faire* approach is gradually being replaced by a more interventionist approach, as manifest in the centralization of activities.

Madrasah
Islam is known to have been established in Singapore at the end of the thirteenth century. Around this time, the established mode of religious teaching was private tuition, either in the homes of pupils or teachers. In the early nineteenth century, Qur'an schools were known to have existed in mosques, *surau*, and teachers' homes.[26] *Madrasah*, as we know of them today, made their appearance from the early twentieth century. Established by wealthy Arabs, these *madrasah* were endowed with some of their properties, the income from which provided the finance for their management and maintenance.[27] These early *madrasah* are described as being Arab-centric: the early teachers came from Arabia and the curriculum was focused largely on Arabic (including Islamic) Studies. They thus not only helped spread literacy and education, but simultaneously helped preserve the cultural identity of the Arabs. Additionally, as pointed out by one study,[28] Singapore gained eminence as an Islamic examination centre for the southern part of West Malaysia in those days.

This early Islamic education had two characteristics: it was almost wholly non-secular and was financed by individuals either through *waqf* or donations.

The *madrasah* continue to exist today: as at June 1986, there were nine, five primary and four secondary. Even though there is a paucity of both studies and data on them, the available statistics suggest that their numbers and thus their role have dwindled considerably (see Table 15). The preference for secular education has evidently taken its toll on full-time Islamic education, which at present is not wholly non-secular and also receives financial assistance from the Singapore government. Nominal fees are charged to students to defray costs, especially teachers' salaries, which are also supplemented by MUIS.

TABLE 15
Islamic Schools in Singapore, 1967–86*

| Year | Government Aided | Private |
|------|------------------|---------|
| 1967 | 25 | n.a. |
| 1968 | 20 | n.a. |
| 1969 | 24 | n.a. |
| 1970 | 23 | n.a. |
| 1971 | 18 | 5 |
| 1972 | 19 | 5 |
| 1973 | 19 | 5 |
| 1974 | 19 | 4 |
| 1975 | 19 | 4 |
| 1976 | 17 | 5 |
| 1977 | 15 | 5 |
| 1978 | 13 | 5 |
| 1979 | 13 | 4 |
| 1980 | 13 | 4 |
| 1981 | 13 | 4 |
| 1982 | 12 | 5 |
| 1983 | 12 | 5 |
| 1984 | 10 | 5 |
| 1985 | 9 | 4 |
| 1986 | 9 | 3 |

* As at June.
n.a. — not available.
SOURCE: *Directory of Schools and Educational Institutions*
(Singapore: Ministry of Education, various years).

Aside from providing grants to approved *madrasah*, the Singapore government's role with respect to Muslim religious education in the 1960s was to make it compulsory for all Malay schools to provide religious instruction and some scholarships to the Muslim College in Klang, West Malaysia, and Al-Azhar University in Cairo.[29] With the publication of the Goh Report in 1978, the teaching of religion as an examination subject became compulsory for secondary schools.[30] Muslim secondary students are thus offered Islamic religious knowledge.

However, the government's role is larger than may be suggested by the above remarks since MUIS is vested with power under AMLA to control all Muslim religious schools. Under the law, it has the power to register, control, and approve curricula, inspect schools, and examine teachers. Apparently all sections of AMLA, except Sections 81 and 82 which pertain to religious schools and grants to religious schools respectively, have been brought into force.

*Madrasah* have featured regularly among the queries raised on Muslim affairs in Singapore's Parliament. These have centred on a number of issues:[31] the absence of a common curriculum and unified administration of Islamic education, the quality of its teachers, and the limited finances of the *madrasah* which are largely dependent on donations.

Perhaps equally critical is the fact that 95 per cent of the full-time *madrasah* students are female.[32] The majority of students who pursue tertiary Islamic education are also female. Since *ulama* and *imam* are traditionally male, this has certain implications for Islamic religious leadership in the country.

With respect to *madrasah* management, a ministerial reply in 1973 indicated that MUIS was not yet ready to take over the management of all religious schools in Singapore.[33] In 1982, it was pointed out that there was a lack of manpower in MUIS to set up a special unit to supervise and inspect *madrasah* and examine their teachers.[34] More recently, the Minister in charge stated that MUIS, with the assistance of MENDAKI, was making a comprehensive study of various aspects of the *madrasah* system with a view to implementing Sections 81 and 82 of AMLA.[35] This study has been completed and accepted by MUIS, and steps are being taken to implement a common curriculum in the *madrasah*.

Although formal full-time Islamic education has declined in importance, there is a great deal of interest in part-time education. There are some thirty part-time *madrasah*.[36] Many are located in mosques where religious instruction using a standard syllabus compiled by MUIS is provided three to five times a week for two to three hours a day. This instruction is available to both children and adults. According to the MUIS 1984 *Annual Report*, more Muslims are participating in such activities, which is indicative of the growing religious awareness.[37]

Religious instruction is also offered by the JAMIYAH Singapore. Some 7,000 students are reported to be taking religious and secular courses organized by it in fifteen educational centres.[38] Included in these is Qur'an reading for the blind. This and JAMIYAH's other activities are funded from donations and other fund-raising projects and supported by a group of volunteers many of whom are professionals (who help run medical and legal activities). To some extent, the activities of this and other similar groups are symptomatic of welfare activities in Islam.

## Financial Support for Education

Somewhat different in scope is the regular financial support for education in the form of bursaries and study grants provided by MUIS and Lembaga Biasiswa Kenangan Maulud (LBKM). The latter, as its name suggests, was established in 1965 to commemorate the *maulud* (Prophet's birthday) celebrations. It derives its funds solely from donations and fund-raising activities. During 1983–85, it received S$15,000 annually from the Saudi Arabian Embassy for its bursaries which are granted to secondary-school and tertiary-institute students. It also disburses bursaries on behalf of Wakaf Angulia which started with a contribution of S$4,500 in 1970; this has now reached around S$60,000 per year.[39] To provide a notion of the magnitudes involved in the support of education, the disbursements are listed in Table 16. Taken together, the amounts involved appear substantial, but as in most welfare activities, they may barely scratch the surface. Still, particularly in the case of the LBKM, its activities represent a major voluntary effort.

TABLE 16
**Bursary and Study Grant Awards by LBKM and MUIS, 1966–85**
(Singapore dollars)

| Year | LBKM | LBKM for Wakaf Angulia | MUIS | |
|------|------|------|------|------|
| | | | Bursaries | Study Grants |
| 1966 | 3,900 | | | |
| 1967 | 12,052 | | | |
| 1968 | 17,361 | | | |
| 1969 | 22,180 | | | |
| 1970 | 23,855 | | | |
| 1971 | 17,650 | | | |
| 1972 | 14,900 | 39,000 | | |
| 1973 | 19,475 | | | |
| 1974 | 19,505 | | 107,300 | 5,130 |
| 1975 | 19,060 | | 89,545 | 17,173 |
| 1976 | 18,875 | n.a. | 93,250 | 17,751 |
| 1977 | 20,470 | n.a. | 98,480 | 14,300 |
| 1978 | 44,397 | n.a. | 98,100 | 17,446 |
| 1979 | 32,768 | n.a. | 100,000 | 18,530 |
| 1980 | 32,023 | 50,000 | 100,000 | 29,795 |
| 1981 | n.a. | 50,000 | 130,210 | 32,271 |
| 1982 | n.a. | 50,000 | 139,360 | 39,695 |
| 1983 | 42,075 | 48,024 | 139,360 | 40,336 |
| 1984 | 55,300 | 53,050 | 141,960 | 31,373 |
| 1985 | 66,700 | 55,375 | 157,420 | 44,905 |

n.a. — not available.

SOURCES: LBKM Souvenir Publications; and MUIS, *Annual Report* (Various years).

*MENDAKI — Its Genesis and Activities*

From our discussion of the socio-economic profile of Muslims in 1980, the following features were noted: 90 per cent of the Muslims were Malays; both the educational attainment and economic status of Muslims were generally significantly lower than the rest of the population. This is not a new development. Ever since Singapore attained self-government in 1959, the People's Action Party (PAP), the ruling party forming the government, has shown a keen awareness of the problem, recognizing its political overtones. This awareness is reflected in a number of ways and at different levels. First, the special position of the Malays is enshrined in Article 89 (2) of the Constitution of Singapore which states that the government

> shall exercise its functions in such a manner as to recognize the special position of the Malays, who are the indigenous people of the state, and accordingly it shall be the responsibility of the Government to protect, safeguard, support, foster and promote their educational, religious, economic, social and cultural interests and the Malay language.[40]

Accordingly education (at all levels) is free for the Malays, and there is provision for special Malay bursaries at the tertiary level.

Second, after Singapore's independence (separation from Malaysia) in 1965, no less than the Prime Minister assured that

> government, with the support of the non-Malays, is prepared to concentrate more than the average share of their resources to our Malay citizens.[41]

Third, in the PAP organization, there has always been a Malay affairs bureau to channel matters to the leadership; there is at present a Minister in charge of Muslim affairs. Fourth, recognizing the separateness of Muslim law, there is AMLA, the establishment and support of MUIS and its activities, and more recently MENDAKI.

Since independence, the Singapore economy experienced rapid economic growth and structural transformation. Significant improvements in the standard of living followed. Yet, as noted, Malay-Muslim problems remain.

The Council for the Education of Muslim Children (MENDAKI) was formed in August 1981. Its prime movers, all nine Malay Members of Parliament and representatives of eleven major Malay organizations, saw in it a consolidation of effort and a national movement for the educational advancement of Muslims, especially children. Its strategy is comprehensive in two ways: resources are pooled and the problem to be addressed has a pyramid approach. Following the example of the Mosque Building Fund, it calls on every working Muslim to have a small monthly contribution deducted from his salary (the present rate is 50 cents) or to make GIRO contributions. These schemes began, respectively, in October and September 1984. The amounts collected were: S$1.6 million through the Central Provident Fund machinery and S$0.27 million through GIRO for the period 1984–86.[42] Over and above these, the following amounts were donated to the foundation:

|      | S$         |
|------|------------|
| 1982 | 457,373.84 |
| 1983 | 289,933.10 |
| 1984 | 151,427.88 |
| 1985 | 432,949.18 |
| 1986 | 120,730.55 |

Between 1984 and 1987 the only foreign donor, the Aga Khan, contributed S$500,000. Thus, the sources of funds are largely local. The bulk of the funds are used to support students to remain in school longer so that they can improve their educational attainments.

With respect to education, a pyramid approach is adopted. This term is used to denote its coverage[43] (all levels of formal, especially secular, education), parental involvement, and student counselling. Past efforts of other Muslim organizations providing support for education, as discussed earlier, have taken the form largely of financial assistance through bursaries, study grants, and other aids. True, some Malay organizations (such as the Malay Teachers' Union and the Malay Literary and Youth Organization) were providing tuition classes, but only on a rather limited scale. MENDAKI is thus attempting to marshall not only larger financial but also manpower resources (principally teachers) to assist in its special tuition classes. It is worthwhile to note that in organizing its activities care has been taken not to duplicate the efforts of other organizations.

The former Prime Minister, speaking at the opening ceremony of the MENDAKI Congress, noted that

> Mendaki's real achievement will be to raise the educational levels, and thus living standards of the majority, and not the minority who make it to the top.[44]

Thus far, tuition classes (which are heavily subsidized) have been started for students taking the Primary School Leaving Examination (PSLE) and A-level (pre-university) students in English, the General Paper, and Economics. These and the foundation's financial assistance and post-graduate bursaries have been well patronized.[45] Other aspects of its wide-ranging programme are at various stages of implementation.

With respect to enlarging its financial resources, MENDAKI hopes to obtain government approval to double the rate of contribution from S$0.50 to S$1.00.[46] Other possible sources which the foundation hopes to tap are the *fitrah* and *zakat* accounts, and the development of *waqf* properties.[47]

The MENDAKI programme, while broad based and ambitious, is geared towards improving the educational attainment of potential entrants to the labour market. However, the educational attainment of those in the labour force also demands attention. According to the 1980 census of population, 25 per cent of the working Malays had no qualifications, while 59 per cent of them had only primary education. A variety of programmes exist for the skill enhancement of the labour force. MENDAKI could usefully encourage and assist Muslim employees to participate in these programmes, so that they can earn more. This, in turn, will place them in a better position to enhance the education of their children.

Finally, the MENDAKI exercise, described as "a serious and unprecedented experiment of self-help and self-reliance", will be watched with interest both within and outside Singapore as the foundation attempts to realize its ambitious goals.

## Welfare and Missionary Activities

Owing to space constraints this section in the main highlights the activities of only two prominent private or voluntary organizations in the area of welfare, defined broadly to include missionary activities. MUIS, more recently, has established missionary activities with a comprehensive organizational frame-work to parallel the spatial distribution of Muslims. This is also examined in this section.

### Muslimin Trust Fund Association

The Muslimin Trust Fund Association (MTFA), established in 1904, is the oldest Muslim welfare organization in Singapore. Its most significant activity is the establishment of two orphanages, Darul Ihsan for boys (in 1904) and Darul Ihsan Lilbanat for girls (in 1980). Funded entirely from voluntary dona-tions, these institutions have been self-sufficient since 1964.[48] Apart from taking care of the maintenance and educational (religious and secular) needs of the orphans, Darul Ihsan also provides educational assistance to non-resident Muslim orphans. This takes one of two forms:

1.  Free textbooks and stationery to primary, secondary, and pre-university students and book allowances to vocational, polytechnic, and university students. When this scheme was started in 1977 there were 380 recipients. This had more than doubled by 1983.
2.  Begun in 1980, the external aid scheme aims to help non-resident orphans meet their daily school needs. Starting with 12 recipients in 1980, the number increased to 115 by 1984.[49]

In addition to the above, the MTFA arranges for the burial of unclaimed Muslim dead and manages four mosques and the Madrasah Alsagoff, as noted earlier.

## Other Welfare Societies

There are numerous other benevolent, welfare societies whose activities are little known. Even an exact number is not easy to come by. A JAMIYAH publication[50] listed sixty-six benevolent societies in 1985. Their number increases to eighty if so-called religious societies (fourteen), which probably do some welfare work, are included.

## Missionary Activities

The Muslim Missionary Society (JAMIYAH) is one of the most prominent Muslim organizations spearheading a multifaceted programme for the preservation and promotion of Islam. Founded by an Indian missionary from Meerut (Maulana Hafiz Abdul Aleem Siddique, with a small mosque standing to his name), the founder committee members included prominent Arabs, Indians, and Malay royalty. This group represented the then Muslim élite. Membership appears to have increased by leaps and bounds since 1970 — from 190 then to 24,000 in 1984.[51] The wide-ranging programme,[52] based entirely on voluntary[53] efforts, does overlap with those of several other prominent Muslim organizations, but this is to some extent unavoidable. On the one hand it may be argued that competition is necessary for the efficient conduct of organizations. This also avoids undue centralization and thus control. Yet, on the other hand, some specialization of functions may be useful to economize on scarce funds and manpower.

As would be expected, MUIS has also been organizing a *dakwah* (missionary) programme.[54] In conjunction with seven other Muslim organizations,[55] the Islamic Missionary Committee was formed in 1974 with the following main functions: (1) to organize religious lectures and forums, and religious and kindergarten classes in mosques; and (2) to prepare texts for Friday sermons. District committees were set up with a view to assisting the main committee and to involve wider grassroot participation of Muslims in *dakwah* movements.

To streamline the above activities and reduce duplication of effort, a MUIS Islamic Missionary Committee (JHD) was inaugurated in 1981. This organization is similar to its predecessor except for the following: it is organizationally more elaborate and complex; its twenty-six district committees now made permanent, compared to the previous sixteen, encompass new Muslim population nodes; and two district committees, unlike the others, do not have a residential basis but rather are work related. The *modus operandi* of this formalized co-operation between a government body and voluntary organizations clearly reflects a statement made by the Minister in charge of Muslim affairs in Parliament:

> ... a more useful approach would be for MUIS, in addition to financial contributions, to associate and involve itself more closely with grassroot Muslim/Malay

organizations ... essential and beneficial for both MUIS and Muslim organizations to maintain good rapport with one another. Only in this way can the MUIS be kept informed of the functions, work and opinions or problems encountered by the organizations.... Conversely, the rapport so established will enable the MUIS to explain the relevant government policy decisions to the Muslim public to assist them whenever possible.[56]

### KEMAS (Kongres Ekonomi Masyarakat Melayu — Islam Singapura)

The third post-1975 initiative, coming close upon the heels of MENDAKI, was another congress, KEMAS. At the congress, held in 1985, it was noted that Malay businesses had difficulty in obtaining bank credit, and Malays in obtaining employment in major banks, industries, and trading and shipping organizations at managerial and executive level even if they were suitably qualified academically.[57] At the core of the congress proposals was the establishment of a financial institution, DANAMIS, to mobilize funds and to use these to increase the involvement of Malays/Muslims in the business sector.[58]

Specifically a two-fold function is envisaged for DANAMIS: (1) it would serve as a voluntary saving scheme for the *hajj* (along more or less the same lines as the Tabung Haji Malaysia) with monthly contributions ranging from S$3 to S$20; and (2) to build up an investment fund, again through voluntary contributions to promote the economic interests of its members. Proposing to use the same collection machinery as the MBF and MENDAKI and based also on the mass resource pooling principle, the KEMAS projections indicate that a S$100 million fund could be built up in around ten years. Thus, the volume of resources to be mobilized is far greater than in the other two schemes. Unlike the other two schemes, where participants do not expect direct (monetary) returns, this scheme is somewhat different. It will have to generate adequate net returns to allow it to carry through its ambitious proposals. Thus, considerable management and financial skills will be demanded. Further, to economize on manpower and other resources, its proposals should be carefully dovetailed with those of other existing programmes.

The emergence of DANAMIS can play an important role in the voluntary sector. By providing Islamically permissible avenues of investment, it should be able to close the void existing at present and at the same time assist Muslim businesses. If successful, it will be among the first to break new ground in a Muslim-minority country.

### Conclusion

Reflective of the principle of *ibadat* (worship), Singapore Muslims have mobilized funds statutorily and voluntarily for good works. As the preceding discussion has shown, many of the earlier good works are embodied in *waqf*. Others have been more *ad hoc*, while still others, especially the post-1975 MUIS and other initiatives which are quite innovative, have employed the principle of mass resource pooling to take advantage of economies of scale. In the aggregate, the volume of financial resources mobilized appears fairly substantial. If *zakat* collection is enforced, fund mobilization would increase to a great extent and dependence on voluntary efforts may be reduced.

Much of the effort in fund mobilization is for the purpose of education. This is partly a result of the socio-economic status of the Muslim population. It is firmly believed that education is the engine of growth which will allow Muslims to compete effectively with the rest of the population.

With the inception of MUIS in independent Singapore, the management of Muslim affairs has moved from *laissez-faire* to intervention. The MUIS type structure is not unique to Singapore, since similar institutions exist in neighbouring Malaysia and Indonesia. The particular paradigm employed is reminiscent of the role of community centres in planned social development. In Singapore, they have been used to foster national integration and also as a control variable. Unlike the community centres, MUIS is a statutory board but it has also been used to initiate and foster change and attain national goals. With MUIS at the helm of Muslim affairs, two types of effects may be observed. First, there is the declining importance of traditional, smaller Muslim organizations. Second, there is the centralization and consolidation of organizations since a policy of co-optation is often practised by MUIS. In the main the trend towards centralization, especially in a small Muslim-minority country, should promote efficiency and also cohesiveness.

The potential of the voluntary sector in performing a redistributive function is especially important in Muslim-minority countries. This redistributive role has traditionally found concrete expressions in *zakat* and *waqf*. In the light of the ongoing resurgence in Islam, these and non-traditional initiatives need to be promoted vigorously.

NOTES

\*   I am grateful to Mr Sidek Sanif, the discussant of this paper, and other participants of the 24–25 August 1987 Workshop for their helpful comments.

1   Defined in the census to include all persons of Malay or Indonesian origin. This corresponds with the Malayo-Muslim group referred to earlier.

2   In 1966 the Malay female labour force participation rate (FLFPR) was only 9 per cent compared to 20 per cent for Chinese women. By 1980 the Malay and Chinese rates were 38 and 39 per cent respectively.

3    This is again reflected in the Muslim share in the manufacturing sector (Table 5[b]).

4    See *Census of Population Singapore 1980*, Release No. 7, Income and Transport (Singapore: Department of Statistics, 1981).

5    One of the amendments presently being proposed is to allow MUIS to take over the entire management of pilgrimage services. *Straits Times*, 3 February 1987.

6    Dr Ahmad Mattar, "10 Years of Majlis Ugama Islam", *Speeches* 2, no. 2 (August 1978): 28.

7    Its other activities are discussed in the section on education and welfare.

8    MUIS interview.

9    Singapore Parliamentary Debates, *Official Reports* 37 (4 June 1978), cols. 1581–84.

10   See K.L. Ter, *The Law of Charities — Cases and Materials: Singapore and Malaysia* (Singapore: Butterworths, 1985).

11   Ahmad bin Mohamed Ibrahim, *The Legal Status of Muslims in Singapore* (Singapore: Malayan Law Journal, 1965), especially Chapter 5.

12   Ibid., p. 47.

13   A recent study on the Arabs in Singapore puts the number of "large Arab wakafs at around 30 and their worth to be in the region of $50 million". The largest Indian *waqf* — Wakaf Angulia — is reported in the same study to hold fixed deposits of S$29 million. The reliability of these estimates cannot, however, be independently ascertained. See Lim Lu Sia, *The Arabs of Singapore: A Sociographic Study of their Place in the Muslim and Malay World of Singapore* (Unpublished academic exercise, Department of Sociology, National University of Singapore, 1986/87), pp. 42–46.

14   Muslimin Trust Fund Association, *80th Anniversary Publication* (Singapore: 1984).

15   MUIS, *Annual Report 1976*, p. 6.

16   Ibid., p. 5.

17   MUIS interview.

18   *New Generation of Mosques in Singapore and Their Activities* (Singapore: MUIS, 1986), p. 6.

19   MUIS, *Annual Report 1973*, p. 3.

20   Ministry of National Development, Singapore. *Annual Report*, various years.

21   MUIS interview.

22   *New Generation of Mosques in Singapore and Their Activities*, op. cit., p. 5.

23   Mansor Haji Sukaimi, *Dynamic Functions of Mosques — The Singapore Experience* (Singapore: MUIS, 1982).

24  Ibid., p. 28.

25  Ibid., p. 33.

26  Ahmad bin Mohamed Ibrahim, "Islamic Education in Singapore", *World Muslim League* 3, no. 11 (January 1967): 13.

27  For details on some of the *madrasah*, see Abdullah Alwi Haji Hassan, "Islam di Singapura: Satu Pengenalan", in *Islamika* (Kuala Lumpur: Sarjana Enterprise, n.d.), pp. 164–68. One of the *madrasah* is reported to be receiving financial assistance from the Brunei government as several of its nationals are attending the institution.

28  Ibid., p. 165.

29  Ahmad, op. cit., p. 14.

30  *Report of the Ministry of Education* (Goh Report), 1978.

31  These issues are also mentioned in: Abdullah Alwi Haji Hassan, op. cit.; Zubaidah Ghani and Fauziah Soeratman, "The Madrasah System in Singapore — A Brief Survey", *SEDAR*, 1975, pp. 44–49; M. Kamal Hassan, "Some Dimensions of Islamic Education in Southeast Asia", in *Islam and Society in Southeast Asia*, edited by Taufik Abdullah and Sharon Siddique (Singapore: Institute of Southeast Asian Studies, 1986), pp. 46–48. The lack of higher Islamic education has long been lamented as well. However, since the government has always regarded education as an investment good, the limited employment opportunities available to such graduates would hardly justify its support.

32  *Straits Times*, 1 July 1987.

33  Singapore Parliamentary Debates, *Official Reports* 32 (14 March 1973), col. 849.

34  Ibid. 42 (3 December 1982), cols. 322–24.

35  Ibid. 43 (19 March 1984), col. 1309.

36  MUIS interview.

37  MUIS, *Annual Report 1984*, p. 18.

38  *History and Activities of JAMIYAH Singapore* (Singapore: JAMIYAH, n.d.), p. 77.

39  LBKM interview.

40  *Singapore Constitution*, Order in Council, 1958.

41  Alex Josey, *Lee Kuan Yew* (Singapore: Donald Moore, 1968), p. 555.

42  MENDAKI interview.

43  See Schematic Chart for Analysis and Planning of MENDAKI Projects and Activities, "Pelejaran final", in *Kongres Pendidikan Anak-Anak Islam Singapura* (Singapore: 1981), p. 55.

44  See *Speeches* 5, no. 12 (June 1982).

45   MENDAKI interview.

46   MENDAKI interview.

47   "A Report on MENDAKI's programmes and activities for the period August '81 to May '82", in *Koleksi Kertas MENDAKI* (Singapore: MENDAKI, 1982), p. 56.

48   Muslimin Trust Fund Association, *80th Anniversary Publication* (Singapore: 1984). Funding is also provided by the SMA Alsagoff Wakaf Fund.

49   Ibid. See also *Directory of Social Services* (Singapore: Singapore Council of Social Service, 1985), p. 78.

50   Souvenir publication for the opening ceremony of the Islamic Centre JAMIYAH and 50th anniversary of JAMIYAH (Singapore: JAMIYAH, 1985).
     A list of registered societies is provided annually in the supplement to the Republic of Singapore, *Government Gazette*. As the societies listed here are not classified by specific religion, only their names provide an indication as to whether they are Muslim or otherwise.

51   *History and Activities of JAMIYAH Singapore,* op. cit., p. 83.

52   Among its credits — the conversion of over 11,000 persons between its founding and 1984. Ibid., p. 80.

53   The sources of its funds are: donations, walkathons, fairs, *zakat* and *fitrah* collections (before the inception of MUIS), and Rabitah Al-Alam-Al-Islami.

54   The World Muslim League is reported to make an annual donation of 50,000 rials to MUIS to support missionary activities. *Straits Times*, 17 January 1980.

55   See *Singapore Islamic Missionary Committee* (Singapore: MUIS, 1985), p. 11, for details. See also "Singapore Muslim Religious Council: A Review", in *Annual General Meeting of Regional Islamic Da'wah Council of Southeast Asia and Pacific* (Kuala Lumpur: 1982), pp. 210–11.

56   Singapore Parliamentary Debates, *Official Reports* 27 (22 March 1978), cols. 1398–99.

57   Ridzwan Dzafir and Ahmad Mohd Don, "Development of the economic well being of the Malays in Singapore", KEMAS (Singapore, 13–15 September 1985), p. 40.

58   For details see the KEMAS proceedings, especially pp. 212–14.

**REFERENCES**

Abdullah Alwi Haji Hassan. "Islam di Singapura: Satu Pengenalan". In *Islamika*. Kuala Lumpur: Sarjana Enterprise, n.d.

Ahmad bin Mohamed Ibrahim. *The Legal Status of Muslims in Singapore*. Singapore: Malayan Law Journal, 1965.

_____. "Islamic Education in Singapore". *World Muslim League* 3, no. 11 (January 1967).

*Annual General Meeting of Regional Islamic Da'wah Council of Southeast Asia and Pacific*. 12–14 June 1982, Kuala Lumpur.

Department of Statistics. *Census of Population Singapore 1980*. Release No. 9, Religion and Fertility. Singapore: 1981.

Hooker, M.B. *Islamic Law in Southeast Asia*. Singapore: Oxford University Press, 1984.

Josey, Alex. *Lee Kuan Yew*. Singapore: Donald Moore, 1968.

Kongres Ekonomi Masyarakat Melayu-Islam Singapore. *Proceedings*. 13–15 September 1985, Singapore.

Kongres Pendidikan Anak-Anak Islam Singapura. *Kertas binchang*. 25–30 May 1982, Singapore.

Lim Lu Sia. *The Arabs of Singapore: A Sociographic Study of their Place in the Muslim and Malay World of Singapore*. Unpublished academic exercise. Department of Sociology, National University of Singapore, 1986/87.

Majlis Ugama Islam Singapura (MUIS). *Annual Report*. Singapore: Various years.

_____. *New Generation of Mosques in Singapore and Their Activities*. Singapore: 1986.

_____. *Singapore Islamic Missionary Committee*. Singapore: 1985.

Mansor Haji Sukaimi. *Dynamic Functions of Mosques — The Singapore Experience*. Singapore: MUIS, 1982.

_____. *Koleksi Kertas MENDAKI*. Singapore: MENDAKI, 1982.

Ministry of National Development. *Annual Report*. Singapore: Various years.

Muslim Missionary Society of Singapore. Souvenir magazine for the opening ceremony of the Islamic Centre JAMIYAH Singapore and Commemoration of the 50th Anniversary of JAMIYAH. Singapore: JAMIYAH, 1985.

———. *History and Activities of JAMIYAH Singapore*. Singapore: JAMIYAH, n.d.

Muslimin Trust Fund Association. *80th Anniversary Publication*. Singapore: 1984.

Regional Islamic Convention. Papers presented at the Regional Islamic Convention at the Islamic Centre JAMIYAH, Singapore, 24–27 April 1986.

*Report of the Ministry of Education* (Goh Report). Singapore: 1978.

Singapore Council of Social Service. *Directory of Social Services*. Singapore: 1985.

Singapore Parliamentary Debates. *Official Reports*. Singapore: Various years.

*Straits Times*. Singapore: Various issues.

Taufik Abdullah and Sharon Siddique, eds. *Islam and Society in Southeast Asia*. Singapore: Institute of Southeast Asian Studies, 1986.

Ter, K.L. *The Law of Charities — Cases and Materials: Singapore and Malaysia*. Singapore: Butterworths, 1985.

Zubaidah Ghani and Fauziah Soeratman. "The Madrasah System in Singapore — A Brief Survey". *SEDAR* (1975).

# 10 MOBILIZATION OF RESOURCES THROUGH *WAQF* IN THAILAND

*Preeda Prapertchob*

## Introduction

Though it is historically well recognized that Sheik Ahmad from Persia was among the early Muslims who came to Thailand and was appointed as the highest ranking officer in the court of Ayuthaya, then the capital of Thailand since 1602, he was probably not the first Muslim who came to this Buddhist kingdom. It was noted that there was significant trading relation between Sukhothai rulers and the Persian empire since the thirteenth century. Already, there was a major Muslim settlement in the present south Thailand centring around Pattani. The long process of interaction between Muslims and Buddhists allowed Islam to spread throughout the kingdom, from the south to the north and northeast. At present, there are Muslims in all provinces of Thailand. In Bangkok alone, the number of registered mosques (*masjid*) stands at 155 out of the total of 2,573 mosques in all Thailand. Therefore, the typical impression that Muslims are people of south Thailand belonging to the Malay stock is not accurate. The structure of Muslim societies in Thailand is more complex. In the northern provinces, there are a large number of Muslims of Chinese origin, while in many provinces of the Central Plain and the northeast the descendants of Indo-Pakistanis dominate the local Muslim communities. Most of the Muslim communities in the Central Plain provinces, which could be traced back to Malay origin, no longer have any apparent Malay culture.

Although it cannot be said that there has been a smooth relation between Muslim and Buddhist Thais, one cannot deny that, in the greater part of Thai history, the ruling regimes had been receptive and generous to the Thai

Muslims. Legally, the freedom of religious belief is recognized and guaranteed in Thailand. There are some laws which have been specially issued for the Muslim citizens in this predominantly Buddhist society. The Masjid Act (1947) and the Royal Decree on Patronization of Muslim Citizen (1945) are the two major laws issued in this country in modern times. Muslims in the four southern provinces of Thailand are also entitled to be governed under the *Shariah* law on matters relating to family and inheritance. The Ministry of Education, with the good service of Islamic scholars, has designed a special Islamic education programme to be incorporated in the general curriculum, in addition to providing support for the *pondok* school system in the form of subsidy. Of course, there is no unitary view about the Thai government's intervention in the affairs of the Muslims in Thailand. Some have viewed these government programmes as part of the assimilation scheme of the government aimed at de-Islamizing the Muslim society in Thailand.

Unlike the politics of Muslim minorities which so far has dominated the interest of the scholars and Muslim activists in Thailand, the economics of Muslim minorities has not been much discussed. Most Muslims in Thailand are still poor and live below the poverty line. Muslims in this country, similar to elsewhere, are proud of their religion and consider Islam as the perfect way of life. They speak of the God-given economic system which is superior to other man-made system, be it capitalism or socialism. References are often made to the welfare institutions such as *zakat* and the interest-free banking system. Nevertheless, there have been no major achievements in translating such ideals into practice. In the four southern provinces where Muslims are the majority, Muslims are only smallholders of rubber trees, small fishermen, and small farmers. Many of them are only farm labourers or wage workers in the modern non-Muslim fishing enterprises. The area is rich in minerals, but Muslims work as labourers in the non-Muslim owned mines. In the Central Plain, where the economy is more developed, Muslims in town serve as vendors, petty officers, unskilled workers, etc. In Bangkok, a large number of Muslims live in the slum areas. During the past two decades, thanks to the rapid expansion of the city, a number of Muslims who owned large pieces of land (because they themselves were farmers) could become millionaires by selling their land. But soon after spending lavishly, many of them have become poor again. In the northeast, a number of Muslims have become cattle dealers and butchers, while a few have developed their own ranches and gone into the tanning industry.

Though Muslims have not been very successful in running their own private businesses and in institutionalizing the *zakat* and interest-free banking, they were quite successful in establishing *waqf* (endowments) for the good of their communities.

## Voluntary Resource Mobilization through *Waqf*

*Waqf* property is defined as one which is permanently dedicated by a person professing Islam for any legitimate purpose recognized in Islam. It has played an important role in the voluntary resource mobilization of the Muslim communities in Thailand. Despite being a minority in most parts of the country (except the four southernmost provinces) Muslims in Thailand have tended to live together. This has been the most effective measure to immunize themselves against the non-Islamic practices of the large majority. In a typical Muslim village there is a *masjid* or *surau* at the centre of the village. Adjacent to the *masjid* site there is a *kubur* or burial ground. The *kubur* is sometimes located outside the village so that the Muslims in other neighbouring villages might share it. The land for the *masjid* and *kubur* is donated by the voluntary sector. The construction of the *masjid* is also a voluntary sector affair. Funds for this purpose are raised from among the people. The mosques, more often than not, are very utilitarian in design, mainly to provide shelter during prayers. The cost of construction tends to be very low, since most of the material (mainly wood) could be procured within the community, and labour is provided free for the construction of the mosque. Nowadays, there is a tendency to construct bigger mosques based on modern architecture and this requires more resources than what the local people could pool together. Therefore it is quite common to see several missions from a village making long trips to other Muslim areas to raise funds for the construction of the mosque. Needless to say, lots of efforts are taken by *masjid* committees, all of which come on a voluntary basis.

In addition to the land for the *masjid* and the *kubur*, some pious Muslims also donated productive land to the *masjid* in order that the *masjid* might earn some income which will help meet the cost of administration and maintenance. The land might be an arable land in a rural location, the produce of which could be sold, or a lot in an urban area which could yield regular rental incomes. There have also been many cases of land being donated by wealthy Muslims for Islamic schools (*madrasah*) or the *pondok* schools in south Thailand.

*Waqf* is one of the better known Islamic institutions found in all Muslim communities. It has also been institutionalized by law and rules governing several aspects of it. However, *waqf* has been ignored by the present Muslim leaders and activists to such an extent that information on *waqf* hardly exists. The contemporary Muslim activists seem more ready to discuss how to establish *zakat* and Islamic banking, but only a few of them, if any, actually realize the importance of *waqf* and its potential for the economic development of the Muslim community. Many in the *masjid* committees do not know what to do with the *waqf* properties that were given for some specific purposes which could not be realized. The *waqf* properties cannot be put to alternative uses without clear sanctions from the donors.

In this study,* the *waqf* situation in Thailand is reviewed and its prospects in terms of future development are considered. This is no easy task, as not much data are readily available in documented forms. There has been no previous empirical study of *waqf* in Thailand. For the purpose of the present study, a field survey was undertaken, involving extensive trips throughout the country, from the north to the south and from the Central Plain to the plateau of the northeast. These trips were necessary to interview the *masjid* committees and to gather information on the *waqf* properties in their communities. The data were speedily analysed by micro-computers at Khon Kaen University. The results are reported in the next section.

Under the Masjid Act of 1947, the *masjid* affairs are administered by the *masjid* committee, consisting of not less than seven persons. Its function also includes the management of the *masjid* property (Article 7). This was more specifically restated in Rules for Masjid Committee Appointment and Dismissal and Regulation for Masjid Administration (1949), that the committee is responsible for the management and maintenance of the *masjid* and its *waqf* in good order and the committee must submit a financial report as well as a list of *waqf* properties to the Provincial Islamic Committee within January every year. The section on *waqf* property of the same rules gives the authority to the Provincial Islamic Committee (PIC) as well as the Central Islamic Committee (CIC) to inspect and control or give any advice to the *masjid* committee on matters relating to *waqf* property.

Under the Land Code of 1954, mosques (as well as Buddhist temples and Christian churches) are not permitted to hold land of more than 50 rai** (about 8 hectares or 20 acres) but this ruling does not apply to land holdings before 1 December 1954 or to the *masjid* in the four southern provinces (Pattani, Satul, Yala, and Narathivat) (Article 84).

The general framework of the *waqf* property is thus stated in both special Muslim laws and general law. But, in practice, it was found that neither the PIC nor the CIC has the complete list of *waqf* properties of all mosques under its supervision. It was found that no mosque in Thailand abides by the law requiring it to submit expenditure reports and *waqf* property lists to the PIC or CIC every year. As the PIC and CIC were unable to provide data on *waqf* property, a field survey was undertaken for the purpose of the present study, involving a number of mosques throughout Thailand.

Besides the mosques, there are foundations (i.e., non-profit organizations) which are entitled to hold land and other *waqf* properties. The establishment and administration of the foundations are regulated by the Civil and Commercial Code (Articles 81 to 97). There are three types of foundation in the Thai Muslim society. The first one consists of foundations attached to the mosques, which enable them to cover a wider range of activities than what the mosques themselves can. The second type comprises foundations associated with educational institutes, mainly the Islamic schools or the *pondok* schools. The third type consists of foundations for the general welfare and service of the society, which are often named after particular personalities/philanthropists. The Muslim foundations work mainly, if not solely, for the benefit of the Muslim community, while several non-Muslim foundations do offer their services to wider beneficiaries.

It is discouraging to note that, of late, *waqf* land in Thailand is subjected to taxation in that the donors who donate the land to non-profit organizations have to pay a tax equivalent to 2 per cent of the value of the land. Under this rule, donors would feel reluctant to donate the land, because they have to pay in cash to the authority in addition to giving away their land. In many cases, the beneficiaries or the community has to raise funds in order to pay the tax on behalf of the donors.

**Survey Results**

As it was not possible to get the record of *masjid* assets from both PIC and CIC, the interview survey was designed. Given the time and budget constraint, a sampling survey of 175 mosques throughout the country was conducted, which represented about 7 per cent of the total in Thailand. Much effort was put in selecting the samples to make them truly representative of the mosques in Thailand. The five regions were stratified according to their geographical and cultural setting: north, central, northeast, upper south, and lower south. The number of *masjid* in each province is shown in Table 1.

A larger number of provinces were chosen for the Central Plain, because this region consists of many provinces and the character of the Muslim population in this region is relatively diversified. From the northeast, where there are only four registered *masjid* for the whole region (although there are a number of non-registered mosques in many provinces), only two were chosen. In the south, two regions were classified: the upper south where Muslims are still a minority and the lower south where they are a majority. There are altogether four provinces in the lower south, out of which two provinces were chosen. The total number of samples for these two provinces was as many as 56, as the number of *masjid* in these two provinces added up to 642.

The survey was first conducted by interviewing the chairmen of the PICs for the provinces where such committees exist. The general conditions of the Muslim community and the mosques in these provinces were queried through the structured questionnaire. Then the *imam* (or their representatives) of the mosques were interviewed, using a more detailed questionnaire. Questions

TABLE 1
**Number of Mosques in the Sample by Province**

| Region | Province | Number of Mosques |
| --- | --- | --- |
| North | Chiengmai | 5 |
| | Lampang | 1 |
| | Tak | 1 |
| Central Plain | Bangkok | 30 |
| | Nonthaburi | 4 |
| | Prathumtani | 1 |
| | Samutprakarn | 3 |
| | Chachoengsao | 10 |
| | Ayuthaya | 10 |
| | Rayong | 6 |
| | Petchburi | 2 |
| Northeast | Khon Kaen | 1 |
| | Udornthani | 1 |
| Upper South | Ranong | 3 |
| | Nakorn Srithammarat | 10 |
| | Songkhla | 20 |
| | Krabi | 11 |
| Lower South | Satul | 12 |
| | Pattani | 44 |
| Total | | 175 |

relating to *waqf* property, management of the mosque, Islamic education, and income and expense of the mosque and *madrasah* were raised during the interviews. The field survey experience indicates that most *imam* responded positively to the survey team after being given a good explanation of the objective of the survey and receiving the introduction letter from the chairman of the PIC. It is interesting to note that the *imam* hardly had any previous experience of being interviewed, which shows how little the Islamic society in Thailand has been researched upon.

*Community Profile*
Out of the 175 mosques, 119 or 68 per cent are in the rural areas and 56 or 32 per cent are in towns. Most of the mosques in the north and all of them in the northeast are located in urban areas. In the upper and lower south, most mosques are in the rural areas (Table 2).

In the past, Muslims have tended to live in relatively closed communities, but recent trends indicate that they are increasingly scattered. In most cases,

TABLE 2
**Number of Sample Mosques Classified by Location**

| Region | Town | Rural | Total |
|---|---|---|---|
| North | 5 | 2 | 7 |
| Central Plain | 27 | 39 | 66 |
| Northeast | 2 | – | 2 |
| Upper South | 13 | 31 | 44 |
| Lower South | 9 | 47 | 56 |
| Total | 56 | 119 | 175 |

mosques are surrounded by Muslim households, but Muslims do freely inter-mingle with non-Muslims. In several communities Muslims are only a minority.

According to the survey, Muslims in the north and northeast are either thinly concentrated or scattered, while in the other regions they tend to be highly concentrated (Table 3). In the Central Plain, there is a tendency for scattered patterns to develop. Due to rapid socio-economic development, many Muslim households had to leave their own community and move into new residential compounds close to their working place, with the non-Muslims replacing them. Inheritance is also a factor contributing to the increased geographical dispersion of Muslims in Thailand. Families which could not well settle in the subdivided portion of the inherited assets sell their proper-ties, distribute the proceeds among themselves and buy a home-lot elsewhere. It should be noted that even in the Muslim-majority area like the lower south, only 70 per cent of the Muslims live in a highly concentrated fashion. In general, at present, about one-half of the Muslim community live in the highly concentrated Muslim areas. The relationship between Muslims and non-Muslims in most communities is very good and they both live together on the basis of mutual respect and understanding. Problems mainly arise from the lack of good cohesion among Muslims in those areas where they are scattered. It is in such environments that the Muslims tend to steer away from Islamic values and to adopt a care-free attitude toward Western culture.

As regards the major occupation of the Muslims in these areas, it was found that about one-third of the total households depend on farming (Table 4). Rubber growing accounts for about 20 per cent of the total house-holds, followed by trading which is the mainstay of the livelihood of about 18 per cent of the Muslim households in these areas.

The average number of Muslim households per *masjid* in Thailand is 183 (Table 5). In the northeast, this average falls to 53, while in the Central Plain it rises to 223. Given an average of eight members per household, it would mean that each *masjid* is surrounded by about 1,464 Muslims.

TABLE 3
**Number of Sample Mosques Classified by Concentration**

| Region | Highly Concentrated | Thinly Concentrated | Scattered |
|---|---|---|---|
| North | — | 2 (28.6) | 5 (71.4) |
| Central Plain | 29 (43.9) | 18 (27.3) | 19 (28.8) |
| Northeast | — | — | 2 (100.0) |
| Upper South | 23 (52.3) | 11 (25.0) | 10 (22.7) |
| Lower South | 39 (69.6) | 10 (17.9) | 7 (12.5) |
| Total | 91 (52.0) | 41 (23.4) | 43 (24.6) |

( ) Percentages are shown in parentheses.

TABLE 4
**Major Occupations of the Households in the Sample**

| Region | Farming | Fishing | Rubber Plantation | Employee | Trading |
|---|---|---|---|---|---|
| North | 2 (28.6) | — | — | — | 5 (71.4) |
| Central Plain | 23 (35.4) | — | — | 23 (35.4) | 14 (21.5) |
| Northeast | — | — | — | — | 2 (100.0) |
| Upper South | 7 (15.9) | 9 (20.5) | 16 (36.4) | 4 (9.1) | 8 (18.2) |
| Lower South | 24 (42.9) | 12 (21.4) | 18 (32.1) | — | 2 (3.6) |
| Total | 56 (32.2) | 21 (12.1) | 34 (19.5) | 27 (15.5) | 31 (17.8) |

( ) Percentages are shown in parentheses.

TABLE 5
**Average Number of Muslim Households per Mosque**

| Region | Number of Households |
|---|---|
| North | 79 |
| Central Plain | 223 |
| Northeast | 53 |
| Upper South | 162 |
| Lower South | 169 |
| Whole Thailand | 183 |

Mosques serve as centres of Muslim community activities. The structure of the *masjid* and the way it is furnished reflect the socio-economic status of the people in the community. A huge and well-furnished building is indicative of the affluence of the people around the *masjid*. However, sometimes the well-built *masjid* lack good maintenance, which suggests either that affluent Muslims have migrated or that the management of the *masjid* is not in capable hands. The extent to which a *masjid* is used is an indication of the level of spiritual development of the Muslims around it. The degree of utilization of a mosque can be gauged by the number of Muslims who come to the place of worship for prayers. Table 6 shows the average number of people who come to each *masjid* for prayers on different occasions.

TABLE 6
**Average Number of Worshippers per Mosque**

| Region | Masjid Capacity | Daily Prayers | | | Friday Prayers | Eid Prayers |
|---|---|---|---|---|---|---|
| | | Zubh | Dhuri/Asr | Maghrib/Isha | | |
| North | 410 | 19 | 19 | 38 | 170 | 403 |
| Central Plain | 531 | 27 | 27 | 37 | 221 | 635 |
| Northeast | 180 | 6 | 6 | 11 | 60 | 225 |
| Upper South | 339 | 29 | 29 | 51 | 144 | 353 |
| Lower South | 333 | 33 | 33 | 50 | 169 | 330 |
| Whole Thailand | 410 | 29 | 29 | 44 | 181 | 452 |

The number of people who come for prayers varies from time to time and from region to region. The turn-out is low for *Zubh-Zuhur-Asr* prayers as the people have to be engaged in their own occupation. It increases during *Maghrib-Isha* prayers. The turn-out for the Friday prayers is lower than one-half of the capacity of the *masjid*. However, the turn-out for Eid prayers invariably exceeds the capacities of the mosques. It can be inferred from all this that mosques are underutilized and that there is a great need for *Da'wah* activity to encourage more people to make full use of the *masjid*. It is of interest to note that the Friday congregation accounts for only about 12 per cent of the total population, which is too low, even if we exclude women and children for whom the prayers in the *masjid* are not obligatory.

*Land Holdings*

The major *waqf* properties in Thailand are in the form of land donated to *masjid*. The land size varies from a few square metres just big enough to accommodate the mosque to some hectares of land, including paddy land and rubber holdings. In the survey it was found that the average land holding for all samples was 12.3 rai (about 4.86 acres or 1.97 hectares). (See Table 7.) There are also great variations between regions and locations (urban vs rural). In the Central Plain, the average size of land holding of a *masjid* is as high as 23.2 rai whereas in the upper south it is only 4.7 rai. In the Central Plain, the Muslims in many locations are large land holders, because they are farmers and their lands were largely inherited. Many of the pious Muslims have donated a part of their land for the construction of new mosques or as asset assigned to a mosque so that income from the land can help meet the general expenditure of the mosque. It is not uncommon for mosques which are located in towns to own some pieces of land in the rural areas.

TABLE 7
**Total Land Holding per Mosque**
(In rai)

| Region | Town | Rural |
|---|---|---|
| North | 13.4 | 3.0 |
| Central Plain | 19.3 | 25.9 |
| Northeast | 6.4 | — |
| Upper South | 6.9 | 3.8 |
| Lower South | 16.5 | 3.7 |
| Whole Thailand | 15.2 | 11.0 |

In the southern region of Thailand, land is more fertile and more scarce. The cultivated land consists mainly of orchard, and rubber and coconut holdings. The size of land holding per household is generally small and the land donated to mosques is not big, with a few exceptions. In general, mosques in the lower south have small *waqf* land holdings, averaging about 3.7 rai per *masjid*, which is sufficient for the *masjid* building, its compound, and the *kubur*. Some mosques have no adjacent *kubur*, in which case there is usually a common *kubur* shared by two or more mosques.

## Masjid *Building*

The construction of a *masjid* building is often based on voluntary resource mobilization. The building may take the form of make-shift arrangements or a grandiose structure with sophisticated architectural design. There are some mosques which were constructed with government allocations (especially the central mosques in the four southern border provinces) and there are some with funds from foreign donors. But most mosques were constructed by the local people with locally mobilized funds. The cost of the building ranges widely, from a hundred thousand bahts to several million bahts. Table 8 shows the present value of mosques in our sample. The average value of *masjid* buildings all over Thailand is about 1.7 million bahts; this rises to 2.6 million bahts for *masjid* in urban centres and 1.3 million bahts for *masjid* in the rural areas. Mosques in the Central Plain generally have higher values than the ones in the rural north, while the mosques in the towns of the lower south have the highest value, because the latter include central mosques which were constructed with government allocations.

TABLE 8
**Present Value of an Average Mosque Building by Region**
(In million bahts)

| Region | Town | Rural |
|---|---|---|
| North | 0.660 | 0.250 |
| Central Plain | 2.691 | 2.481 |
| Northeast | 1.400 | — |
| Upper South | 1.938 | 0.660 |
| Lower South | 4.811 | 0.666 |
| Whole Thailand | 2.629 | 1.252 |

The conditions of the *masjid* as discovered by the survey are depicted in Table 9. Mosques which are already old or dilapidated account for about 5.7 per cent of the total, while new ones under construction form 18 per cent. There are some mosques which have been under a long period of construction, with some portions left unfinished owing to lack of funds. To be sure, the number of mosques in Thailand is gradually increasing. Some of these new mosques have come about because of the migration or dispersion of Muslims in the country. But some new mosques have been put up as a result of internal conflicts within the community.

TABLE 9
**Number of Mosques Classified by Condition**

| Region | Old/ Dilapidated | Under Construction | Under Expansion | Newly Built | Normal |
|---|---|---|---|---|---|
| North | — | — | — | — | 7 (100.0) |
| Central Plain | 4 (6.1) | 11 (16.7) | 6 (9.1) | 2 (3.0) | 43 (65.2) |
| Northeast | — | — | — | — | 2 (100.0) |
| Upper South | 5 (11.4) | 8 (18.2) | 2 (4.5) | — | 29 (65.9) |
| Lower South | 1 (1.8) | 13 (23.2) | 4 (7.1) | — | 38 (67.9) |
| Whole Thailand | 10 (5.7) | 32 (18.3) | 12 (6.9) | 2 (1.1) | 119 (68.0) |

( ) Percentages are shown in parentheses.

It was found that most mosques had standard structures with only one storey (69.7 per cent). There are some mosques with two storeys, in which case the first floor is mostly used for class-rooms, meeting hall, store-room, etc. (see Table 10).

*Other Assets*
In addition to the *masjid* buildings, and the land on which they are situated, *masjid* normally do own other assets such as rent houses. All mosques possess a certain amount of utensils and furniture which were purchased by the *masjid* committees or donated by the public. These include carpets, public address system, kitchen utensils, electric fans, etc. Some of these items may be borrowed by individuals for ceremonies or festivities. In Bangkok, some mosques own

TABLE 10

**Number of Mosques Classified by Type of Building**

| Region | Wooden Structure | Temporary Brick Building (One floor) | Standard Concrete Building (One floor) | Standard Concrete Building (Two floors or more) | Others |
|---|---|---|---|---|---|
| North | — | — | 6 (85.7) | 1 (14.3) | — |
| Central Plain | 8 (12.1) | — | 33 (50.0) | 21 (31.8) | 4 (6.1) |
| Northeast | — | 1 (50.0) | — | 1 (50.0) | — |
| Upper South | 3 (6.8) | 3 (6.8) | 34 (77.3) | 3 (6.8) | 1 (2.3) |
| Lower South | 3 (5.4) | 1 (1.8) | 49 (87.5) | 2 (3.6) | 1 (1.8) |
| Whole Thailand | 14 (8.0) | 5 (2.9) | 122 (69.7) | 28 (16.0) | 6 (3.4) |

( ) Percentages are shown in parentheses.

micro-buses which are used for general transportation and carrying the dead. The average value of these assets is shown in Table 11.

Only a few mosques in the Central Plain and the north have rent houses but none of the sample mosques in the other regions own them. As for other assets, mosques in the Central Plain possess more than their counterparts elsewhere, while those in the upper south have the least.

TABLE 11
**Average Value of Rent Houses and Other Assets per Mosque**
(In baht)

| Region | Rent Houses | Other Assets |
| --- | --- | --- |
| North | 88,571 | 36,800 |
| Central Plain | 118,181 | 90,620 |
| Northeast | — | 40,000 |
| Upper South | — | 19,434 |
| Lower South | — | 30,500 |

*School and Islamic Education*

Most mosques incorporate class-room facilities for Islamic education. Attention is focused on teaching the children how to read and understand the basic tenets of Islam. Only a few mosques offer more advanced studies on Islam. Almost all of these Islamic classes are conducted in the *waqf* property, i.e., within the *masjid*, or in separate premises. These schools start their sessions in the evening during weekdays, after the children return from their secular schools, or in the morning during the weekends. The number of pupils per school is about 124, with about 4 teachers (Table 12). The management of the Islamic classes is generally vested in the hands of the education subcommittee of the *masjid*. The management handles the recruitment of Islamic teachers, class-room arrangements, fund raising or collection of school fees, etc. The survey results reveal variations in the costs of school buildings between regions (Table 13). The north has the highest average value of school building per *masjid*. This is because a large investment was made at the school attached to Masjid At-takwa in Chiengmai, which offers both elementary and advanced Islamic courses. The low level of investment in Islamic schools in the northeast reflects the community's lack of interest in Islamic educational pursuits, as a consequence of which a large number of Muslim youths in the region know very little or nothing about Islam. Many of them have been de-Islamized and assimilated into the large majority. Recently, there was an attempt by the Committee for Muslim Development in the northeast to dispatch Islamic

TABLE 12
**Number of Teachers and Pupils by Region**

| Region | Number of Teachers | Number of Pupils | Ratio of Pupils to Teachers |
|---|---|---|---|
| North | 3.6 | 70 | 19.4 |
| Central Plain | 4.1 | 135 | 32.9 |
| Northeast | 1.0 | 30 | 30.0 |
| Upper South | 2.7 | 101 | 37.4 |
| Lower South | 4.9 | 140 | 28.6 |
| Whole Thailand | 3.9 | 124 | 31.8 |

TABLE 13
**Cost of School Building or Class-room per Mosque**
(In baht)

| Region | Value |
|---|---|
| North | 501,429 |
| Central Plain | 381,635 |
| Northeast | 30,000 |
| Upper South | 57,396 |
| Lower South | 144,471 |

teachers to some communities in the region but this project is just at the initial stage.

The cost of Islamic education in each community is shown in Table 14. The honorarium paid to teachers represents the biggest slice of the total. Highest expenditures are incurred in the northern communities, which indicates how enthusiastic the Muslims in this region are about Islamic education. However, it should be noted that the expenditure distribution is uneven, as much of the costs are concentrated in Masjid At-takwa (Chiengmai). The upper south region spends very little on Islamic education. Many school teachers in this region are either poorly paid or not receiving any remuneration at all for their services.

The major source of finance for Islamic education is either the parents of the children who study in these classes or the public via fund-raising activities (Table 15). In the Central Plain, fund raising is the major source. Fund-raising campaigns are organized annually. Public lectures and panel discussions are given by well-known Islamic scholars, and exhibitions and other activities are organized during the campaign. It should be noted, however, that in all cases the proceeds, as disclosed by the respondents, have fallen short of the expenditure. The balance is presumably met from donations by some individuals inside or outside the communities.

TABLE 14
**Annual Expenditure on Education per Mosque**
(In baht)

| Region | Teacher Honorarium | Janitor Payment | Water Supply and Electricity | Material | Total |
|---|---|---|---|---|---|
| North | 43,471 | 3,771 | 10,286 | 857 | 58,385 |
| Central Plain | 26,079 | 793 | 785 | 59 | 27,716 |
| Northeast | 21,000 | 0 | 600 | 250 | 21,850 |
| Upper South | 7,893 | 0 | 0 | 0 | 7,893 |
| Lower South | 21,404 | 7 | 57 | 5 | 21,473 |
| Whole Thailand | 21,871 | 536 | 890 | 74 | 23,371 |

TABLE 15
**Funds for Islamic Education per Mosque**
(In baht per year)

| Region | Parents | General Donors | Fund-Raising Activities | Others | Total |
|---|---|---|---|---|---|
| North | 0 | 6,000 | 5,714 | 0 | 11,714 |
| Central Plain | 16,161 | 932 | 17,991 | 583 | 35,667 |
| Northeast | 9,000 | 0 | 0 | 0 | 9,000 |
| Upper South | 1,256 | 0 | 1,481 | 0 | 2,737 |
| Lower South | 226 | 238 | 0 | 0 | 464 |
| Whole Thailand | 7,408 | 781 | 8,332 | 251 | 16,772 |

## Income from Waqf Property

Of course, there can be no income from the land used as sites for *masjid* and *kubur*, but many mosques do possess other pieces of land which generate income for the mosques. Unfortunately, in most cases these *waqf* properties have not been efficiently managed. For example, most pieces of *waqf* land are simply rented out, generating no more than minimal rental incomes. A mosque in the outskirt of Bangkok owns a large piece of land (17 rai or about 2.7

hectares), the present value of which is about 8.1 million bahts. It has been rented out for the purpose of putting up private houses, from which the *masjid* earns a rental income of about 14,000 bahts annually, while a similar piece of private land can earn four to five times more. Of course, it can be argued that the *waqf* land is allotted to the poor in the community and, therefore, it should be seen as part of the welfare programme. But it was found that, in many cases, the more well-to-do people have set up homes on the *waqf* land. This *masjid* also possesses a larger piece of paddy land (41 rai or about 6.6 hectares) which is rented out to Muslim farmers, yielding an income of 2,000 bahts a year as rental fees, which is far below the market rate.

But there are a few mosques which enjoy a more lucrative income from house rentals on *waqf* land. One *masjid* in Chiengmai could earn as much as 60,000 bahts a year from renting four compartments of business premises.

### Other Sources of Income

Since the income from *waqf* properties is inadequate to meet all expenditures incurred by a *masjid*, there is a need to raise the funds through other means. The major source of income consists of donations made during the major Islamic festivities, such as the Eid festivals and *Mauludin-Nabi* (birthday celebrations for the Prophet). The *masjid* committees usually organize the various activities and these occasions are used to collect substantial sums from the Muslims who participate in them. Some mosques, mainly in the lower south, do get allocations from the government budget as well as from Members of Parliament (as part of the special budget for development allotted to Members of Parliament).

Some mosques have organized the *zakat fitr* (*sadaqah al fitr* or *fitrah*, which is a poll tax) by setting up a central body to facilitate the collection, the proceeds of which are disbursed either to the Muslims themselves or to the needy. Thus, *zakat fitr* represents yet another source of income for the mosques. The number of mosques which have organized *zakat fitr* collection through the central body is shown in Table 16.

However, this central body so far has not extended its activity to cover the collection of *zakat*, which is based on income/property, although there is consensus that such organized *zakat* collection is essential. *Zakat*, in general, is disbursed individually and personally to the needy. There are a few mosques which have established the formal Zakat and Charity Fund, but such organized *zakat* collection is an exception rather than the rule.

### Expenditures of Mosques

The cost of maintaining and repairing the *masjid* building constitutes the major expenditure item, accounting for 90 per cent of the total expenditure (Table 17). Mosques in the Central Plain seem to incur the highest expenditures

TABLE 16
**Number of Mosques with Organized** *Zakat Fitr* **Collection**

| Region | With | Without | Don't Know/ No Response |
|--------|------|---------|------------------------|
| North | 3 (42.9) | 4 (57.1) | — |
| Central Plain | 35 (54.7) | 29 (45.3) | — |
| Northeast | — | 2 (100.0) | — |
| Upper South | 9 (20.9) | 33 (76.7) | 1 (2.3) |
| Lower South | 25 (44.6) | 31 (55.4) | — |
| Whole Thailand | 72 (41.9) | 99 (57.6) | 1 (0.6) |

( ) Percentages are shown in parentheses.

to the tune of 194,083 bahts per *masjid* per year, followed by mosques in the upper south region (68,487 bahts per *masjid* per year).

From the list of expenditure, it appears that the major concern of the mosques is the upkeep and maintenance of the buildings. Some might question the role of *masjid* in the development and welfare of the people within the community. It should be noted that for Islamic education, a separate budgeting is kept, as discussed earlier.

## Waqf *Property Management*

In general, a *masjid* committee would assign one particular member to take care of the *waqf* property to account for it but the whole committee is reponsible for major decisions. According to the survey results, most mosques have rules and regulations for the borrowing of movable and other assets. But there are no *masjid* financial reports on *waqf* properties submitted to the PIC or the CIC regularly. Thus, *waqf* properties are almost exclusively managed by *masjid* committees without any interference from the PIC or the CIC. The PIC and the CIC would intervene only when there is a conflict or quarrel within the community with regard to the *waqf* properties.

There are some mosques where the land has not been formally transferred to the *masjid*. This is because the donors have already passed away and the heirs are not willing to donate the land.

TABLE 17
**Average Expenditure of Each Mosque per Year**
(In baht)

| Region | Water Supply and Electricity | Janitor | *Masjid* Repairing | Material and Furniture | Donation to the Poor | Land Tax | Total |
|---|---|---|---|---|---|---|---|
| North | 12,600 | 1,600 | 41,667 | 583 | 0 | 0 | 56,450 |
| Central Plain | 7,489 | 3,030 | 176,586 | 5,909 | 306 | 763 | 194,083 |
| Northeast | 6,000 | 12,000 | 2,500 | 500 | 0 | 0 | 21,000 |
| Upper South | 2,285 | 4,811 | 61,368 | 23 | 0 | 0 | 68,487 |
| Lower South | 4,650 | 1,746 | 32,655 | 3,895 | 0 | 0 | 42,946 |
| Whole Thailand | 5,419 | 3,121 | 94,475 | 3,526 | 116 | 290 | 106,947 |

The major problem facing all mosques with some excess land is the low income earned from such land. In most cases, the land is rented out for housing to the poor if it is in town or a suburban area or for cultivation if it is arable land. But all *waqf* land earns only minimal income, often much lower than privately owned land. There is also the problem of rental fee collection. Since the fee collection is carried out by the *masjid* committee on a voluntary basis, the committee members are, in many cases, not very enthusiastic in doing their job. Consequently, the rate of default is high and the income of the mosques remains low. From the interviews during the survey it appears that some *masjid* committees do have the idea of developing the *waqf* land to make it more profitable or productive by building new apartments or housing complexes, but they lack the capital needed for such projects. In most cases, however, the *masjid* committees do not have any plan or idea for developing the *waqf* land, and they seem more concerned with the welfare of the poor who reside on the land and who will have to be displaced if the land is to be developed. They prefer to resort to other means of fund raising to make ends meet. Most of the *masjid* committee members do not have business orientations. They, therefore, prefer not to take risks, especially with the *waqf* land entrusted to them.

Fund raising for mosque construction and maintenance and for financing Islamic schools/classes is actively resorted to by the *masjid* committees. Funds flow in as donations from Muslims within or outside the communities. The efforts in this sphere include annual festivals organized, with generous contributions from the Muslim public.

## Pondok *Schools and the* Waqf

*Pondok* school system is part and parcel of the tradition of Islamic education in south Thailand and north Peninsular Malaysia. Students of all ages, male and female, used to come to seek for knowledge from the *tohkru* (teacher) by building their own huts next to the *tohkru*'s house. They came to the classrooms voluntarily and learnt the subject they wished either from the *tohkru* directly or from the senior students who became the *tohkru*'s assistants. There was no standard curriculum and one might spend more than ten years to master the subject. The land on which the *pondok* schools operated might be the personal asset of the *tohkru*, but in many cases it was *waqf* land donated by the people in the village specially for religious education.

In the old days, when the property right and land title were not officially registered, the right of the *pondok* land was customarily recognized and respected by the people concerned. But as land laws were introduced requiring all pieces of land to be registered and the owners of the land had to be specified, the *pondok* land estates were registered under the respective *tohkru*'s names. There was no problem during the lifetime of the *tohkru*, but when the *tohkru* passed away, the lands were inherited by their children. Thus, *waqf* lands have become private properties in the legal reuse over time. In most cases, however, these lands were treated as public properties in practical terms.

During the past thirty years the *pondok* system has undergone significant transformation and the *pondok* schools have been converted into private Islamic schools registered under the Ministry of Education, but the land ownership has been left intact. There are some famous *pondok* schools which have successfully preserved their identity and still remain public institutions under the ownership of some foundations with some outside help. For example, the Foundation of Islamic Education in Yala operates three Islamic schools. The foundation has been able to attract financial assistance from donors in the Middle East in addition to receiving substantial amounts of government subsidy every year (in 1986, it received a government subsidy of 695,175 bahts). The foundation currently also receives the support of the local people in terms of *zakat* and *sadaqah*. School fees also represent an important source of revenue for the foundation. At present there are 94 teachers and 2,466 students (1,320 for Islamic education and 1,146 for secular education). There are other success stories too. The At-Tarkiyah School in Narathivat, which was registered under its own foundation, has been performing quite well. But most private Islamic schools have not been registered under any foundation, either because they are unaware of the need to do so or because they are afraid of being closely monitored, thereby losing their autonomy altogether.

## Conclusion

This study has revealed that there has been a considerable amount of effort put in by the Muslims in Thailand in building up the institution of *waqf*, although the management of the *waqf* properties has not been efficient. Although the institution of *waqf* was well recognized and legalized by law, few administrators (from the *masjid* level up to the national level of the CIC) paid much attention to the efficiency aspect. There are a number of ways in which *waqf* properties in Thailand can be improved. First of all, there is a need to eliminate the rigidity about the use of *waqf* properties; and the *waqf* management should be given more powers to use them more meaningfully. Secondly, the PIC should place more emphasis on the documentation and record of the *waqf* properties of the mosques under its supervision. There is a need to train the *waqf* administrators on how to manage *waqf* properties in a more efficient manner and how to make and submit returns to the PIC. Thirdly, a local fund should be established for all mosques to collect and to disburse the *zakat*, and a central fund should be created so that each *masjid* can design development

TABLE 18

**Number of Private Islamic Schools and Students and Their Government Budget Allocation, 1984**

| | Islamic Course Only | | Islamic Course and Secular Course | | Islamic Course and Vocational Course | | Government |
| | No. of Schools | No. of Students | No. of Schools | No. of Students | No. of Schools | No. of Students | Budget Allocated* (Million bahts) |
|---|---|---|---|---|---|---|---|
| *Region 2* (Yala, Narathivat, Pattani, Satul) | 80 | 39,663 | 115 | 20,544 | 25 | 1,189 | 9.621 |
| *Region 3* (Songkla, Nakorn Srithamarat, Pattaloong) | 2 | 5,721 | 29 | 3,540 | 4 | 2 | 1.675 |
| *Region 4* (Phuket, Krabi, Pang-nga, Ranong, Trang) | 1 | 1,116 | 8 | 702 | 1 | 16 | 0.381 |
| Total | 83 | 46,500 | 152 | 24,786 | 30 | 1,207 | 11.677 |

* Not including subsidized salary paid to teachers dispatched by the government for secular courses.

SOURCE: Division of Special Education School, Office of Private Education Committee, Ministry of Education.

plans for its *waqf* properties. The principle of self-reliance should be followed by all mosques instead of being dependent upon outside funds. However, in those communities which are really poor, external funds (i.e., at the provincial and national levels), should be made available. Fourthly, the mosques which are quite successful in their *waqf* property management should be treated as models to be emulated by others. It is believed that, if the *waqf* properties are well managed, the *waqf* institution can become a major source of self-reliance for the Muslim minority in Thailand and greatly contribute to the economic development and welfare of the local Muslim communities.

## APPENDIX

TABLE A
**Number of Registered Mosques by Province in 1987**

| Region | Province | Number of Mosques |
|---|---|---|
| North | Chiengrai | 2 |
| | Chiengmai | 11 |
| | Tak | 2 |
| | Pichit | 1 |
| | Prae | 1 |
| | Mae Hongsorn | 1 |
| | Pitsanulok | 1 |
| | Lampang | 1 |
| | Total | 20 |
| Central Plain | Bangkok | 155 |
| | Kanchanaburi | 1 |
| | Chachoengsa | 49 |
| | Chonburi | 21 |
| | Chainat | 1 |
| | Trad | 7 |
| | Nakorn Nayok | 26 |
| | Nakorn Sawan | 1 |
| | Nonthaburi | 20 |
| | Prathumthani | 27 |
| | Prachuab Kirikhan | 9 |
| | Prachinburi | 1 |
| | Ayuthaya | 50 |
| | Petchburi | 8 |
| | Rayong | 4 |
| | Ratchaburi | 2 |
| | Samut Prakarn | 9 |
| | Samut Songkram | 1 |
| | Saraburi | 3 |
| | Supanburi | 1 |
| | Angthong | 1 |
| | Singburi | 1 |
| | Total | 398 |
| Northeast | Nakorn Ratchasima | 1 |
| | Khon Kaen | 1 |
| | Udorn Thani | 1 |
| | Surin | 1 |
| | Total | 4 |

TABLE A (*continued*)
**Number of Registered Mosques by Province in 1987**

| Region | Province | Number of Mosques |
|--------|----------|-------------------|
| South | Pattani | 505 |
| | Yala | 280 |
| | Narathivat | 421 |
| | Satul | 137 |
| | Songkla | 265 |
| | Pang-nga | 70 |
| | Pattaloong | 68 |
| | Phuket | 34 |
| | Trang | 91 |
| | Krabi | 137 |
| | Nakorn Srithamarat | 94 |
| | Surat Thani | 28 |
| | Ranong | 16 |
| | Chumporn | 5 |
| | Total | 2,151 |
| Grand Total | | 2,573 |

TABLE B
**Distribution of Mosques by Age**

| Region | Less Than 10 Years | 11–30 Years | 31–50 Years | 51–100 Years | More Than 100 Years |
|--------|--------------------|-------------|-------------|--------------|---------------------|
| North | 1 (14.3) | 4 (57.1) | — | 2 (28.6) | — |
| Central Plain | 1 (1.5) | 14 (21.2) | 13 (19.7) | 27 (40.9) | 11 (16.7) |
| Northeast | 2 (100.0) | — | — | — | — |
| Upper South | 7 (15.9) | 16 (36.4) | 9 (20.5) | 11 (25.0) | 1 (2.3) |
| Lower South | 14 (25.0) | 18 (32.1) | 20 (35.7) | 4 (7.1) | — |
| Whole Thailand | 25 (14.3) | 52 (29.7) | 42 (24.0) | 44 (25.1) | 12 (6.9) |

( ) Percentages are shown in parentheses.

TABLE C
**Distribution of Islamic Schools by Age**

| Region | Less Than 5 Years | 6–10 Years | 11–20 Years | 21–50 Years | More Than 50 Years |
|---|---|---|---|---|---|
| North | 1 | 4 | 2 | – | – |
| | (14.3) | (57.1) | (28.6) | | |
| Central Plain | 34 | 3 | 7 | 17 | 5 |
| | (51.5) | (4.5) | (10.6) | (25.8) | (7.6) |
| Northeast | 1 | 1 | – | – | – |
| | (50.0) | (50.0) | | | |
| Upper South | 27 | 7 | 9 | 1 | – |
| | (61.4) | (15.9) | (20.5) | (2.3) | |
| Lower South | 38 | 7 | 5 | 5 | 1 |
| | (67.9) | (12.5) | (8.9) | (8.9) | (1.8) |
| Whole Thailand | 101 | 22 | 23 | 23 | 6 |
| | (57.7) | (12.6) | (13.1) | (13.1) | (3.4) |

( ) Percentages are shown in parentheses.

## NOTES

\*    This study received much support and kind co-operation from a number of people. Dr Imron Ma'luleem, the General Secretary of the Central Islamic Committee of Thailand, gave valuable advice and strong support to this project. Mr Ilyas Adam and Mr Yunus Adam, the research assistants, made a long trip visiting a number of *masjid* from north to south and from Central Plain to northeast Thailand. Miss Phanee Thirangoon of the Computer Center of Khon Kaen University also worked laboriously for the data analysis. The *imam* and *masjid* committees of 175 *masjid* as well as the chairmen of Provincial Islamic Committees of several provinces provided valuable information about their *masjid*, contributing to the success of this study.

\*\*    1 rai is equivalent to 0.395 acre or 0.16 hectare.